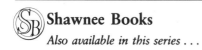

Shawnee Books

Also available in this series . . .

All Anybody
Ever Wanted of Me
Was to Work

The Memoirs of Edith Bradley Rendleman

Edited by Jane Adams

Southern Illinois University Press   Carbondale & Edwardsville

Library of Congress Cataloging-in-Publication Data

Rendleman, Edith Bradley, 1898 -
    All anybody ever wanted of me was to work : the
memoirs of Edith Bradley Rendleman/edited by Jane
Adams.
        p.   cm.—(Shawnee books)
    Includes bibliographical references and index.
    1. Illinois—Social life and customs. 2. Illinois—
Rural conditions. 3. Tenant farmers—Illinois—Social
conditions. 4. Rendleman, Edith Bradley, 1898—Childhood
and youth. 5. Women—Illinois—Biography.
I. Adams, Jane (Jane H.). II. Title.
F546.R46   1996
977.3'903'092—dc20
[B]   94-37252
ISBN 0-8093-1931-4
ISBN 0-8093-2059-2 (pbk.)   CIP

Title page photo: Edith Bradley Rendleman, 1995.
Geneva Wiggs Photography

The paper used in this publication meets the minimum
requirements of American National Standard for Information Sciences–Permanence of Paper for Printed Library
Materials, ANSI Z39.48-1984. ⊗

Contents

Appendixes

Plates

Editor's Preface

In 1984 I undertook a project for the Union County Historical Society to survey the county's old farmsteads. From that survey we selected five farms to study in depth. One of the farms, located in the Mississippi bottoms near the village of Wolf Lake, belonged to Edith Rendleman. Here is what I reported at the time:

There are few farms in the bottoms that have a long history in one family. Much of the land, until the Depression, was owned by merchants and businessmen who lived in town, and was farmed by tenants. This farm was owned by Jesse Ware, who owned hundreds of acres in the bottoms. His son, Charles, lost it in 1932 and Elijah Bradley, who had worked as a tenant on several farms in the immediate

area, bought it. Mrs. Rendleman lived, as a child, on two farms [I was wrong here—she had lived on four farms]; after marriage she lived in four houses, one of which her son W. P. (Bud) now lives in. Her husband's father, Robert Rendleman, was the founder of the town of Wolf Lake.

Mrs. Rendleman has written a history of Wolf Lake (published in the Anna *Gazette Democrat*) and worked on her family genealogy for the Rendleman family book. She has a fine memory, and members of her family are interested in the project.

. . . The farmstead is a good example of the kind of relatively substantial tenant farming in this area in the first third of the century. It has been well maintained and remains a working farm, although the house is strictly a residence (Mrs. R. lives there alone). The farming in the bottoms was distinctively different from that in other areas, in its system of absentee land-ownership, and Mrs. R.'s personal life history provides a great deal of information about this type of farming. She seems to have a strong sense of history, and would contribute a great deal to the project.

In the course of this project Mrs. Rendleman gave me her memoirs. She later stressed, as we prepared the manuscript for publication, "I did not write this book for the general public; I wrote it for my grandchildren." This document is a unique recounting of growing up in a region that was still being cleared for settlement. In her lifetime the landscape has been deforested, swamps drained, rivers channeled and leveed, noxious insects like mosquitoes, flies, and bedbugs brought under control, and diseases like malaria and hog cholera eliminated. Farming has undergone a revolution, with machines and chemicals replacing manual labor, and in the process the farm home has ceased to be a center of agricultural and domestic production. Wolf Lake has gone from a town called "Pistol City" for its frequent fights and numerous rough characters, to a small village for retirees and people who work elsewhere. Edith's memoirs trace these developments through recollections about her life.

In the course of my anthropological work tracing the changes in farm life in Union County, I have had the opportunity to read a number of memoirs; this one is special. Most memoirs tell of childhood through a lens colored with nostalgia. Edith's recollections of her life are unvarnished. She has a vivid eye for detail and the ability to create a scene simply and clearly. Most memoirs I have read were written by people who came from relatively privileged families. Edith, in contrast, came from an extremely poor family, but her parents were ambitious. Many of her relatives and neighbors were, therefore, among the poorest of the rural poor; her family, by dint of extremely hard work and intelligence, was able to move up in the world. In addition, Edith's mother's family was one of the earliest to settle in Union County, and their story provides us glimpses of the dense networks of kinship through which nineteenth-century farmers made a living. Edith's keen memory uniquely recalls many scenes of this rural society. In the South, novelists such as Faulkner have captured the daily life of the common people, but in this region of deep southern Illinois, which belongs to neither the North nor the South, almost no one has given voice to the lives of its people.

These memoirs have had a circuitous career. When Edith was working on a history of Wolf Lake and her family's genealogy in the 1970s, she decided to pass along her recollections to her grandchildren and great-grandchildren. In 1975 she began writing her memoirs in a desk diary. Finally, in 1979 she finished the story with the horrific events of 1947–48 and a list of friends who died in

1978. This book then vanished. In 1981 she took up the task again, this time writing in a notebook. She lent me this version in 1984. I made a photocopy, returned the book, and typed the manuscript into my computer.

Around 1988 Edith's son Lee Roy turned a recliner upside down while looking for Edith's hearing aid, and the lost book with the first draft of her memoirs fell out. They lent it to me; I photocopied it, typed it into my computer, and returned the book and typescript. The two memoirs were very similar; in some cases stories were recounted almost identically in the two versions, while sometimes one contained more or different details than the other. I merged the two versions into one and added material from many hours of interviews done in connection with the 1984 project and from the subsequent work Edith and I have done together editing this book. Copies of both original manuscripts, along with typed transcriptions of the 1984 interviews and negatives of the photographs included in this book, are available in Special Collections, Morris Library, Southern Illinois University at Carbondale.

I tried to exercise a light hand in editing these memoirs. I reorganized the narrative to follow the chronology Edith laid out, a chronology marked by the farms on which she and her family lived. Occasionally, however, she recollects a series of related events that occurred at widely different times. In these cases I followed her style and abandoned the temporal organization. The only significant material I took out of the text, other than that which Edith judged to be too frank or personal, was a somewhat disjointed genealogical section near the beginning of the 1981 memoirs. For it I substituted an introduction to Edith's ancestors and immediate relatives (chapter 1), drawing on her memoirs, her contribution to a published Lyerla family genealogy, and some original research.

Edith's recollections sometimes presented problems of how best to communicate them to an audience unfamiliar with the locale and the people who inhabit it. Her sense of place—both geographic and social—was created through the people who lived around her. In every place she lived and at every period of her life, she recollects who lived in the area, itemizing who they married and linking them to people the intended audience—her children and grandchildren—might know. Because most of the readers of these memoirs will not know the individuals named and because lists of names of strangers can become tedious, I was tempted to edit out most of them. However, that would have done real violence to Edith's sense of herself as a person deeply connected to the people who live around her. She intended these memoirs to convey "the way it was"; the many people who lived up and down the roads and hollows are a central part of that story. For Edith, each person named is a fully fleshed-out human being, some of whom she knew virtually all her life. It became clear, as we worked on these memoirs, that calling the names of these people and identifying where they lived evoked for her, and was expected to evoke in the reader, a larger experience of the people named. It is important to recognize that each vignette and anecdote she tells about the people she lived among is embedded in a continuing relationship, even if it is one that most readers will only understand very superficially. To have further developed the biographies of the many people who populate Edith's memoirs would have drastically altered the rhythm of her work, and our time together did not allow us to undertake such a project.

I was faced with the problem of how to represent the many names in Edith's story so that the average reader, lacking specialized historical knowledge of the Wolf Lake area, could still follow her account. I therefore created a series of genealogical tables of her extended family, included as appendixes to her text; and I drew a map showing the various places she and the people she remembers have lived (see map 3). These illustrations, combined with Edith's photographs and my editorial notes on her text, should enable the reader to follow the large cast of characters and places Edith writes about, allowing the specialist to study the interrelationships closely but not burdening the general reader with the need to remember every person named. In some places, I edited out the names of people whom she had identified primarily because of their relationship to other persons being discussed (so-and-so's mother, etc.).

Edith also referred to some people by a variety of names. For example, she refers to her late husband, William J. Rendleman, as W. J., Wm. J., and Bill; she refers to her father's partner in a thrashing outfit as Mr. Jones, Will Jones, Wm. Jones, and so forth. In some cases, particularly in the earlier part of the memoirs, I added identifying references (for example, "my future husband") or made all the references to the same person consistent in a given passage. In the first version of these memoirs, she often wrote specifically for her intended audience, referring to her parents as "Grandma" and "Grandpa." I have changed these to "Mom" and "Dad," to conform with her second version and to avoid confusion.

I also made minor grammatical and spelling changes that conform to standard English or, in the case of place names, to contemporary maps. For example, I changed *set* (the barn set in the flat) to *sat* or *sit,* and *come* to *came* when used in the past tense. In the southern Illinois hill dialect, a number of pronunciations vary from Standard American English. Among these, an *a* at the end of a word is generally pronounced like a long *e,* as in *Sarah,* pronounced "sar-ey." Other local pronunciations include *Vienna,* pronounced "vie-an-na"; and *Cairo,* pronounced "kay-ro." Edith sometimes spelled names phonetically, as in *Peet* (the name Peter was commonly known by), and *Rilo* (pronounced "rye-lo") for the cemetery that appears on maps as *Rallo.* She spelled *Hutchins Creek* in an archaic form, *Hudgeons',* and sometimes used other archaic spellings common in the area. In all such cases,

I standardized the spellings to those currently in use. Some names appear with diverse spellings, both in the historical record and in Edith's memoirs; I have standardized them, using published genealogies or common usage as my authority and leaving a variant spelling only in direct quotes. I also made some editorial changes in punctuation, such as occasionally breaking up long, compound sentences that speak well but do not read as comfortably. Edith's narrative was not broken into chapters; I have divided the memoirs into chronologically based sections and added chapter titles.

Edith tends to identify places according to the names she knows them by. This makes part of her recounting of the settling of the area confusing, since she tends to refer to places by the names of recent owners. For example, the Lyerla cemetery is located on land that Henry Lyerla Sr. bought from the government in 1832, but Edith refers to the land as the "Uncle Calvin Smith farm." I therefore changed her terminology or added clarifications to make it easier for the reader to identify the places named. Sometimes she identifies places according to a succession of owners or residents who never appear again in the narrative. In these cases I simplified and made consistent the identifying place-names. I have also occasionally inserted information in endnotes and photo captions that were relevant but that were not included in Edith's account.

Most of the photographs are from Edith Rendleman's collection, which, along with other photographs donated by southern Illinois families, have been placed in the Union County Farmsteads Project, Special Collections, Morris Library, Southern Illinois University at Carbondale. One photograph was contributed by Dan Wilson. Photographs from a source other than Edith Rendleman are noted thus in the captions.

This project would not have been possible without Edith's enthusiastic participation. In preparing the manuscript for publication, I read all of the 1975 version and all of the edited manuscript to her. She corrected and clarified many passages and added new material as we worked. Because of failing eyesight, she could not proofread the maps and genealogies, but they were compiled from detailed instructions she provided and from two tours, with her son Lee Roy and archaeologist Mark Wagner, during which we located sites from her childhood on USGS topographic maps.

An editor rarely has the opportunity to work so closely with the author or with such a unique body of material. Anthropologists and historians usually have the difficult task of representing people who are unable to speak for themselves, perhaps because they lived in a time that has passed or in a culture that did not provide the means for them to speak for themselves in a literary form. Most anthropological life-histories or "autobiographies" are heavily shaped by the dialogues between author and editor, so that authorship becomes blurred. People who work closely with interview materials are keenly aware of how much the interviewer's interests and social position determine the information the interviewee gives them. The fact that Edith wrote two versions of these memoirs before we met assured that they represented *her* interests and concerns rather than mine. My role remained clearly that of editor, not author. In Edith's memoirs, we have the opportunity to glimpse a now remote world through the eyes of one who has lived it. I am deeply thankful to have been allowed to be part of the process of making this world accessible to a larger public.

This book also would not have been possible without the help of a number of other people whose contributions I gratefully acknowledge. Ronald Rich and Elaine Rushing ran down many factual details, and Lee Roy Rendleman and W. P. (Bud) Rendleman assisted in many ways. Lester Lyerla was also helpful. Mark Wagner identified sites on maps; Professor Gary Kolb and members of the 1992 field school in ethnohistory and documentary photography at Southern Illinois University at Carbondale made copy negatives of Edith Rendleman's photographic collection; and the extremely helpful staff at the Research Photography and Illustration Facility, SIUC, printed the photographs. Kevin Davie at Morris Library, SIUC, scanned maps so I could trace them. Thanks also to Valerie Yow, Ronald Rich, and anonymous readers, whose comments enabled me to revise the manuscript; to James Simmons, editorial director at Southern Illinois University Press, who helped initiate this project; and to the sensitive and careful editing by freelance copyeditor John Wilson, Managing editor Susan Wilson, assistant editor Tracey Sobol-Hill, and the rest of the staff at SIU Press. Any errors and oversights in editing are, of course, entirely my own.

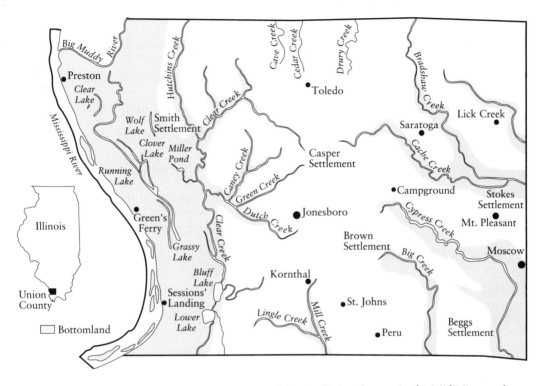

Map 1. Union County in the Mid-Nineteenth Century

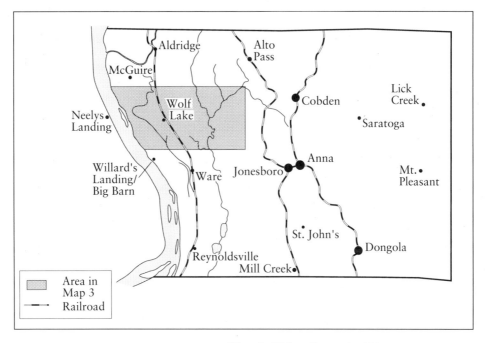

Map 2. Union County in 1900

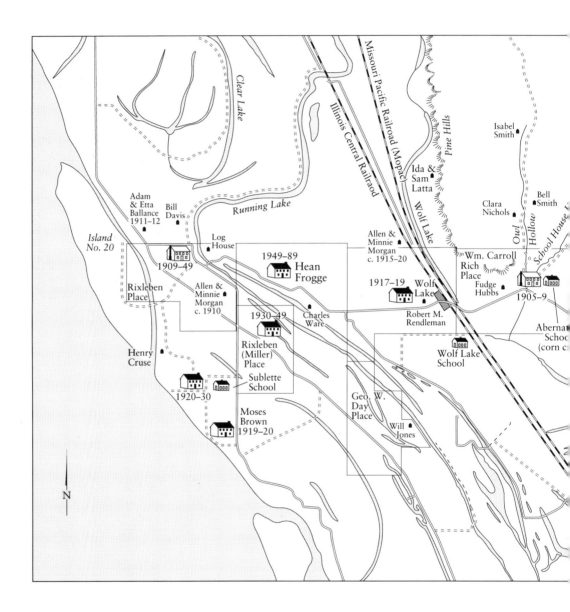

Clear Lake

Running Lake

Missouri Pacific Railroad (Mopac)

Illinois Central Railroad

Pine Hills

Wolf Lake

Owl Hollow

School House

Isabel Smith

Ida & Sam Latta

Bell Smith

Clara Nichols

Adam & Etta Ballance 1911–12

Bill Davis

Log House

1949–89 Hean Frogge

Allen & Minnie Morgan c. 1915–20

Wm. Carroll Rich Place

Fudge Hubbs

1905–9

Island No. 20

1909–49

Rixleben Place

Allen & Minnie Morgan c. 1910

Charles Ware

1917–19 Wolf Lake

Robert M. Rendleman

Aberna[] Scho[] (corn c[])

Henry Cruse

1930–49

Rixleben (Miller) Place

Sublette School

1920–30

Moses Brown 1919–20

Geo. W. Day Place

Will Jones

Wolf Lake School

N

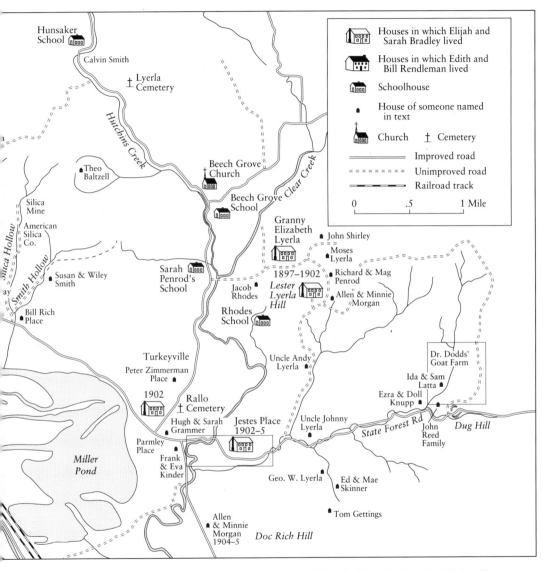

Map 3. The World of Edith Bradley Rendleman's Memoirs

Hunsaker School

Calvin Smith

Lyerla Cemetery

Hutchins Creek

Theo Baltzell

Silica Mine

American Silica Co.

Silica Hollow

Smith Hollow

Susan & Wiley Smith

Bill Rich Place

Beech Grove Church

Beech Grove School

Clear Creek

Granny Elizabeth Lyerla

John Shirley

Moses Lyerla

Sarah Penrod's School

Jacob Rhodes

1897–1902

Lester Lyerla Hill

Richard & Mag Penrod

Allen & Minnie Morgan

Rhodes School

Uncle Andy Lyerla

Turkeyville

Peter Zimmerman Place

1902

Rallo Cemetery

Hugh & Sarah Grammer

Jestes Place 1902–5

Uncle Johnny Lyerla

State Forest Rd

Dr. Dodds' Goat Farm

Ida & Sam Latta

Ezra & Doll Knupp

John Reed Family

Dug Hill

Parmley Place

Frank & Eva Kinder

Miller Pond

Geo. W. Lyerla

Ed & Mae Skinner

Tom Gettings

Allen & Minnie Morgan 1904–5

Doc Rich Hill

Legend:

Houses in which Elijah and Sarah Bradley lived

Houses in which Edith and Bill Rendleman lived

Schoolhouse

House of someone named in text

Church ☩ Cemetery

Improved road

Unimproved road

Railroad track

0 .5 1 Mile

All Anybody Ever Wanted of Me Was to Work

Introduction

JANE ADAMS

The Settling of Union County, Illinois

Edith Rendleman's account of life in the early twentieth century is set in the western hills and Mississippi bottoms of Union County, in deep southern Illinois (see map 1). Part of the upland South, this region is more similar to Appalachia and the Ozarks than it is to the prairies that lie to the north.[1] Edith's family descended from three of the several streams of immigration that settled Union County. The first two groups of settlers, of which Edith's mother's family was a part, were German-ancestry Lutherans and Dunkards (German Baptists or Brethren) who arrived in the early nineteenth century from east of the Appalachian Mountains. The third stream was made up of upland Southerners who migrated into Illinois after the Civil War and included Edith's father's family.

Immigrants from other areas also populated the county. Quakers of English ancestry settled on the eastern side of the county in the early nineteenth century, later becoming Universalists. Other settlers established Methodist, Cumberland Presbyterian, Christian (Cambellite), and Baptist churches. Austrians formed a colony south of the county seat in the 1840s and organized their own Lutheran church; German Catholics arrived with the railroad in the 1850s, as did Yankees and business-oriented immigrants from England, Scotland, and other areas, who established Presbyterian and Congregational churches in the towns. A few African Americans settled in the area before the Civil War, some coming as slaves, others finding the antislavery sentiments of the Dunkards and their descendants congenial.[2] After the Civil War, Southern freedmen joined impoverished white

Southerners seeking better lives in the North. However, by this time racial sentiments had hardened and, except for the area around Cobden and in the bottoms around Ware, few African Americans created a home in Union County.

During the eighteenth century, many Germans settled in Pennsylvania seeking religious freedom. The Lutherans who settled in Union County had followed the mountain ranges southward from Pennsylvania to what are now Rowan and Cabarrus Counties in the Yadkin Valley in the North Carolina piedmont in the mid-1700s, moving, a generation later, west to Illinois. The Dunkards who migrated to Union County moved out of Pennsylvania after the Revolutionary War. The pastor of the Union County Dunkard congregation, George Wolf, was representative of this migration. He was born in 1780 in Lancaster County, Pennsylvania; by 1800 he had joined a Brethren community along the Green River in Tennessee. Around 1813 a number of families from this community, including Wolf, moved to what is now Union County, where they became active in forming the new county in 1818. Their importance in the early political culture of the county is indicated in the county's name: "Union" referred to a camp meeting jointly held by George Wolf and a Baptist minister around 1817. Despite being active in local affairs, including being a founding member of the Masonic Lodge in 1822, Wolf stayed only two decades in the county, leaving for Adams County in northwestern

Illinois in 1831 with some members of his flock. Those who remained behind appear to have become core members of the Clear Creek Baptist Church, organized in 1820.[3]

Union County was attractive to these early settlers because of its elevation from the malaria-ridden bottom lands, its many springs flowing from limestone bedrock, and its rich forests growing from a thick mantel of loess (windblown) soils, left by the glaciers whose advance ended some miles north of the Shawnee Hills that stretch across the southernmost part of Illinois. They began hewing out homesteads and establishing landings on the Mississippi while Illinois was still a territory, and their relatives joined them in the decades following statehood in 1818. By 1837 John Mason Peck noted eight settlements plus the "seat of justice," Jonesboro, in his *Gazetteer of Illinois*, and the federal census listed the county's population as 5,524 in 1840, up from the 2,362 enumerated in 1820.[4]

Preemption records place settlers in the area along Clear Creek and Hutchins Creek, where Edith was born, as early as 1807,[5] although denser settlements lay to the east, where Jonesboro would later be located. Only a few sites in the bottoms were initially purchased from the government, largely along the banks of the Mississippi where ambitious settlers—with both German and English surnames—opened landings on the river. Despite early settlement by some people of British ancestry, the county quickly became known as a Dutch (German) settlement.

The ancestors of Edith's mother, Sarah Penrod, were part of both the Lutheran and Dunkard migrations: her great-great-great-grandfather John Christopher Lyerla[6] (1710–86) had been one of the delegates sent by his Rowan County community to Germany to recruit a Lutheran minister. One of his sons, John Christopher Jr., with his wife, and two sons, a daughter, and their spouses and children, moved to Union County around 1821 and settled near St. John's Lutheran Church, founded in 1816 by earlier migrants from Rowan County. John Christopher's brother Zachariah, Sarah's great-great-grandfather, had apparently led a more dissolute life. His father instructed the following in his 1784 will: "to my eldest son, Zacharias Lyerly, because he reached his majority, received a mare, a cow and calf, but shamefully lost them gambling and drinking and entered upon a life of godlessness and even cursed his father and laid hands on him and threw him to the ground. I leave him one shilling, and exclude him from everything else."[7] Zachariah migrated with his family to Union County in 1818–19, but rather than joining the other settlers from Rowan County in the south of the county, he settled along Hutchins Creek in an area that would later be known as the Smith Settlement and the site of the Lyerla Cemetery. A number of Dunkards settled along the upper reaches of Clear Creek and Zachariah's descendants married into these families, some of them becoming Dunkards and following George Wolf to Adams

County.[8] Sarah's father's surname was Penrod and her first husband was a Grammer;[9] both were descendants of members of the original Dunkard community. The ancestors of Edith's husband, William Rendleman, were important members of the Lutheran settlement on the Yadkin; Christopher Rendleman of Organ Church went with Christopher Lyerla of St. John's Church to Germany to recruit a minister for the two churches.[10]

Edith's father, Elijah Bradley, and his parents and siblings came to Union County in the third wave of migration from the upland South. After the Civil War the economy of the South in general, and Kentucky and Tennessee in particular, was severely disrupted. Many people migrated out of the eastern hills, crossing southern Illinois on their trek westward. In the process many settled in Union County. Some came in extended family groups, much as had the earlier settlers; others, like the Bradleys, came alone. Unlike the earlier settlers, these migrants found that the good lands were already claimed and that thriving, labor-intensive, commercial agriculture and timber industries needed their labor.

Elijah's parents worked as day laborers; when Elijah first married he also supported his young wife by working on area farms and in timber. After his first wife and two infant children died, Elijah married Sarah Penrod Grammer, who had been widowed two and a half years earlier with four small sons. It was not uncommon for recently arrived men, like Elijah Bradley, to marry women from old established families. Edith's memoirs reflect the fact that although people tend to trace kinship through their father's line more than their mother's, the mother's ancestral line is sometimes better known (see, for example, appendix B).

The Clear Creek/Hutchins Creek area, where Edith's family settled, lies well west and north of the main centers of settlement. Nonetheless, during the nineteenth century these fertile creek bottoms provided a stable livelihood for the people who owned the farmland, and the oak-hickory forests that covered the unfenced, rugged hills nourished the farmers' free-ranging hogs and cattle. In the 1850s, with much of the more desirable land already purchased, the government gave large tracts of the hilly woodland to the Illinois Central Railroad to help finance the building of the railroad. Although the land was grazed and timbered, much of this land found no buyers until 1904, when George W. Fithian bought eight thousand acres in western Union County from the railroad for fourteen cents an acre.[11] Most of this land was later purchased either by the state of Illinois for a state forest or by the U.S. Forest Service as part of the Shawnee National Forest.

In the post–Civil War decades Union County became one of the major suppliers of fruits and vegetables for the burgeoning industrial cities like Chicago. These crops along with wheat, which was one of the major crops in the bottoms, required large amounts of sea-sonal labor. During the winter, many poor laborers eked out a meager livelihood from the great hardwood forests that blanketed the rugged hills and swampy Mississippi bottoms. The tall trees were hewn into railroad ties for the expanding railway system and into timbers to support the walls and ceilings of coal mines just north of Union County, while the rapidly growing cities created an ever-increasing market for lumber.

An 1881 atlas of the county shows a settlement at the juncture of the road paralleling Clear Creek and the road now known as the Trail of Tears State Forest Road—the site of the earliest preemption claims in the area.[12] The atlas shows two sawmills, a box mill, a store, and several residences scattered around the junction. Edith recalled this settlement as Turkeyville; her father lived there with his first wife, although by 1890 the timbering had played out. Rallo Cemetery, where many of Edith's relatives are buried, lies on a low ridge between the road and Clear Creek (see map 3).

By the 1890s logging had moved west into the Mississippi bottoms. The broad bottoms, cut by swampy meanders of old river channels, were subject to annual flooding and occasional massive floods, like one in 1844 that drove many settlers from the area. The bottoms had always been distinct from the rest of the county. Malaria-infested, subject to inundation, swarming with snakes, turtles, and other reptiles in spring and fall, but also the home of giant nut trees and the wintering ground for huge flocks of geese and ducks, it was not attractive to families who wanted to farm in stable communities. Its fertile soil was, however, well suited to commercial wheat-growing, and by the late nineteenth century much of the land was owned by investors, rather than resident farmers.

Early Towns and Landings

The earliest settlers had established landings along the river where county produce, particularly in the prerailroad era, could be shipped to commercial markets. One of the first acts of the county government when it broke off from Johnson County in 1818 was to site a road from Penrod's Ferry to the old Johnson County seat, Elvira. Early maps of Illinois show a town of Hamburg variously sited along the river,[13] but it does not appear on post–Civil War maps. Early in the county's history a small group of Jonesboro merchants improved a road west to a landing known as Willard's or, later, Big Barn, and other enterprising ferrymen and merchants built landings at promising sites, varying according to the river's shifting banks. One of the more stable communities, Preston, was laid out in 1841 at the north end of the bottoms, just south of the mouth of the Big Muddy River at the Union Point landing. Two years later eighteen-year-old Massachusetts native Samuel Spring settled there, eventually buying large tracts of land, establishing substantial businesses in the village, and, in 1867, moving to Cobden where he continued to operate his several businesses and farms. Edith would later live about four miles southeast of this landing. Following the Civil War, as the government established postal routes from Preston and Willard's Landing, aspiring businessmen tried to boost the town, with only limited success due in part to competition from the more accessible railroads.[14] The Preston correspondent's reports in the *Jonesboro Gazette* give a sense of the enthusiasm with which boosters promoted their projects. The reporter wrote in the September 17, 1867, edition,

> This village is situated in the north-west corner of Union County on the Mississippi river, in one of the best farming parts of the state. It has two stores, one saloon, one blacksmith shop, one wagon maker's shop and a cabinet shop. It has a permanent Landing all the year round, where freight can be shipped for one-third what it can be shipped on the I.C.R.R.; to any part of the United States. All it wants to make a large place is enterprising men to come in. . . . Spring and Bro. are at present putting up a large new house for the benefit of the country at large. The politics are purely Democratic.

A few months later, in the December 5, 1868, *Gazette*, the correspondent boasted that the village had a dry goods store, blacksmith shop, family grocery, and drugstore. He continued,

> Nothing is anted to insure the rapid growth of the town but a mill. I think it would be no hazard of economy for some enterprising man to invest his money in this way as the yield of corn and wheat cannot be excelled by any part of the state. The nearest milling point is Jonesboro, and the mode of conveyance being very inconvenient. A great quantity of flour and meal is shipped from St. Louis, and consequently cannot be retailed at as low rates as at the mill.

By August 20, 1870, the *Gazette* could report that a miller had established a flouring mill and the Springs had put up a warehouse "capable of holding fifteen thousand bushels of grain, and are about to build another." The Springs also opened a dry goods store that year. The village, however, was eaten up by the river's shifting course and thirteen years later, when a massive county history was compiled, it had been swept away. Only the post office, a small store, and a steamboat landing remained.[15]

An 1883 Union County history, in its chapter on Preston and Union Precincts, sketches the area fifteen years before Edith's birth:

> Most of the land is owned by a few individuals, who, with one or two exceptions, live back in the hills, or in Jonesboro and Anna; hence, the inhabitants are nearly all renters, and of a kind of migratory character, flowing back and forth with the tide, as it were; retreating back into the hills during the overflow of the bottoms, and returning when the waters abate. Could the river and other streams be so leveed as to prevent overflow, and the swamps subjected to a perfect system of drainage, these bottoms would soon become the most valuable lands in Union County. . . . The population of Preston in 1880 was 283, and Union 827, and a large proportion of these are transient. The precincts are without railroad communication, and are dependent on water transportation to get rid of their surplus products.[16]

Despite the relatively transient character of the population, there were nine schoolhouses in the two precincts in 1883: Parmley, Frogge, Hamburg, Reynolds, Brumitts, Abernathie, Sublet (also spelled Sublette), Grading, and Big Barn. Church services were also held in these schools.

Around the time that Edith's father first married, in the early 1890s, influential landowners prevailed on the county commissioners to dam and drain a section of the swampland just south of Miller Pond, near where Edith would later live. Known as the "Goodman Ditch," the project faced strong opposition by some neighboring landowners who challenged it both in court and by direct action, repeatedly dynamiting or attempting to dynamite the dam. The conflict came to a head in February 1894 when the sheriff and his deputies confronted a group of men hired to destroy the dam. After a chase they arrested two men who implicated several large landowners; a third man was found some weeks later drowned behind the dam. The affair finally went into the courts.[17] The first drainage district was formed in 1908, and year by year more land was drained. When Edith's family moved into the bottoms around Miller Pond on the Carroll Rich place in 1904, and then further down to Running Lake on the Rixleben place in 1909, the area was largely wooded and had only begun to be drained.

By the turn of the century, urban businessmen had begun to consolidate not only their control over land in the bottoms, but also to develop a variety of clubs that helped establish themselves as the town and county "fathers." They bought land in the bottoms where they and their families would take brief vacations, hunting ducks and geese, fishing, nutting, and relaxing. Two hunt clubs built houses on the western edge of Miller Pond, another claimed Grassy Lake, and three more were established on Bluff Lake.[18] Around this same time silica mines were opened in the western hills.

Edith was a teenager in 1914 when the old river bed beside which she lived, known as Running Lake, was dredged. The first levee, "no higher than a potato hill," was built at the same time. The first application for a levee specified that it was to "reach three feet above the highest stage of 1903 flood" on both the Mississippi and Big Muddy Rivers.[19] It was raised repeatedly until the great flood of 1943 breached it and flooded most of the bottoms. The levee was rebuilt higher and stronger to its current strength, which withstood major floods in 1973 and 1993.

Plans to drain the bottoms were part of larger developments in the area that were directly tied to the growth of urban-based industries elsewhere. Cities in the U.S. and, increasingly, in Europe needed wheat for bread, which the rich flood plain could provide. The railroad system, growing cities, and coal mines continued to demand wood. Shortly after a railroad was built through the bottoms and the station of Wolf Lake established, an item in the *Jonesboro Gazette*, dated January 24, 1891, noted that a sawmill had begun operating near the station and stated that "Wolf Lake is on the boom." According to Edith's history of the community, Moses Cook operated this first sawmill. Her future father-in-law and founder of the town, Robert Rendleman, and another man named Ran Sides bought Cook out and operated the mill for many years.

Rendleman came from an old and influential family in southern Illinois. As noted previously, the family was among the earliest settlers from North Carolina. Edith wrote, in her history of Wolf Lake, that in 1889 Robert

Plate 1. The Illinois Central Depot at Wolf Lake in 1909 or 1910.

donated land at the north end of what is now the village for the Grand Tower and Cape Girardeau Railroad, later bought by the Illinois Central Railroad, or ICRR, for a branch line. He then platted the town. Between 1900 and 1904 the St. Louis, Iron Mountain and Southern Railroad built a line parallel to the original line. It was bought in 1917 by the Missouri Pacific, known as the MoPac.[20] The

ICRR operated until the late 1960s; the MoPac still operated its branch line in 1995.

Edith's life spans nearly the entire period of development and decline of the Wolf Lake area. She was born in 1898, just nine years after the town was platted, when most of the area was still in swamps and forests. Her parents' generation, born in the 1860s, had experienced the advent of steam-driven machinery, which replaced handicrafts such as spinning and weaving, and the hand thrashing of wheat. In Edith's lifetime most of the drainage systems were dug; the levees built and rebuilt; telephone lines installed, destroyed, and reinstalled; and electric lines, all-weather roads, and city waterlines constructed throughout the area. She experienced the arrival of the first automobile and the first tractor in the area. She grew up during the Golden Age of Agriculture, in the years just before World War I, when her parents were building up their estate; she set up housekeeping during the Great Depression that began for farmers after World War I; and her children set up housekeeping during the long period of economic expansion following World War II. During this period she and her family reaped the benefits of a wide range of government social programs aimed at bringing urban amenities to rural areas.

At the same time, farming became ever larger and more dominated by expensive technologies, and it also became increasingly marginalized by the expanding industrial and service sectors of the economy. Her grandchildren's generation—those who came of age during the Vietnam War and stayed in farming—have largely lost the farms their grandparents were able to buy. The Mississippi bottoms in the first third of the century comfortably supported renters and provided a surplus to support urban landowners and in the middle third of the century comfortably supported landowning farmers; but in the 1980s most landowning farmers there were fighting bankruptcy. In the 1990s only a handful of farmers operate the land that once supported hundreds of people.

Kinship and Neighborliness

During Edith's childhood, people relied on complex networks of neighbors and kin to maintain most aspects of daily life. Families were large and, despite a tendency to move frequently, they generally moved within a fairly limited area. This meant that most people were related to one another, either by blood or by marriage or both. Sometimes these connections were lost, even when social relations were maintained. Despite the importance of kinship, Edith's memoirs indicate that most people traced their kin relations to others in fairly simple terms. Except for close relatives like siblings, uncles, aunts, and cousins, relations between neighbors seem to have been more important than kin relations, although the ability to trace a blood connection might make the connection stronger. Where these relationships were strong, they would be called aunt or uncle, or grandmother or grandfather, without regard to the specific genealogical relationship. For example, Edith called one landlord "Uncle Carroll Rich," and another landlord "Grandpa Rixleben."

Kinship did not define the circle of those who had access to relationships of reciprocity or could expect kindness. Edith's mother,

Sarah, was charitable to poor people in her area, not just those who were her relatives. As Edith understood it, a neighbor loaned money to her father because her father was a man of good character and a hard worker, not because the lender was a relative, although they were related through marriage.

Marriages between relatives were common in the hills where Edith was born, in part because the pool of possible marriage partners was relatively limited and the webs of kinship extensive. Neither Edith nor any of her brothers married people they were related to, perhaps because of the greater diversity of the people who lived in the bottoms, where they moved as the children reached marriageable age, and because several of her brothers left for urban areas, where they found wives. In the early years of settlement, sisters occasionally married their widowed brothers-in-law, or vice versa. For example, John Cauble married three daughters of Henry and Mary Lyerla, the first generation of Lyerlas to settle in Union County. When Elizabeth died in 1833 or 1834, he married her sister Malinda; when she died three years later, he married a third sister, Delilah.

At the time Edith and her brothers were growing up, marriage linked families together, in addition to joining two young people. When parents depended on their children for their support in old age, and when many of the necessities of daily life were provided through kin networks, parents had a strong interest in seeing that their children married into families that could provide this security. Edith's mother actively intervened to encourage her sons to marry well, and Edith's parents and older brother made sure that inappropriate boys did not court her. In addition, marriage was a path to social mobility for both men and women. Edith's father, for example, who came from a family of transient laborers and was himself penniless, married a woman who had considerable farm equipment and livestock and was closely related to most of the landowners in the Hutchins Creek area. His sister Martha married Moses (Mose) Lyerla, uncle to Sarah. While Edith's family was not as "up in society" as the resident landlords in the Wolf Lake area, her family was obviously well respected by these families and she and one brother married into one of them.

Since many people died at an early age, children often experienced remarriage by one parent or another. Edith's maternal grandmother lost her husband during the Civil War and remarried, having several children by her second husband. Edith's mother also lost her husband and married the man who would become Edith's father. Edith therefore had only one "own" brother and four half brothers. These families did not always blend well. Edith remarks, "I always knew Mom thought more of the Grammer boys than she did of me and Leora. He was gone by the time he was eighteen and he didn't notice it like I did." But, conversely, Edith and her brother were favored as their father's only legal heirs, because he had not put their mother on any of the property deeds and legal adoption of children by a previous marriage apparently was uncommon. Edith's generation tended to live longer than their parents and grandparents, and unlike the older generations, divorce was much more common. Several of her brothers and cousins divorced, a pattern that has persisted with their children and grandchildren.

Edith's generation also significantly reduced the size of their families. Tracing back through her mother's lineage, Sarah Penrod bore eight children to two husbands (see appendix E). Sarah's mother, Ritta Lyerla, bore eleven children (five died as infants or young children), also to two husbands;[21] Sarah's grandparents, Catherine Elizabeth and Henry Lyerla Jr., bore five children; Henry's mother, Mary Fite Lyerla, bore ten children, and Henry Sr.'s father, Zachariah, had nine children by three wives, while his father, John Christopher, the first Lyerla in the United States, had five known children (see appendix B). Edith, in contrast, bore four babies, but only had her fourth child after the third one died in infancy, and most of her generation had similarly small families, another pattern that her children and grandchildren have continued (see appendix H).

Women of Edith's mother's generation nursed their babies for two years, Edith recalled. This prolonged nursing usually (although not always) kept women from getting pregnant again. As the children grew older, childcare became somewhat less of a problem, as the older children, especially daughters, took over many responsibilities. Edith, for example, recalled that her oldest daughter, Bonnie, "practically raised" her youngest son, Lee Roy.

Since at least the turn of the century, many people recognized and valued the breadth and strength of family ties, organizing formal family reunions to gather in the descendants of specific ancestors. One of the largest and most enduring of these is the Rendleman family reunion, which began informally in 1899. In 1902 family members formed an organization to coordinate the annual affair, and it has been held every year since. In 1983 they published a massive, 1,070-page compilation of the descendants of the first Rendleman/Randleman/Rintelman in the United States. Edith helped research the Union County branch of the family, as well as the Lyerla family with whom members of the Rendleman family intermarried.[22] Large family reunions became increasingly common and well organized as the century progressed; now, during the summer and early fall the county newspapers are full of their announcements. Genealogical research has also become a widespread activity.

Patterns of Social Life

In this area marked by dense networks of kin and interdependencies among neighbors, social life tended to revolve around such relations. However, social life in the hills, where Edith was born, appears to have been somewhat differently organized from social life in the bottoms, where she grew up. In the hills many people lived on small farms that they owned or rented. These farms often were too small to support a family, and with timbering playing out, many of the poorest renters—like Edith's father before he married Sarah—lived in acute privation. Edith's early memories are populated with such people, families who relied on more well-to-do neighbors, like her parents, for survival. Very few farmers owned large amounts of land, and most larger landowners farmed their own ground, even if they had a number of tenants on their land. In addition, many renters were related to their landlords and reasonably expected to buy land as they grew older. Sarah and her first husband, Hugh Grammer, were amassing the stock and equipment that, when their boys became old enough to help on the farm, would allow them to buy land. In this community, landownership was a mark of status, and soon after she married Elijah Bradley they began buying a small farm on top of a hill. Edith recalls that her mother never wanted to sell that farm and move into the swampy, flood-prone, malarial bottoms, but her father saw opportunity there and so the family moved.

In the bottoms most of the land was owned by absentee landlords and was rented as sizeable commercial farms. Families like the Bradleys often settled on one farm and stayed there for many years, developing the kinds of political and social ties that come with lengthy residence; reflecting this, most of the road

and school commissioners were renters, offices rarely held by tenants in the uplands. Nonetheless, clear class differences persisted between renters and landowners and between these two groups and people who depended on day labor in farming, timbering, and the silica mines. While the lines could sometimes be crossed, especially by young people (as evidenced by Edith's marriage), people tended to socialize mainly with people of their own class.

The few formal organizations that existed reflected the flexibility of class standing: All children attended rural schools, although the most prosperous families often maintained a house in town or sent their children to live with urban relatives so the children could attend high school; the churches, although of specific denominations, were open to everybody. Beech Grove Church, organized in 1876, was initially a Christian (Cambellite) church;[23] it later became Baptist. The Wolf Lake Methodist Church was organized in 1896, seven years after the town was founded; not until 1935, when the Assembly of God Church was founded, did church membership divide the community. Community baptizings were major events and they tended to mark a change in behavior in the person who was saved. Many of the saved were young people, for whom the rite marked the end of childhood frivolities. After Edith and her cousin Grace Ballance were baptized when Edith was seventeen, she writes, "that ended our going to dances."

Plate 2. A typical log house in the Mississippi bottoms in the early twentieth century. *Courtesy of the Union County Farmsteads Project Papers, the Walton Family Collection, Special Collections/ Morris Library, Southern Illinois University at Carbondale.*

While many people did not attend church, the churches, like the schools, provided public arenas where people could come together without regard for personal background. In contrast, the IOOF (Independent Order of Odd Fellows) and the women's counterpart, the Rebekahs, like other fraternal and sororal organizations, generally included more prosperous and settled members of the community. These national organizations created networks that linked members to others throughout the county, state, and nation.

Within the immediate area, people generally knew one another well and so could use a wide array of characteristics to evaluate one other. As some of Edith's recollections demonstrate, the multiple criteria of status—primarily landownership, personal character (which included one's immediate family), and ancestry—allowed people to compete with and judge one another in terms that were not always kind. People who were thought to act as if they were superior to others were referred to as "snooty," "high and mighty," and by other pejorative terms. People looked down on by others might be referred to as "lazy," "moochers," "bums," or maybe "crude" or "rough." No matter what their economic standing, people could also be "mean," a term that includes the attributes of stinginess, bad temper, and cruelty. Most people were "common" and, with more or less success, made a living for themselves and their families.

Edith's memoirs reveal that, despite their relative cultural homogeneity, people held to very different standards of appropriate male and female behavior, ambition, cleanliness, and other values. She recounts that her father and her husband wouldn't allow a woman in the field. On the other hand, she says, "My neighbor, Roy Belcher, his wife worked in the field like a man." Her parents did not believe in physical displays of affection and her mother never discussed sex with her. This reflected a common pattern of hiding the facts of pregnancy from children, but some people were more frank about such things than others. Edith, for example, says that "Mrs. Lockley told me all I knew, as she was a rough talker and knew the score." Women's bodily functions were mysterious and in the medical knowledge of the day, any ailment a woman had might be attributed to the onset of puberty or menopause. One doctor speculated that Edith's mother, sick nearly to death with what Edith later believed to be tularemia (rabbit fever), was undergoing the change of life. When in her adolescence Edith had a paralyzing seizure, the doctor attributed it to her menstrual cycle.

Women's bodily functions were hedged by silences. Such topics as menstruation and the indications of pregnancy were not spoken of in public, although networks of women and girls communicated needed information. For example, a girl might have her first menses and tell her closest girlfriend, who might tell her own mother, and eventually the word would get back to the first girl's mother, who would then give her the appropriate instruction. Patent medicines, such as wine of cardui, were sometimes given at first menses to regulate the flow. Similarly, early signs of pregnancy, such as weight loss by a nursing infant, might be noted by an observant female relative, who might tell the inexperienced mother why her baby was not thriving. Experienced women passed on information on a need-to-know basis, although there was little public, or general, circulation of such lore.

Women did not always welcome evidence of pregnancy with joy. One woman recalled that when the doctor confirmed that she was pregnant with her second child, while her first child was still nursing, she cried all the way home, wondering how she could take care of two babies while washing by hand, carrying all the water from an outside pump, cooking for a hired hand, and so on.

Women who bore children out of wedlock and the children they bore were strongly stigmatized. Wills occasionally show a wayward daughter cut out of the estate with an inheritance of only one dollar. Edith recalls some girls in her school whose mothers, unmarried sisters, had a reputation for being prostitutes. Edith and her friends picked out the eyes of these girls in the school photograph. On the other hand, one of Edith's best friends was illegitimate. Until her friend was grown she believed that her grandmother, who raised her, was her mother. Most adults in the community undoubtedly knew the truth since both families were well established in the area. If a couple got married the child bore no stigma of illegitimacy: genealogists often comment on the number of "premature" babies born to newly wed couples.

Despite the racial and religious homogeneity of the area, race and religion were ever present as lines of cleavage and prejudice. Edith said of her father that he would not tolerate Blacks or Catholics; she believed that he might have overcome his prejudice against Blacks but never would have given up his hatred of Catholicism. Racial attitudes seem to have changed and hardened between the 1860s and 1890s: Turner Brown, who had once owned the farm on which Edith grew up, was a mulatto who married a white woman and appears in the historical record as a well-respected man whose home was used for church services; and early records of the Clear Creek Baptist Association include some Black members.[24] However, by the time Edith was a young girl, Blacks were so uncommon and so stigmatized that when an African American junk buyer appeared at their gate, she and her brother fled in terror. Gypsies, who came through from time to time, were also stigmatized, apparently because of their alleged tendency to steal things and trick people.

Families varied greatly in ambition, as evidenced by Edith's aunts and uncles. Some of her relatives were hard working but unfortunate; others she perceived as lazy and slovenly. Compared to other relatives of the Bradleys, Edith's parents were the most successful. Extremely hard working themselves, they communicated their belief in, and respect for, hard work to their children. People who believed in the "work ethic" and ambition did not necessarily also adopt urban middle-class standards of personal and household appearances and cleanliness. Edith's mother, for example, cared deeply that her children marry well and be successful, but she placed a low value on her personal or household appearances. Edith, in contrast, always wanted the "finer things of life" and worked hard to achieve them.

Members of the Country Life movement, a major reform movement at the turn of the century, believed that farm women, in addition to being overworked, felt isolated. A study carried out under their auspices by the U.S. Department of Agriculture in 1914 states, "The loneliness, isolation, and lack of social and educational opportunity on the farm form the text of letters from all parts of the United States."[25] This may have been true in some regions, but it does not seem to have been true in this area. Edith Rendleman's memoirs testify to close relationships among the people who lived in every neighborhood in which she lived. While her memoirs recount mainly those relationships between neighbors and kin, she and her parents before her were also involved in a large number of organizations: the local school and church; fraternal organizations like the IOOF (Odd Fellows), Rebekahs, and Modern Woodmen; the Farm Bureau, which organized in Union County in 1918; the Rural Electrification Administration (REA) organized as part of the New Deal;

the Home Bureau organized in 1949; and a variety of other activities. In addition, many people were members of the Masons and Order of the Eastern Star and other fraternal and sororal organizations.

When interviewed February 9, 1984, Edith recalled, "In the bottoms and lower bottom, we knew everybody in the country, much more than I do today. . . . You had meetings and gatherings where you would all come together more." In contrast to her parents' time, during Edith's life various government agencies that had been influenced by the Country Life movement or were created by the New Deal spurred development of organizations that aimed to enhance the quality of rural life. These organizations also reflected the far denser population of the bottoms before World War II. Population peaked in 1910, with the census listing 1,864 people living in the three precincts making up the bottoms. Thereafter it declined, then peaked again in 1940 with 2,110 people. It then declined steadily, reaching a low of 913 in 1990.[26]

American communities have always been characterized by a great deal of immigration and emigration; the nineteenth-century immigrant streams described previously did not end in southern Illinois, and some inhabitants of Union County moved west to Missouri, Kansas, Texas, and the Gold Rush states of Colorado and California. Nonetheless, in areas dominated by local landowners, those who stayed formed multigenerational bonds, while in areas like the bottoms, largely owned by absentee landlords, people tended to be more transient, or "migratory," as the 1883 history stated. With Edith's generation, young adults in both areas tended to emigrate at high rates, as employment by railroads and industry provided greater security and affluence than did farming. World War I also seems to have given young men experiences outside their natal communities; in Edith's family, in what appears to be a common pattern, all her brothers except one left the area, while she married into a landowning family and stayed.

By the time Edith's children reached young adulthood, social patterns had shifted dramatically. The automobile and all-weather roads made it possible for young people to go to high school in town and led to school consolidation. In 1943 Sublette and Big Barn schools consolidated to form the Wolf Lake District; in 1949 Wolf Lake consolidated with the remaining schools in the area, Ware, Morgan, McGuire, and Beech Grove, to form the Shawnee School District No. 84. This, combined with out-migration, led to far more diversity in marriage partners among Edith's children, grandchildren, and great-grandchildren than in her own and her parents' generations.

Cemeteries appear prominently in Edith's memoirs. This is partly because like many genealogists she uses tombstones for genealogical information. But it also reflects the attachment many people feel to the burying grounds of their ancestors. This sentiment is not, however, universally shared. Many farmers, like the man who built a barn and hog lot on the old Rallo Cemetery, use old graveyards for other, utilitarian purposes. Some farmers use tombstones for flagstones or clear them away and then plow the field. In the 1970s Union County passed a small tax to maintain cemeteries so that many of the abandoned graveyards could be cleared. Those associated with active churches are generally well maintained, but those associated with disbanded churches or family graveyards generally rely on family members for upkeep. In the 1990s the sites of Edith's ancestors' burials, Rallo, Beech Grove, and Lyerla Cemeteries, exist in various states of repair. Rallo, as noted above, was destroyed; Beech Grove remained an active church and is well maintained; and family members, sometimes with county support, occasionally cleared Lyerla Cemetery.

The Household Economy

In the mid-nineteenth century, as industrial manufacturing stripped the urban home of many of its productive functions, educators and the mass media began to promote a new ideal of family life. This new ideal portrayed the home as the site of private domestic activity, divorced from the "public" realm of money and politics. The farm home Edith grew up in was nothing like that prescribed by these urban reformers, although she did, as resources permitted, remodel her own house, so that by the 1960s it appeared largely indistinguishable from an urban or suburban home. The dramatic changes that occurred can be marked in the small technologies of daily life: Edith's mother grew up in a household in which cloth was still made from their own sheep's wool; she did not use yeast until Edith was ten years old; and Edith did not own a ready-made dress until after she went to college. By her parents' death in 1948, a refrigerator had replaced the well and cellar for cold storage, and a locker in town replaced the smokehouse for preserving meat. Edith's parents, Elijah and Sarah, born in the 1860s, lived on the cusp of an economic and cultural shift that would, by their death in the mid–twentieth century, completely transform the farm home. The urban reformers saw farms as "backward." Edith, growing up in a time when the links between urban and rural cultures were increasing, felt the sting of such prejudice. She frequently mentioned that "Mother never modernized with the times." As a child she was often embarrassed by her mother's lack of attention to appearances and later felt considerable anger toward her father for his failure to pay for comfortable furnishings for the house.

But the farm household Edith lived in was not old-fashioned: her parents, drawing on values often at variance with urban middle-class values, kept up with the times. Elijah kept up with developments in agricultural production, buying the most modern farm equipment and the best draft stock available, and her mother must have kept abreast of poultry-raising practices, because she raised a large flock for market sale. At a time when markets for poultry and butter were just developing, Sarah aggressively sought buyers for her goods. At least as early as 1889, when the first railroad was being built, she walked six miles to the commissary at Wolf Lake to sell her produce to the workmen. Despite her geographically remote location, Sarah was among the earliest Union County women to develop a commercial poultry operation. Between 1880 and 1890 the number of chickens produced in the county more than doubled—from approximately 43,000 to 100,000—and egg production nearly doubled—from 175,000 to 337,000 dozen. By 1910 the number of chickens had increased to 157,000, but the number of eggs had risen only to 451,000 dozen, indicating the increasing importance of birds raised as meat.[27] Sarah also sold butter, but it does not seem to have been as lucrative as poultry, since she did not invest in a cream separator during Edith's childhood. In a small operation a separator did not save much labor since it had to be carefully cleaned with hot water, but it did extract more cream from the milk than could be skimmed by hand.

Like many farm women Sarah did virtually all her own marketing. She established business relations with merchants to whom she sold her butter and poultry products, and she decided how to spend her earnings. In the process she established strong ties with a few town families such as the Rixlebens, who were both landlords and merchants. She also traded butter and eggs at specialty stores such as Alden's for men's clothing; bought shoes at

Gams, coats at Sanford's, and yard goods at Matthais's General Store; and traded for other goods at The Racket and Nusbaum's General Store. Elijah, although he shopped for his own suits, almost never made purchases for his wife. Despite these business dealings, few social bonds existed between townspeople and farmers. Edith recalled, "We never associated with the town kids—they were way up above us country kids."

Sarah's strong orientation toward market production and Elijah's propensity to invest heavily in good draft stock and equipment indicate that despite shunning fashionable appearances, they were anything but "backward." However, their values, and particularly Sarah's, did point in some "traditional" directions. Unlike her husband, Sarah highly valued landownership. Edith recalls that her mother always regretted giving up a small hill farm they were buying for a larger, potentially more productive rented farm in the nearby bottoms. Sarah was a member of a well-rooted community in which landownership and marriage represented key avenues for achieving respected social standing, while Elijah seems to have been more like a harbinger of a new order in which individual economic achievement loomed large.

Despite the "entrepreneurial drive" Elijah exhibited, Edith's parents maintained strong economic as well as social bonds with their relatives and neighbors. Elijah arranged for his in-laws to rent farms near his own and he employed them when they needed work. He entered into formal partnerships with wealthier neighbors to operate thrashing equipment and relied on neighborhood swap work as well as hired labor to thrash his wheat. In an era before Social Security and welfare, Edith's parents housed an elderly woman and various old men; her mother gave milk and other food to poor neighbors, relatives, and hoboes; and they relied on neighbors for help during illness and other distress.

These demands often meant that housing was extremely cramped: When Edith was very young, Elijah's three siblings and an elderly woman lived with the eight Bradleys in a three-room log house. Hired hands, relatives, and others always lived with the Bradleys; her parents gave transient laborers and peddlers a pallet on the floor when they came by late in the evening. The openness of the immediate family to the larger community and the acceptance of having others in the household was part of the fabric of daily life. The fact that the household included many others only becomes obvious when Edith tells a particular story involving one of the residents or when she names the succession of hired hands who lived in the house. Although Edith valued privacy in a way her parents did not, as long as her husband was alive she, too, cooked and washed for resident hired hands, because her husband liked having the men around to socialize with.

The kind of farming Edith's parents practiced required all the family's labor, in addition to resident and seasonal hired hands.

Children were required to work hard from an early age and their obedience was often coerced with whippings. Women, too, worked long and hard, sometimes, like Sarah's sister-in-law Maggie, driven by their husbands with threats and beatings. Elijah, in contrast, helped his wife with her chores, hoeing the garden and carrying water if he came in early from the field; and unlike some mothers, Sarah does not seem to have used the switch against her children. Elijah, however, did beat his sons if they did not work hard enough, and Edith greatly feared her father.

Women's labor was essential to farm prosperity. Edith persistently marveled at how well her mother managed and at the table she was able to set, with little contribution from her father. Virtually all the family expenses for food, clothing, and maintenance, and one-fourth of the resident hired hand's expenses, were borne by the women, with no paid assistance. Only those few people who were "up in society" regularly hired help for the wives, although household wages were far below farm wages: a dollar a day for men (less twenty-five cents if they lived in the house); a dollar and a half a week for a girl. Although the women in Edith's family did not work in the fields, their labor included responsibility for the gardens, poultry, and dairy, virtually all food preservation and preparation, and procuring and cleaning the household's clothing.

In addition to being a workshop, the rural home was a center for neighborhood social life. Edith recalls the square dances, ice cream socials, and afternoon gatherings that took place in her childhood home and at her neighbors' homes. Funerals and weddings were held in the homes of the family. Many economic transactions also occurred on the farm. Although distant markets increasingly set prices for farm products and most grain and livestock were sold in markets such as the East St. Louis stockyards, farmers bought goods and services from one another, dickering over the prices.

By the time Edith set up housekeeping, family life had become more private and most public gatherings, such as recreational activities and religious rituals, had moved to other locations. Edith seems to have relied less on local merchants than did her mother, buying many of her family's clothes from the Sears Roebuck catalogue. The school, with its organized basketball teams, provided a new and geographically larger focus for entertainment, as did the access to town nightlife that automobiles and all-weather roads made possible. This greater mobility decreased the significance of the annual county fair, although in the 1990s the fair continues to be a popular event. Social Security and other New Deal programs, instituted some years after Edith's marriage, made it possible for elderly people to live independently. Except for the laborers and boarders who lived in her home until her husband's death in 1949, after World War II Edith's household was similar to urban and suburban ones, housing only immediate relatives. After her daughter divorced she stayed for a time with Edith; Edith's ailing brother stayed with her during his later years; and from time to time grandchildren stayed with her, partly to keep her company and partly for housing near their jobs. The household, still open to immediate family, was no longer a place of public accommodation and activity.

As the home became more private, it also lost many of its manufacturing functions. Most food processing moved outside the home. In the 1940s the county extension service promoted the development of cooperative packing plants to butcher beef and hogs and lockers to store frozen meat and home-packed fruits and vegetables. As farming became increasingly dependent on expensive machinery and purchased materials and virtually all acreage was planted to cash crops, families also became increasingly reliant on purchased clothing, food, and services. Unlike her parents' house, which would have appeared alien to an urban visitor, Edith's house would have felt familiar. Nonetheless, Edith continued to be an agricultural producer—if anything, on a larger scale than her mother, as she milked more cows and raised more chickens for meat and for eggs than her mother had. Shortly after her husband's death, she gave up her poultry and dairy operations; by the late 1950s, as markets centralized and large-scale chicken and dairy enterprises displaced women's small-scale operations, virtually no women supported their households from their poultry and dairy operations.

Among property-holding people, inheritance is always a time fraught with potential difficulties.[28] In the period of earliest settlement, women were completely excluded from operating as "persons" in a legal sense: they could not make contracts or engage in other legal arrangements but had to be represented by their husbands or other male representatives. By the late nineteenth century a series of reforms had given women the right to represent themselves in legal contracts, although they still did not have the right to vote. When Sarah's first husband, Hugh Grammer, died in 1891, Sarah was named administrator of the estate and she was able to retain virtually all of their property, except for a binder that was repossessed by W. Deering and Company. Sarah's stepfather "wasn't much of a manager" and, according to family tradition, by the time her mother died her inherited farm was heavily mortgaged to Jesse Ware, a major property-owner in the county, so the land was sold to pay the debt and Sarah and her siblings inherited nothing.

Divisions of land can, however, lead to enduring enmities between siblings when one sibling feels the other received the lion's share. This cleavage often seems to occur between brothers when one remains on the home place, caring for aging parents, and receives a somewhat larger share of land than his brother who settles nearby. In some cases brothers cease to speak to one another, in others the enmity appears as a conflict between brother and sister-in-law. In some cases daughters, who rarely keep farming family land, are left with a disproportionately small share of the estate, although state law gives each child an equal share if the parents die without a will. Women, with a history of leaving major financial and legal decisions to their husbands, often make unwise decisions regarding disposition of their estates. During the years I worked with Edith on this book, she frequently stressed the importance of not partitioning one's estate before death. She dictated the following caution for inclusion in this book: "Parents, stop, look, listen. Don't be stupid and give your land and property to your kids before you die because they can't be trusted. If you do, you may get the biggest fooling you ever got in your life. Some may get it all and some may get none."

That Edith does not say much in her memoirs about political activities may be an indication of women's general absence from local political affairs. She once stated that her mother probably never voted. Her father, a "hot" Republican who "hated Democrats, Catholics, and Negroes," while living in a largely Democratic area, stayed out of local politics, although renters often held local offices such as road commissioner. Her husband, Bill, in contrast, was active politically, as were many of his relatives. His father had helped organize one of the earliest drainage districts in 1908, and Bill served as a director on the drainage district board, as well as on the Rural Electrification Administration board. Her sons, too, were politically active, with both serving as county commissioners

and holding a variety of other political and civic offices. Edith was a charter member of the Home Bureau but remained a local leader, never working on the county level.

Nonetheless, with radio and, later, television, national and world affairs are part of her consciousness in a way they could not have been to her parents: She recalls Franklin D. Roosevelt as a great hero of the common people, a champion of farmers and poor people, the man who brought electricity to rural areas. She followed the great dramas of the century such as the Lindbergh kidnapping. The world wars affected her firsthand: her husband was drafted for World War I and her sons served in World War II. Edith does not write of the Vietnam War, which happened during her older years, but many of her grandchildren and other relatives were deeply affected by it. Edith has also traveled widely, visiting her brothers in California, her son in New York, and other relatives in Louisiana. She has joined groups organized by a local tour company, visiting Disney World and many other places. Although her recollections are strongly rooted in a few square miles of Union County, unlike her parents who, as adults, traveled no farther than the Missouri Bootheel, St. Louis, and western Kentucky, Edith's intellectual universe embraces the world.

Recalling the details of a long and well-remembered life, these memoirs communicate a way of living far different from that lived now. In the small and large details of daily life, this account reveals many of the changes that worked a revolution in farm life. It is told neither to celebrate the past—that life was far too difficult and loveless to wish to return to—nor to celebrate the present—there is too much heartache and loneliness for that. Rather, Edith seems motivated by an urge to communicate across the generations, to break through the loneliness imposed by being formed in a different time, a time that those raised since World War II have difficulty imagining. Edith views her life like a historian: as a part of our reality that needs to be documented to rescue it from oblivion and perhaps, in the telling, shed more meaning on our present and how we got here. These memoirs represent a conscious effort to collect the past and to cast it into the present, where it may live on in our lives and the lives of those who come after us.

1 The Hard World I Was Born Into

John Bradley, my grandfather, was born in Kentucky in 1848. My grandmother, Mary Curtis Bradley, was born in 1850 in Tennessee. Grandpa Bradley was a small man with red hair and red mustache. He didn't seem to have any relatives except an uncle Sol. My dad took my brothers Albert and Leora and my mom and me where my father lived as a small boy near Morganfield, Kentucky. He showed us where the house stood and the coal mines were. Dad always told us how a big boy used to whip him every evening when he went to get coal at the mine to burn. After many fights his father told him if he didn't hide a piece of coal under his sack to protect himself he would whip him that night. Next evening when Dad went after coal, he hid a chunk of coal under his sack and when the bully started for him, he let him have it be-tween the eyes and knocked him out cold. After that he was Dad's best friend.

They came to Illinois when my dad was a boy in his teens, in the 1880s. My dad said his father was a coal miner and they used to travel up and down the Ohio River on a boat. My father wouldn't eat the food cooked by Negroes, and his mother had to fix his food to take along. He also said he got so tired of moving from one place to the other that as a small boy he said if he ever got to be a man he would have a home where he wouldn't have to move all the time.

When they came to Illinois from Kentucky they settled at Bloomfield, a little town north of Vienna that was the home of transient fruit-pickers. Also they raised vegetables. They lived in a barracks, which was a long row like horse stables of one-room houses. They had one window in the back and a door in the front. Each family had a room. Dad took us out there and showed us where the old barracks and town stood. They had this barracks for strawberry pickers, and that's what my dad and his family did, they worked in the fruit and vegetables. I don't know how long they lived here but it must have been a few years, as I don't know anything of Dad's whereabouts until he was in the Miller Pond area around 1890.

Dad never went to school a day in his life. He learned to read and write after we kids started to school. He would study my spelling book every night, even after we moved to the Rixleben farm. He would spell words and ask me what they spelled. If I had only realized how bad he wanted to learn I could have taught him so much. He said we must all go to school and get as much education as we could, and not one of us was allowed to miss a day. Even when we were so poor, not one of the boys ever missed school to work.

John and Mary Curtis Bradley had seven children, Cynthia, Lou, Martha, Florence, Maud, George, and my father, Elijah [Lige] who was the oldest [see appendix A]. Two of their children, Cynthia who married Joe Returno, and Lou who married James Rogers, moved to Grays Ridge, Missouri, near Hornersville, in the Bootheel. The rest stayed in the area. Uncle Jim Rogers was a Baptist preacher. He had three small children when Lou married him, and then they had three children. He was a miracle man to me because

he could blow fire out of a burn so that it didn't hurt at all anymore. He could stop a rising of a boil, and he could stop blood, all with verses from the Bible. He taught me to do it but I told my brother and that caused me not to be able to do it. You aren't supposed to tell your blood kin. One time my cousin Orville Morgan and his family was at my mother's house and Uncle Jim was there. Orville wasn't over three or four years old. We had an oblong woodburning stove that had a door in the front and a hearth under the door. But there was three or four inches under there, where he could stick his hand up under there. He was running and playing and he fell down and stuck his hand under the door in the coals. Oh, burned it bad. And in just a few minutes Uncle Jim had blown the fire out of it, and he was back playing again.

Martha married Mose [Moses] Lyerla, Florence married Ade Holder, Maud married John Weiss, and my father married Sarah Penrod Grammer.

John Bradley was only fifty-one or fifty-two when he died of pneumonia January 6, 1900, on Hutchins Creek near Beech Grove on the Jacob Rhodes farm. They had boxed in a slat double crib and lived in that.[1] My grandmother died two years later in Anna, on April 5, 1902. She was cleaning onions to ship and just fell over dead. Dad was very poor in those days, but records at Norris Funeral Home in Jonesboro show that he paid for all his family's burials. His father's funeral cost

$16.00 for casket and $7.50 for shoes and clothes and his mother's clothes and casket cost $17.50. I believe he had to haul his parents to the cemetery because there was no other way. My grandfather and grandmother, and all the rest of both my father's and mother's families who stayed in the area, beginning with my half sister Mevia, are buried in the old part of Beech Grove, except my father and mother. Maud, Florence, and Uncle George, Dad's youngest brother, came to live with us when Grandma Bradley died in 1902, and Maud and Florence stayed with us until they married.

George was the youngest and retarded. He lived with us after Grandma died until he got to where he wouldn't mind Dad and he had to send him to the home for the feeble-minded at Lincoln, Illinois. He was nearly grown when he went there. Seva Arnold told Dad he became a real good dancer. He died during the flu epidemic in 1918 and was sent to Wolf Lake in a casket and was buried at Beech Grove. His burial cost Dad $250. Norris was called.

My father was nineteen when he married sixteen-year-old Ritta Etta Josephine Lanham, the daughter of Bill Lanham, August 14, 1890 [see plate 3]. They lived in a log house on a little hill on the right side of the road just after you cross the bridge as you go up the hill. To me it is the Pete [Peter] and Mary Zimmerman place just past the Parmley place and old Rallo Cemetery [see map 3]. Mom and Dad called it Turkeyville. Dad said

he walked six miles and made railroad ties for fifty cents a day when he lived there. He said he plowed one summer with a one-horse plow, with a big boil on his leg, and never missed a day's work. He also lost both children and his first wife while living there.

They had two children, Raliegh Harris and Ada Gustavia, who died as infants. They and their mother, Etta, died of TB. They are all buried at Beech Grove, but my father could not afford a marker for their graves.

My mother, Sarah Penrod, was born October 6, 1861, and died February 14, 1948, on the Thomas Rixleben farm. She married Hugh Grammer July 27, 1878. He was born May 6, 1851, and died November 4, 1891.

My mother's family were among the first settlers in Union County and along Hutchins Creek. My mother's mother, Ritta Lyerla, was the daughter of Henry Lyerla Jr., who was born in 1809 in North Carolina and came to Illinois around 1818 with his father, Henry Sr., and mother, Catherine Elizabeth Smith, who was also born in North Carolina in 1804. Henry Sr. and his brother Jacob came to Union County by the way of Kentucky with their father, Zachariah [see appendix B]. It took them two years to make the trip. Zachariah went on into Jackson County and then joined other members of his family in Adams County with other members of the German Baptist or Dunkard church. Henry settled north of Beech Grove on what I knew as the Uncle Calvin Smith place.[2] The family graveyard is on this farm, although we have never

Plate 3. Tintype of Elijah Bradley and his first wife, Ritta Etta Josephine Lanham, probably on their wedding day, August 14, 1890.

Plate 4. The old Lyerla place, built by Henry Jr. and Elizabeth Lyerla in the mid-1800s. Sarah Bradley grew up here with her mother, Ritta, and grandmother, Elizabeth. The property is now owned by the Rhodes family. Photo taken in 1984 by Jane Adams.

found a marker for Henry Sr. Henry Lyerla's daughter Belveritta married George Smith and they settled south of his father, on the farm I knew as the Uncle Charlie Smith place.[3] Then they left there and moved across the creek in front of what I call Uncle Jake Rhodes's place.[4] There was more land over there than there was on the Calvin Smith place, so I guess that's why they moved over there.

Henry Jr. and Elizabeth built a house east of Hutchins Creek on land Henry Jr. bought from the government [see plate 4]. My grandmother Ritta inherited it from her father and after her death her husband, Lum Ballance, sold it to Ritta's brother Zachariah, who gave it to his son Jacob. That stayed in the Lyerla family until about 1965 when the heirs of Jacob Lyerla sold it. My grandmother Ritta must have lived with her parents since my mother was raised there and often spoke of [Catherine] Elizabeth as "Old Granny Lyerla." Uncle Zachariah's daughter Bertha and Zachariah's grandson Lester Lyerla told me that Henry Jr. left his wife Elizabeth, but no one seems to know what became of him. My mother never said anything to that effect. I do know that he was gone when his father's estate was settled in 1857, because the court gave his share to his children.[5] I never heard my mother speak of her grandfather.

My grandmother Ritta was born January 1, 1841, and died January 24, 1897, at her home on the Jake Lyerla farm. She is buried in Beech Grove Cemetery on Hutchins Creek. She married my mother's father, William Penrod Jr., in 1857. He was born about 1834 and died April 5, 1865. He was a Civil War veteran and died from chronic dysentery he contracted as a soldier in the Civil War. He was mustered out at Mound City, Illinois, with sick leave in November 1864. He was never out of bed again. He was buried in what was once Rallo Cemetery. Ted Wilson destroyed this cemetery in 1980. He buried all the tombstones and used it for a hog lot. My people's graves were on a point running south and he built a hog barn over their graves. My people buried there were my grandfather Wm. Penrod, Mom's brother David and his wife, Martha, and five babies of Grandma Ritta Ballance. All the rest of the family (except Mom and Dad) are buried at Beech Grove.

My mother had two full brothers: David, who married but he and his wife both died young, and W. Richard, who married Maggie Donavan. He was some character. He was drunk in his younger days and the wickedest man you ever heard swear. But he got religion in his old days and was just as religious as he was wicked. He used to make Aunt Mag sit up half the night and read the Bible to him after she had plowed new ground all day. He was so overbearing nobody could live with him. All of his kids left home as soon as they were old enough to make their own way. Aunt Mag left him in 1915. She and Uncle Richard are buried in Carbondale but not together.[6]

After Will Penrod died, Grandma Ritta married Christopher Columbus Ballance in 1867. Everyone called him "Lum." He was from Vicksburg, Mississippi.[7] He and my own grandfather Penrod were in the trenches together and he asked Lum to come back and marry his wife and take care of his children if anything happened to him. And he did. Altogether Ritta and Lum had eight children, but only three, Adam, Minnie, and Christopher Columbus Jr. (called Lummie), grew up. Their first child, Samuel Earnie, was burned to death as he fell into a wash kettle of boiling water as Grandma was making soap, when he was two years old,[8] and the other four died as infants. Adam married Etta Bittle and they lived near us. Minnie married Allen Morgan and they also lived near us [see appendixes C and D]. Lummie Jr. thought he had killed a man and left in 1904.

When my mother was a young girl in her teens, they had a big dog named Tige. He must have stayed in the house some. He was a biting dog and people were afraid to come to the house without somebody coming out to guard the dog. One day Grandma and Grandpa went to town and left Mom at home alone. Somebody came up and hollered and Mom started through the house to see who it was. Tige must have been asleep and thought she was someone else as he lunged at her, knocking her to the floor, biting and chewing her in the chest. She finally hollered, "Tige, you Tige," and he realized who she was and stopped and crawled under the bed. Mom had scars all over her chest. When Grandma and Grandpa came home they had the dog killed.

They all had to work hard. Mom helped card the wool from which their clothes were made. That carding was done to roll the wool into a thread so it would go through the spinning wheel, making a yarn that could be made into clothes, which were sewn by hand, as they never heard of a sewing machine at that time. They also raised a lot of geese and used the feathers to make their beds and pillows. Many trips had to be made to the springhouse. The spring was located quite a ways northeast of the house. There was a house built over the spring and a large stream of beautiful clear water flowed from it. That was where Grandmother kept her milk, cream, butter, eggs, etc. The old spring is still there today. They called the place the old Mill Race as Henry Lyerla (Jr. or Sr.) used to operate a gristmill close by where people came and got their corn ground into meal.[9]

There was a school on the Willis Rhodes farm from which my mother received a fair education, as she could read and write.[10] The seats in the school were logs split in halves with legs attached. They just had two books, a reader and arithmetic.

My mother told about the old witch that lived up the hollow from them. Her name was Hailie Journagen. When things went wrong they went to her to make them right. Mother told of so many things she did, such as dry up the creek where her enemies' cattle got water and make the water spring up on her side of the creek. She would also boil a half-dollar in the tea kettle to change your luck.

My mother married Hugh Grammer in 1878, when she was sixteen years old. They had six children, Phelix Everett, Mevia Belveritta, Curtis Elmer, Ellis Elbert, Albert Elvin, and Orville Claudius [see appendix E].

Mom's oldest son, Phelix, was killed in 1891 when he was twelve years old, in a hunting accident. He and his cousin Walt Penrod were duck hunting on Miller Pond. Walt pulled a gun out of a boat by the barrel, causing the gun to discharge and striking Phelix in the stomach and groin. He died that night, March 26, 1891. Mevia, her second child, was sleeping on a pallet on the floor and took a congestive chill and died August 21, 1889. She was almost eight years old.

Curtis, the third child, was a good looking young man and loved a good time. All the girls were crazy about him. He said they walked to Anna for band concerts, the Anna Fair, etc. They attended Church and Sunday school at Beech Grove. They walked every place as there were nothing but lumber wagons in those days. There were always several of them in the bunch. Curtis married Dora Myers, the daughter of George and Kate Myers, in 1904. They had six children. They lost their first baby, a boy, and lost another boy when they lived in Cairo. He borrowed one hundred dollars from Bob Rendleman to go to Vienna and study telegraphy. He got a job as operator and ticket agent in many small towns on the MoPac Railroad and later a good job in Cairo, Illinois. They lived there several years until 1918, when he moved to Sacramento, California, and worked many places on the Southern Pacific Railroad. His children still live there. Curt came and lived with me from 1959 to 1965, when he went back to California and lived in a retirement home till he died in 1966. He is buried in Sacramento.

Ellis was never so full of life as Curt. He was the quiet, still type. But he had a temper. He married Dora Rendleman, daughter of Julius and Ella Walker Rendleman.[11] They had two sons, Quentin and Robert. Quentin lives in Denver, Colorado, and has four children, Billie, Carol, Gene, and Patricia. Dora and Ellis lived for years in East St. Louis, where he was a clerk for the Southern Railroad. He died November 14, 1954, and is buried in Valhalla Cemetery, Belleville, Illinois.

Albert was a good looking, dark-headed, dark-complexioned young man. He was always the stubborn type. Never talked much except to argue. He never was girl crazy and never married until he was forty-four years old. He and Ellis both went to school until they were nineteen and twenty-one years old. Because there was no high school, a lot of people took eighth grade over and over. Their last year was 1907 in old Wolf Lake school. They both took the teachers exam at Jonesboro and both became school teachers. Then you could take that exam at Jonesboro after you completed grade school and if you passed you could teach school. Ellis taught a year at Sublette and Albert taught two years, first at Hunsaker and then at Mountain Glen. They saved enough money that year (Ellis got thirty-five dollars a month, Albert a little more) to go to college in Valparaiso, Indiana. Albert went on to more schooling, working his way by washing dishes in a restaurant and finally teaching in college, until he put himself through law school and became a lawyer there in Chicago for fifty years. He married Emily Kuska in 1933. They had one daughter, Barbara, who married a Littell and had two sons and a daughter, Jeffery, David, and Susan. They lived in Chicago until he retired, when they moved to Florida. He died there March 1, 1979, at the age of ninety years and twenty-eight days. He is buried in Chicago.

Orville never had as much interest in school or work as his brothers did. I think he quit school before he finished the eighth grade. He took a trip with another young man to Oklahoma to look for work and found none and had to hobo it back home. He married Della Smith and had two sons, Cyril and Merle. Orville and Della were separated; she took the youngest son, Merle, and went to Ohio with another man. Orville went back home and Mom wasn't able to take care of Cyril, so he stayed with my husband, Bill, and me for two years, from 1920 to 1922. We always went to church and Sunday school at Wolf Lake and one Sunday we—Bill and Mom and Cyril and I—stopped at Bill's mother's, Mrs. Rendleman's, for dinner. About 4 P.M. Mom asked Cyril to go down and tell Dad she was ready to go home. A truck was taking a baseball team to Neelys Landing on the river after the game between Neelys Landing and Wolf Lake, and Cyril tried to jump on the running board to ride home. It was raining and slick. His foot slipped and he went under the truck. It ran across his stomach, and he lived about two hours. That was September 10, 1922. He is buried at Beech Grove beside his grandpa Grammer. That was my first experience with death. His brother Merle died in August 1981 with a heart attack.

Orville married a second time, to Martha Glotfelty. They had six children. The first baby, Imogene, died at six weeks old and was buried beside Mr. Grammer at Beech Grove. They then had Hugh Dean, Jewel, Alta, Carol, and Georgia May. Hugh has several children and lives in Florida. Jewel has several and lives in Chicago. Alta lives in Indiana, Carol in West Chicago, and Georgia in Murphysboro. Orville died at their home out from Murphysboro, August 5, 1958, with a heart attack. He nor Ellis either one would go to a doctor when they needed one.

Mother and Mr. Grammer lived on the Parmley place, now owned by Ted Wilson. The house was bulldozed down in 1980 and Ted's son Eddie put a nice trailer there. Dad said Mr. Grammer died from locked bowels but Mom always said, after we knew about appendicitis, that perhaps was what killed him.

Dad used to work for Mr. Grammer and Mom occasionally. A little anecdote that happened one day when he was working there: In those days all ladies that rode horses rode sidesaddle. One day they were in the yard at the house and someone looked up and saw a woman coming on a horse riding astraddle. They hollered, "Don't let her see you looking!" My dad brought out a big oath and said, "I'm going to look if it puts both eyes out."

They had equipment and livestock to run that farm. Somebody sued Mom for a binder and won their case after Mr. Grammer died.

Plate 5. The Elijah and Sarah Bradley family in 1899. *Left to right*: Curt, Leora, Elijah, Ellis, Albert, Sarah, Edith, and Orville.

But Mom said they were not behind on their payments. She broke up housekeeping and moved back to her mother's house. I don't think she sold her livestock and tools, as I think she had them when she married Dad.[12]

After Hugh died in 1891 Mom married Wm. Elijah Bradley, March 19, 1894. She really loved Hugh Grammer. I think she buried her heart when she buried him. I don't think

she ever loved my dad; she just needed a home. She loved the Grammer boys more than she loved me and Leora. Leora was gone by the time he was eighteen and he didn't notice it like I did. In fact, I don't think she, or Dad either, ever loved us, as she always told us Dad never wanted any kids and he never touched us unless it was to have a case. He loved me after I was grown, but that couldn't repair the damage that was done when we were kids. Mom never loved anybody but the Grammer boys and their families. But she did love my kids.

I'm sure their marriage wasn't a marriage of love but of necessity. My father needed a housekeeper and my mother needed someone to help raise those four boys. I made a remark to Mr. Plott[13] that my dad did something wonderful to marry a woman with four kids and he said, "Now your dad done all right when he married your mother." So I know by that she still had her farming equipment and he might have had his eye on that farming machinery.

My brother Leora Adam was born May 14, 1895, and then I was born August 2, 1898 [see plate 5]. Leora was the youngest of the five boys and did not have to work as hard as the older boys. He attended college in Valparaiso, Indiana, learned telegraphy, and worked for the railroad. He was one of the first called in by the army in World War I. He was stationed at Fort Campbell, near Louisville, Kentucky, and was in the Signal Corps. He was sent overseas for a year. When he was discharged from the army in 1918, he went to California where Curt was. He loved California and never came home again except for a few visits. Leora never took life serious and just believed in having a good time, which he always did. He first married Lolita and then

Ethel Browne. She had one son, Donald Henderson.

Mom was a wonderful Christian person. She joined Beech Grove Baptist Church when she was sixteen or seventeen years old and remained a Christian woman the rest of her life. She must have joined when it was organized in 1876.[14] She still belonged to Beech Grove Church when she died February 14, 1948. She always came up with her part of the work raising chickens, milking cows, and selling butter and eggs to supply the table with groceries. She told me she walked to Wolf Lake from the Parmley place (more than six miles) and carried butter and eggs and sold (or traded for groceries) to the Commissary when they were building the Illinois Central Railroad in Wolf Lake in 1889 and before. And walked back carrying her groceries. She continued her work up until the year before she died. Then she would get something for a walking stick and go to the barn to look for eggs.

She never turned anyone away from her door hungry. Up until Social Security and nursing homes came in for people to have a place to stay, there were lots of tramps, hoboes, and bums coming to the door and asking for something to eat. She always fed them and helped orphan children and anyone in need. She always (or both of them) visited the sick and went to every funeral.

Plate 6. The Elijah and Sarah Bradley family, around 1926. The portrait was taken on the occasion of Curtis's visit home after eight years in California. *Front row*: Elijah and Sarah Bradley. *Back row, left to right*: Orville Grammer, Albert Grammer, Leora Bradley, Edith Bradley Rendleman, Ellis Grammer, and Curtis Grammer.

2 First Memories of Home

My mother, as I said, wasn't happy living back at her mother's with four small boys and my dad needed someone very bad. So they were married, March 19, 1894, and moved to this small house on the Pete Zimmerman place where Dad was living. While they were there Ellis had typhoid fever. Ellis was sick for six or eight months with typhoid fever. He was eight years old. His head became soft and that was when his ear became shriveled up. Old Dutch Doc came and stayed for days. No telling what it was really.

I don't know if Leora was born there or not. But they had bought a place on top of a high hill in front of the Mose Lyerla farm for three hundred dollars and we moved there shortly after he and Mom were married because I was born there. You go through where the CCC or Boys Camp used to be and go back on top of the highest hill and that's where I was born, August 2, 1898. It was a three-room house. It belonged to the Jake Lyerla place in later years; Jake's son, Lester Lyerla, lived there a long time; he added two more rooms to the house.[1]

Lester Lyerla and his wife, Edith (Edith was my dad's niece, the daughter of his sister Florence), raised their family up there. But he tended corn ground down under the hill on his dad's place. They lived there until Jake died and the boys sold the farm. We didn't know until then, when they had to clear the title, there were two Henry Lyerlas. My great- and great-great-grandfathers. That is the second piece of land they bought when they came here from North Carolina. The Jake Lyerla place was where my mother was raised.

In later years, after we moved out, Grandpa

Ballance and his second wife lived in the same house I was born in, and he died there when we were living on the Jestes place.[2] Nobody liked his wife because she was a snooty somebody and wouldn't let him have anything to do with his family. She would hold a parasol between them and the house when they were driving by in the buggy. One time he was sick with the dysentery and she made a pallet on the floor and put him on it. Aunt Minnie heard about it and went up there and gave her so many minutes to get him on the bed. She got most of Grandma Ballance's pretty quilts. My grandma Ballance sat and pieced quilts as she was sick a long time. She died of a heart attack one Sunday morning. Just fell over in her chair, in 1897.

When we lived up on the hill, the big boys would have to take the cows down under the hill to graze every day. They tied a rope around their horns and sometimes the cows would run away with them and drag them a long ways, especially the one Albert took that was named Bute. They teased him for years about him crying and hollering, "Bute."

They grew a lot of strawberries and such up there on top of the hill. Leora, they said, was out in the strawberry patch before breakfast. One morning Uncle Allen Morgan went out where he was and grabbed him by the top of the head. Leora started crying and hollering, "Oh, Uncle Allen, you've hurt my soft spot." Of course, you know every new born baby has a soft spot on top of their head and as you grow it closes up. Uncle Allen would tell that and die laughing as he said, "His (curse word) head was so hard you couldn't have hurt him with a hammer."

Uncle Allen and Aunt Minnie lived back of our house, up on the hill, and Uncle Richard and Aunt Mag Penrod lived out the ridge from us. Uncle Richard was a pretty rough customer. He never liked hard work, drank a lot, *cussed* like a sailor, and sued Grandma Ballance for his part of the pension money she drew on him, as his father died from the Civil War. He finally moved to Missouri and he talked my dad into going down there to look things over to see if he wanted to move down there. We went in a covered wagon and camped at night. The boys walked along behind the wagon to make it easy on the horses. We crossed the river at the Cape [Girardeau] on a ferry. Mom cooked a lot of food up before we left home and Curt ate some of the chicken and dumplings that had started to spoil and it gave him a diarrhea. For two or three days he was awful sick. It didn't take Dad long to see he didn't want any part of Missouri, as Uncle Richard always lived in a swamp. So we came back to the Jestes place. I can't see why he didn't go by himself and not drag us along. Some things puzzle me.

Then Dad sold the farm and moved to the Jestes place in 1902.[3] Mom just thought we were ruined, as we owned a home. She never wanted to move any time we ever moved. We had to wait to get possession of the Jestes place, so we moved in a little house at the top of the hill where you turn off to go to Beech Grove. Right at the top of the first hill, across the road in front of Rallo Cemetery, stood a two-room small log house. We were living there when I was a baby, sitting alone on the floor, as Mother told another anecdote. They were raising the house (they called it house raising when the house was about to fall down and they lifted it up to put a new foundation under it) and I was sitting alone on the floor on a pallet, when Leora ran in the house and hollered at me, saying, "Hun Jay Ba, are you afraid the house is going to fall down on you?" That is where I got the nickname of Jade. The boys would say to me, "Jade, stop looking cross-eyed. Shut your mouth," because I had a lazy eye and I guess I'd sit with my mouth open.

My first remembrance of life was living on the Jestes place. When we lived there we lived in a three-room log house. It consisted of one large living room and bedroom combined and a kitchen downstairs and one room upstairs over the living room. There were only two small windows, one on each side of the house. We had two beds in the living room and three upstairs, one in each corner. The stairs were in the fourth corner. The six boys slept upstairs and Mom and Dad and me downstairs. In the summertime we had what was called mosquito bars over the beds. There were high posts at each corner with a solid piece of material—a canopy—at the top. Mosquito netting hung down all around the bed and

there was an opening on the side to crawl in bed. Often in summer it was hot and someway the mosquitoes got inside the bed also. Every night Dad would smoke out the mosquitoes late in the evening by taking an old iron pot and putting rags in it, setting it afire enough to make a smoke, and setting it in the center of the floor. That would run them out for a while. Many times we all got up and took our quilts and went to the hay loft in the barn that was at the foot of the hill and slept on the clover hay, as the mosquitoes were supposed to not like clover hay. But that didn't keep them all away, as many times we battled them all night. I asked Albert just before Christmas this year [1974] if we didn't have screen doors then, and he said we had screen doors but no screens on the windows. Albert said, "Boy, the mosquitoes were really thick." But I don't believe we had screen doors. Very few people did.

When we lived there there was a cistern out from the kitchen door on the right. We used water out of it to drink, cook, wash, etc. There was also a well in the backyard, down the hill, under the apple trees. We drew water out of the well by the bucket for the stock. Near it Mom had a milk trough eight feet long by twelve inches wide and twelve inches deep, sunk in the ground. It had a lid on hinges. She kept her milk and butter and anything else she didn't want to spoil in this trough. Somebody had to draw fresh water from this well and change the water three times a day. It had a plug called a bung hole in the corner to let the water out. In 1982 those same locust trees were standing in the front yard and the well was still there. They had bunches of white flowers on them that we called "boy breeches." Each petal looked like a pair of breeches. At the foot of the hill there was a big pear tree loaded with big yellow pears. People I knew didn't have toilets or privies. The women went to the chicken house and behind it and the men used the barn.

We were very poor, according to our living standard today, but we were better off than most of our neighbors, as we had two teams. A team of horses—mares—Daisy (we called her "Dais") and Fan. Fan was a big black mare and Dais was a wiry high-strung gray. Dais threw a fit when other horses would pass her. She was also balky. She would take spells she did not want to pull a load and she would not budge, no matter what you did. We also had a team of mules, Jack and Cook. Jack was a big black mule, very slow, and Cook was small and fast. Cook would try to run away but he couldn't get Jack to run. We had two or three cows and plenty of chickens. Very few people had horses, cows, (maybe a few chickens), or much to eat, only what they raised. Nobody else but Uncle Johnny Lyerla had horses and cows.

One time while we lived on the Jestes place Dad tried to borrow ten dollars at the Jonesboro Bank. Dave Karraker was cashier and stockholder and he wouldn't let Dad have it. George Lyerla was standing there and heard

Dad ask for it and he said: "Lige, I'll let you have it." I don't know if George was sheriff then or not, but he was at one time. He was living at State Forest then, up Picnic Hollow,[4] and knew what a hard worker Dad was. I suppose he wanted the money for medicine or groceries. I went to Norris and Son Funeral Home in 1975 and got burial figures for my family that Dad had buried. I later went back to see if the bills had been marked paid and they had. I was sure they had, as there was one thing Dad tried to instill in our head was honesty. He would always say, "If you can pay your bills you can go back and get credit again."

We always had plenty to eat except meat. Very few people had any kind of meat except hog jowls and fat salt pork, once in a while. Mom would buy hog jowls and soak the salt out of them in water, roll them in flour and fry them. They were good.

We didn't always have flour but we always had cornbread. When we ran out of flour we would have cornbread and gravy for breakfast. They used to go to Jonesboro twice a year in the wagon [see plate 7]. They would take three to five two-bushel sacks of corn laid across the back end and Mom and Dad sat in the spring seat across the front for him to drive. Once in a great while they would let Leora and me go along. We sat on the sacks of corn. They took the corn to the Little Red Mill, which stood at the junction of the street to the courthouse and what is now Route 146 [then, Market Street and Willard's Ferry

Plate 7. The public square in Jonesboro, where farmers traded produce with one another, around 1900. *Courtesy of the Union County Farmsteads Project Papers, Thelma Degamore Collection, Special Collections/Morris Library, Southern Illinois University at Carbondale.*

Road]. Mom would take butter and eggs and sell them to Charles Chase's store in Jonesboro and Alden's in Anna.

She would buy cheese and bologna by the piece and we'd get a big pickle, five or six inches long, out of the barrel and we'd split it. We would go in the back room at Charlie Chase's and eat our lunch. Then Leora would have to stop two or three times on the road home to get a drink and Dad would *cuss* every time he wanted to stop. His first stop was at Gum Spring, just this side of Jonesboro one-half mile. The spring is still there; a double-wide trailer sits close to it. Then we stopped at the branches we crossed. We started at near daybreak and never got home till after dark.

If I didn't get to go to town with them, Mom would bring me a small bucket (a pint) with a lid and some dog taller wax. It was really just sweetened paraffin in long sticks, one cent per stick. Also maybe some horehound candy or licorice. Boy, was that a treat. We went through what is now state forest. Dug Hill hadn't been cut down at that time and we always dreaded that hill as old Dais was balky and you never knew just when she would decide to balk on that hill, or anyplace else. She didn't like to pull a heavy load.

One night Dad was coming home through there and she balked on him. He beat her and beat her till he gave up and he unhitched her from the wagon. He took her out in the woods and tied her up and brought old Fan and came on home. He wouldn't tell Mom where she was and Mom made Ellis, Albert, and maybe Curt go hunt her up with the lantern and bring her home. They went back after the wagon next morning.

When we drove her and Fan to church at Beech Grove and started home after night and lots of boys rode horses and would go running past her, she wanted to run too. She would rare up and back up and cut up to run and almost turn the hack over. Many times Mom and I would jump out of the hack, afraid she was going to turn us over. And old Fan would just stand there. She would do the same thing when we drove her to Jonesboro and a train would catch us between the two railroad crossings. That was before they put the highway in; between where Shawnee Motel and Tripp School are now, the road was on the other side of the railroad. Sometimes Dad would jump out and hold her by the bits till the train passed. Dais lived a long time and I rode her lots of times. I was grown when Dad traded her off. She was one I drove to the buggy also.

You have to wonder how we existed when you look at the small fields on that place. This Jestes place, or farm, is hardly large enough to call a farm now. It was once owned by Mother's people, the Penrods, as her uncle Hugh Penrod came back here from Missouri or Arkansas and tried to see if they couldn't claim it, as they thought somebody cheated them out of it. But for some reason he didn't bring suit against anyone. Hugh was Mother's father's youngest brother [see plate 8]. If you think we lived *crude* on the Jestes place, you should hear about them. We lived on the Rixleben place when they visited us. Mom and Dad visited them once and Mom came back and said they really lived rough. Mom said Aunt Lou had a half-gallon bucket she used to stir up the cornbread and she never washed the bucket out. She would hang it up on a nail from the rafters (as the house had no loft in it), with no lid, and use it next time. They had a grown son named Harris and a daughter named Annie when they came to visit us. Annie had a powder puff made from moleskin. They were really soft but I never tried one. Really, you skinned the mole and dried his hide.

At the Jestes place the well and milk trough

Plate 8. Sarah Bradley's uncle, Hugh "Cornbread" Penrod, lived in the Mississippi delta in southern Missouri or Arkansas. Hugh is seated on the far right. This photo of the Penrod family was taken around 1913.

were shaded by apple trees. They were small dark red apples with blackish blotches on them, the inside was sour and had a green cast. That is where Dad got apples he made cider out of. He put it in big fifty-gallon barrels. We kids used pumpkin leaf stems to drink the cider through the bung hole. After four or five days it would start to sour and finally turn into vinegar and it would make you drunk if you drank very much in that stage. John Reed was a friend of Albert's and he lived at the foot of Dug Hill. He stayed at our house a lot and he and Albert would argue all day over anything. One Sunday he drank too much fermented cider and got down under the locust trees, drunk and sick. He wallowed all over the yard and said, "I've eat apples all my life and they never did hurt me before."

Old Granny Neal was there and she went to the door and said, "God drat you, if you don't get up from there I'm going to bring a bucket of water out of there and throw on you." But he didn't get up until late that evening.

Granny Neal was the mother of Uncle Richard's wife, Maggie. Granny and James Neal lived with her daughter Ida and Sam Latta on the goat farm at the foot of Dug Hill. On the left there was a road running back in there to the goat farm. Dr. Dodd from Anna owned the farm but the project didn't turn out as it went broke. He had a large herd of goats at one time.[5]

Frank and Eva (Lyerla) Kinder lived across the creek on the Parmley place.[6] They had eight or nine kids. They used to come over to our house to play with Orville and Leora. They would build a rail fence out of stove wood and put each other in the pens, like they were hogs. They fed you apples for corn. And they played ante-over a lot. When you play ante-over you throw a ball over the house, and someone on the other side would try to catch it. When you throw it over you call out, "Ante-over." That would go on all afternoon. We made our own balls by taking an old heavy sock, we called a sawmill sock, that was worn out. You'd cut off the heel, then ravel out the yarn and wind it around and around to make a round ball. If we had a small rubber ball we'd put it in the middle. When you got the ball the size you wanted, you took a darning needle and twine and sewed it all over to hold it good.

Uncle Johnny and Aunt Vina [Malvina] Lyerla lived where the state forest is now, in a nice two-story house.[7] Uncle Johnny drove a pair of very small mules, a white and a black, to a wagon. He was a small man with long whiskers. Seems like most all the old men had whiskers. Aunt Vina was a pretty high-strung, bossy character. She would get mad at him and sit in the back end with her feet hanging down out the back. The boys would say, "Well, they have had another fight." Seems like she was always with him in the wagon.

Ezra "Cars Durham (Derm)" and Doll Knupp lived on the road just above Uncle Johnny Lyerla. George and Minnie Lewis lived on the Laster farm. He and another man were cutting a tree and it fell on George and killed him.

Uncle Johnny and Aunt Vina's son George lived a short ways up Picnic Hollow, on the left of the road. Farther up the hollow you turned right and went straight up the hill to the top and there was where Tom Gettings lived in an old log house. They had four girls. Two belonged to Mrs. Gettings. Ed and Mae Skinner lived close to George Lyerla's.

Old Uncle Andy Lyerla (a brother to Uncle Johnny) lived up CCC or Boys Camp Hollow. He had a red plum orchard. We also had lots of plum trees. This old Aunt Nancy Giles that lived with us later was their half sister [see appendix B].

In those days the creek hadn't been dredged yet and *every time* it came a big rain the creek would cover all the fields with mud, and Dad and the boys would pull off their shoes and roll up their pant legs and go in there with a big long corn knife and cut the blades loose so the corn could straighten up and make corn. We had what they called a cutting box in the barn and they would run that green corn and sometimes weeds and hay through that to chop it up and mix it with ship stuff and bran for the horses. One would turn the handle while the other fed it hay. Albert has part of two fingers off because he got them in the cutting box.

There was a barn sitting in the flat next to the house. I thought it was a big barn. It had two stalls, a corn crib, a harness room, and a hay loft. It had a wide hall in it where the cutting box stood. The ground on the right just before you get to the house was the cow pasture. That was something, to have a pasture for the cows, because when we lived on the hill where I was born, the boys used to have to take them out grazing.

One time when the pasture was low Dad sent Orville and Leora to cut willows for the cows in the pasture in front of the house and a tree fell on one of the cows and knocked a horn off, but Orville and Leora denied knowing anything about it, till in later years they owned up to it. In those days and many years later they whipped you for nothing.

To get to school we kids went straight up the hill behind the house, on top of the ridge, until we were even with Rhodes School and then we went down the hill to the schoolhouse.

It was real steep, too. All the kids that came from across the creek had to cross the creek on a log. Years later, after I was grown, there was a swinging footbridge across the creek so the kids could get to school. It had chicken wire along the sides so the kids wouldn't fall off. I only went one year to Rhodes School and Charley Goddard was teacher. We didn't have toilets. We girls went away from the school on one side of the path to the briar patch and bushes, and the boys went on the other side above the road to another patch of bushes. Harvey Plott was teacher there when Albert was five years old. He saw Albert had a brilliant mind, as he had him spelling "grass-hopper," "Mississippi," and other big words at five years old. That was when Mr. Plott first knew my mother and dad. He boarded with my mother.

Rhodes School stood directly across the creek from Tommy Rhodes's house, against the foot of the Pine Hills. It was three and a half feet above the ground in the rear, sitting on big white rocks. In the middle it was about two and a half feet and in the front it was sitting on two rocks. Can you imagine, little old Rhodes School turning out two lawyers, Albert Grammer and Will Lyerla; two ministers, Levi and Will Lyerla; and a doctor, Dr. A. J. Lyerla.

There was a spring between the schoolhouse and Aunt Minnie's house. Two boys would go morning and evening (that is, at noon) and get a bucket of water. There would be three or four tin cups to drink from.

Some of the teachers at Rhodes were Harvey Plott, Albert Anderson in 1890, Bessie Postlewait, Seva Arnold, Charley Goddard, George Blevins, a man named St. John, Ida Wallace Choate, and my brother Albert Ballance. After Hunsaker School was washed away by the creek, they combined the two districts and built Beech Grove School. One of my classmates, Mollie Frogge, married Earnest Rhodes and they made the old Rhodes School into a dwelling.

Uncle Johnny Lyerla's kids went to school there also. But they got Uncle Johnny (their father) to move into Jonesboro for the winter so they could go to high school when they finished at Rhodes. They would move back to the farm in the summer. Will Lyerla went on to become a lawyer and also a Baptist preacher, and Andrew Jackson (Dr. A. J.) went on to become a doctor. He paid for his education by teaching school, as Uncle Johnny could not afford to send him. He married Dr. Doty's widow here at Wolf Lake and doctored here for a spell, then moved to Jonesboro. He later built a little brick office between Jonesboro Bank and Norris and Son Funeral Home on the Jonesboro square. After the boys and girls finished school there, Uncle Johnny moved back on the little farm, now the state forest. That is where I remember them.

One more incident. A bumblebee stung me on the head at Rhodes School and it made me so sick I couldn't climb the hill to go home. Ellis carried me up the hill.

Mom was down in bed sick one whole year when we lived there. Ellis took over the cooking and keeping house. He did the washing and raising chickens. Old Dutch Doc doctored Mom a long time and then Dad got a Dr. Goodman from Cobden to doctor her for a long time. He drove two little bay ponies to a buggy. Two neighbor women, Mary Lyerla (George's wife)[8] and Mrs. Tom Gettings (Susan), came every morning and changed mustard plasters on her chest and back until it blistered and sometimes changed her bed and gave her a bath. Mom never forgot their kindness. I used to hang around her bed when she had something good to eat. Sometimes Dad would buy her steak to see if she could eat something. She would give me a bite, now and then. I was only four or five years old. She was awful bad sometimes. She had a bad cough and they thought she had TB. Dad said many days when he went to work he thought they would come after him to tell him she was dead. It took her two or three years to get well. She always said a medicine she ordered out of a newspaper from Yonkerman's cured her. At the end of a year she began coughing up mouthfuls of yellow stuff and began to improve. All this time she was taking a cough remedy she made by the quart bottle. She took a pint of whiskey and a half a pound of rock candy (which looked like rock salt) and a pint of glycerin and put that in a quart bottle and shook it all up, and she took that for years.

It is certain she didn't have TB. The doctors said it was change of life. But now with many diseases diagnosed I wonder if it could have been tularemia—rabbit fever—as Ade Holder, Dad's sister's husband, had something identical. They drained pus from his lung and he lived and got OK, only his formed outside the lung, where they could drain it.

I had pneumonia when we lived there, when I was six years old. Old Dutch Doc came to see me. He gave me a great big doll to get me to take my medicine. I kept it even after I was married, until it just crumbled away.

I will tell about old Dutch Doc here. He was a country doctor that rode a nice black horse and just went from house to house. When anyone got sick you would walk or ride a horse, if you had a horse to ride (many people didn't have a horse), and start out inquiring if anyone had seen or heard of Dutch Doc. Sometimes it took two or three days to find him. He got that name because he spoke with a German accent, very Dutchy. His horse's name was Dickey. When he came to your house he would tell ever who took his horse to give Dickey plenty of oats and corn. He was black and slick as a ribbon. When he came to your house to see the sick, he would stay until you were much better or died. He stayed at Grandma Ballance's a lot. He was married three times. They were at Grandma's house when one of his wives named Delia died suddenly. She was buried at Beech Grove. After she was buried a while, the doctors at Cobden and Alto Pass accused him of poisoning her. They had her taken up and her stomach was examined but they found no poison. They were jealous of him and his practice.

But the people could not afford to pay him and Old Dutch was paid very little. He was up in years as I remember him. He had gray hair. I went to the courthouse and found his first marriage certificate, dated 1886. He married an eighteen-year-old girl from Grand Tower. He was sixty years old. His full name was Fredrich Van Bueghn Galin. Her name was Fannie Frances Boston. His papers said he was from Greece. But Albert said because of a political uprising in Germany they fled to Greece. When he had a sick patient he just walked the floor. I can still see him shaking down a fever thermometer as he walked.

Della Angell, Uncle Charles Smith's daughter, told me every time Dutch Doc came by there he would stop and play the organ for hours. He gave Cora Verble Myers music lessons here in Wolf Lake when she was a girl. After we moved to the Rich place we lost contact with him. At one time he had an office in Wolf Lake, in Grandma Keith's house that was once Dr. Doty and Dr. Lyerla's office. The building sat between the Boys Club and Charley Miller's house. It was the first lot sold (to Dr. Doty) when Wolf Lake was platted out in 1898. Curt, my brother, said, when he came back here in 1959 to live with me, that someone on Hutchins Creek told him Dutch Doc lived in a little shack near Alto Pass on Milligan Hill and lived like a pauper, nearly starving and freezing, after he got too old to doctor. Milligan Hill was the road coming down the creek from Alto Pass. My friend Hester Bridgeman's family, Mort Hunsaker,

Uncle Calvin Smith, Uncle Charlie Smith and Little Zach Lyerla all lived on that road. I'm surprised that Dad and Mom didn't go see about him. We were living on the Rixleben place when he died.

There were lots of incidents that happened when we lived there. One was we were all down in the horse lot one morning and a mad dog came along. Jim Shirley had stopped in a wagon to talk. Dad ran to the house and got the gun and they took off in the wagon and overtook the dog and killed it. Jim was just whipping those mules to make them run to catch that dog. We were all on top of the gate when the mad dog passed. You could tell a mad dog by the way he trotted along, never noticing anybody unless he ran into them and slobbering at the mouth. They said they had a fit when they came to water. It was not unusual for one to come along.

Also, Patch Eye's (Oscar Davis's) mother had just died and left Patch and a brother (Hammer) Arlie and an older sister who was retarded or, as some people said, silly. Patch Eye was called that because he got his eye hurt and had to wear a patch over it. They came to our house a lot, and sometimes Patch would have a hole in the seat of his breeches. The boys would have to run him down to get his breeches so Mom could patch them. He was only four or five years old. They got sent to the orphans' home.

Old Jim Davis took his kids out of the orphanage so he could collect so much money for keeping them, then he kicked them out and drew the money and spent it on himself, and the kids had to make their own way. He only kept them six months and then broke up housekeeping and they had to root for themselves. Patch would live a few months here and a few months there. People took him when they had some hard work to do and as soon as that was done, they would kick him out. One time Patch, when he was ten to eleven years old, was taken in by a family five miles east of Anna. They were so mean to him he slipped out in the night. He was carrying in stove wood and he dropped a piece and the old woman hit him with it. He decided to leave that night and walked to Aldridge, where Arlie was. Took him that night and all next day. His brother Arlie and the people he was staying with had body lice. That is why I think so much of him, he had such a hard time as a boy. Mom and Dad didn't like the way old Jim treated his kids, but they didn't run him off when he stayed with them.

The boys used to walk to Jonesboro, to the county fair or band concert. Also they walked to Beech Grove Church and Sunday school. Sometimes there would be several of them, some had girls and some didn't. Ellis had a temper like a wasp. One night, walking home in a crowd from Beech Grove, Gene Miller made a smart remark about Curt and Dora. Ellis jumped on him and almost bit his ear off before they could pull Ellis off. I don't think they ever spoke again.

Curt had worked out and bought him a new buggy before he was married that cost thirty-five dollars. He would let Orville and Leora drive it to Wolf Lake after groceries sometimes. I remember them driving old Jack (a big mule) and you could get these paper fans you would open up and they would have the harness all decorated with them. You probably got a fan and a stick of dog taller wax or a piece of candy for one cent, yes, one penny.

I can remember wishing I would have a chill so I could get a bottle of soda pop. Sometimes when it rained Dad and the boys would drive the wagon over to Running Lake to fish. Once I came with them and took a chill about noon. They made me a bed in the bottom of the wagon and they had to take me home. And I got a bottle of orange soda on the way home.

Man, those chills used to be very common. Curt was always having chills. These bottoms were full of mosquitoes, snakes, and bullfrogs. And malaria was very common. That's why Mom hated to leave the hill so bad. But you had chills on the Jestes place. There was three-day chills, every-other-day chills, . . . and it was hard to break them. There was Grove's Chill tonic and Mendenhall's Chill tonic. They were made of quinine. Oh! how I hated that chill tonic. You could take it and think you had them broken, and in three weeks you would have them again. Curt had them so much Mom took him to a faith doctor in Anna. His name was Williams and his office was on that street in front of the fair ground

gate, near Davie School. A little old, red brick building. Mom really believed in faith doctors. She said she saw the doctor cure a lot of sick people.

Another thing that happened along about then was that Dad's sisters and brother, Aunt Maud, Aunt Florence, and Uncle George, all came to live with us when their mother died in 1902. Aunt Maud went to school when she stayed with us, and as soon as she was old enough she hired out. Aunt Florence began hiring out, too. Maud was hired out in Alto Pass and was courting John Weiss, whom she later married. One day Maud and John were going to visit Aunt Martha Lyerla. She lived back in there by Jake Lyerla's, across Hutchins Creek. Uncle John had hired a livery stable rig, two small bay ponies to a buggy, and they were going in there to Aunt Martha's. It had come one of those big rains and the creek always overflowed. They thought they could cross it and it washed them—horses, buggy, and all—downstream a long ways, but they stood up in the seat and stayed put. They swam downstream a long ways until they finally found an opening in the trees and bushes that the horses could finally get through. That was right in front of where Loren Rhodes lives now. They still ford the creek there today, the same place that they've crossed for a hundred years. That has been the drawback of that farm. You can't get out or in if it comes a big rain. There was a crossing going in by Leora Smith's and down the side of the creek and you could ford the creek there, but you also had to cross the old Mill Race.

The Miller Pond used to be a pond the year round. All that land in around there was under water until it was drained. Today it's in cultivation. My brothers used to collect seed pods there that we called "yonkee pins." I thought they grew on bushes three or four feet tall, but I learned from my son Lee Roy that they grow on things like water lilies.[9] We used to knock the nuts out of those pods and eat the meat inside of them, all but the little green thing in the middle that was supposed to be poison, so we picked it out. Miller Pond was a playground for the community. The boys skated there in the winter and duck hunted. Also, as I said before, Felix was shot there duck hunting. Patch Eye Davis's oldest brother, Johnny, was killed on Miller Pond. He fell on the ice while skating and hit his head and died from it. There was a red clubhouse back down the hill from the road, owned by families who lived in Cobden.[10]

Miller Pond was supposed to be haunted. You couldn't get Dutch Doc to go by there after dark, as he was riding by there one night and he said a woman dressed in white got on the horse behind him and rode until he reached the other side and she got off. Grandma Rinehart used to drive a big black horse to the buggy and come from Jonesboro and stay a week with Mrs. Rendleman. She usually took one of the kids home with her. She said the snakes were so bad at Miller Pond, many times she would take her whip and lead the horse by the bits and run the snakes out of the road with her buggy whip to keep old Paul from getting snake bit.

This is not a ghost story, now, I'm telling. People were mean then just as they are today. This man lived on this side of the branch, on the DuBois place. His wife told this story after he died. She was afraid to tell it when he was alive, for fear he would kill her. He was known as a mean person. One time a peddler came by late, after dark, with a pack on his back, and asked to stay all night. It wasn't unusual for a peddler to come by with trinkets, table clothes, dresser scarfs, etc. He let him stay and after supper he asked the peddler if he wanted to go down to the dry house with him. The dry house sat down in the field or woods, down toward Mule Hollow, and was where they dried fruits, lumber, or anything else. He had an open fireplace in one end of the shack. The peddler went and they were gone so long the wife knew he was up to something. So she decided to slip down there and see what they were doing. She peeped under the door and her husband was cutting the peddler up in small pieces and throwing him into the fire. It scared her so bad she could hardly get back to the house. She ran back to the house and pretended she had been out. I talked to this man's great-granddaughter about it and she said she bet it was true because he was a mean, mean man. I know his name but don't want to use it.[11]

There was another man in later years disappeared where my son Bud lives now. He was driving a team of nice black horses to a nice wagon. He came by there late and asked to stay all night. He disappeared and was never heard of again. People were sure he was murdered, as the man kept the horses and wagon he was driving. When Uncle Adam Ballance lived there they were always looking for bones when they dug up a place. One time they found some and took them somewhere to see if they were human bones. They turned out to be dog bones.

It wasn't unusual for someone to come by late and ask to stay all night and Dad always let them stay. One time on the Rixleben place, a man with a team of horses to a wagon and a woman and child asked to stay all night and he let them stay. I was always afraid of them.

3 Spice Cake and Fried Squirrel

We moved to the Uncle Carroll Rich place, December 1905, and lived there until January 1909. Harry O. Myers now owns it, but it was a different house than is there now. The house at the Carroll Rich place that we lived in had been a nice house. It was a two-story house, three rooms downstairs, living room, bedroom, and kitchen, with three bedrooms upstairs. That was some space, after moving out of a three-room house. There was a rock well at the back door. It had a pump over it and some way to hang milk and butter in it. The house on the Bill Rich place was built the same way.[1] Mom had washtubs full of moss roses in the front yard and she planted some four-o'clocks. You can see part of the house in the family group picture made soon after we moved there. I am holding my "Dutch Doc" doll and old Aunt Nancy Giles is in the picture [see plate 9]. That far down in the bottoms was really low and wet then. But it was much bigger and better than the Jestes place.

My brother Curt and Dora Myers had gotten married the year before. Curt went to a school of telegraphy in Vienna, Illinois, and was never home again to stay. Dora said her dad sent him to school at Vienna but Curt told me he borrowed the money—one hundred dollars—from Bob Rendleman. Bob Rendleman helped many people and lost money by doing it. I am quite sure my Dad borrowed money—one hundred dollars—from him. In 1907 Curt and Dora were living with her parents when they had their first child, Lella. She was born on my mother's birthday. Later, when they were living in the old Wolf Lake schoolhouse, Dora would go out to her father's place to stay a week and she would take me along to take care of Lella while she sewed.

51

Plate 9. The Bradley family and Aunt Nancy Giles, 1905. *Back row, left to right*: Orville, Ellis, Albert, Edith (with the doll Old Dutch Doc gave her), Dora Myers, Curt, and Leora. *Front row, left to right*: Nancy Giles, Elijah, and Sarah Bradley.

Their third child, Kerma, was born in the old schoolhouse in 1910. Curt was working somewhere on the MoPac Railroad. He worked at nearly all the small towns along the railroad between here and Murphysboro. So did Leora and Dallas Ballance.

When we moved to the Rich farm, Ellis and Albert were still going to school. We all started to the old grade school below Wolf Lake after Christmas, in January 1906. That's the building where Fannie and Dick Davie lived later. Frank Ellis was the teacher our first half-year there, beginning January 1906. Then Ed Angell taught the next year. He was a rough one. He whipped Leora for drawing the picture of a dog, and he made me and Bill[2] stand against the wall with our noses in a circle fifteen minutes because he caught us whispering across the seat. Bill and I used to walk up the railroad from school together. The next teacher was Francis Dillow in 1907–8. He was the last teacher in the old schoolhouse. Will Jones lived in the house I own now and Francis boarded with them. I came home with Zora Jones, who was in my class at school, that winter. They built the new two-room school up in Wolf Lake and the Maxwell sisters taught in it. Leora and I went to school there until January 9, 1909, when we moved to the Rixleben place.

In 1905 to 1907–8 there were five of us in school at one time, as you can see by the picture of old Wolf Lake School in 1907 [see plate 10]. After Ellis and Albert took the teacher's examination in 1907, Albert taught

at Hunsaker, north of Beech Grove. The creek washed the school away later. Ellis taught Sublette in 1908 and 1909 and rode a bicycle to Sublette from the Rich place, until we moved to the Rixleben place, January 14, 1909. None of the roads were even graveled then. The sand was so deep, sometimes he would have to get off and walk, pushing the bike. Albert walked to Hunsaker till winter came. He would go across Mary Lyerla Hill, as Hunsaker was a few miles north of Beech Grove. He boarded with the Calvin Smith family in the winter.

Ellis got thirty-five dollars a month at Sublette. School lasted only six months. For years it was six months, then seven months, and finally, nine months. Albert taught Mountain Glen School the next year. The boys there had been running the teachers off but they tried Al and he took on the parents and all and came out on top. He boarded with the Crit and Lizzie Rendleman family. She had two sons and a daughter and she used to take a buggy whip and go after them at night if they didn't come in when she told them to.

It was common in those days for the big boys to run the teacher off. They ran two teachers off at Beech Grove until Lawrence Sitter stood up to them. At Big Barn, they tried to run off the teacher, John Northern, but he knocked one of them in the head with an iron poker and that ended it.

Ellis and Albert both went on to Valparaiso, Indiana, to college the next year. Later Leora and Dallas went there, too. Somehow Ellis got

Plate 10. Wolf Lake School class picture, 1907. Edith was nine years old. *First row, left to right*: Raymond Brothers, Ted Jones, August Brown, Bill Smith, Virgil Smith, unidentified boy. *Second row, left to right*: Blanch Fox, Lula Fox, Mabel Brothers, Willie Owens, Harry Walker, Charley Landers, Ida Randles, Marie Miller, Minnie Vancil (holding slate), Clarence Vancil, Oscar Duty, Earl Tweedy, Jack Farmer, Rolla Smith, Bob Smith. *Between second and third row, left to right*: Ethel Stone, Mary Smith, Mattie Randles, Howard Rendleman, Minnie Williams. *Third row, left to right*: Myrtle Brothers, Ben Vancil, Jessie Randles, Zora Jones, Ruth Brown, Edith Bradley, Edna Rendleman, Archie McMahan, Chas. Jones, Virgil Stone. *Fourth row, left to right*: Wm. Rendleman, Harvey Owens, Edith Newbold, Mary Rogers, Mae Roberson, Leora Bradley, John Vancil, Chas. Jones, Warren Chandler. *Back row, left to right*: Cliff Robertson, Fannie Davie, Maud Smith, Orville Grammer, Albert Grammer, Bill Landers, Ellis Grammer. *Center rear*: the teacher, Francis Dillow.

a job as railway clerk in East St. Louis and worked there until he died, November 14, 1954. Albert taught school in Kankakee. He also taught law in Chicago while studying to become a lawyer. They put themselves through school. Dad could have helped Albert some but he didn't. He didn't help any one of his kids, except me and Leora.

Dad gave each a horse if he would stay home until he was twenty-one years old. Only Curt and Ellis stayed. Curt's mare was the color of a palomino and named Fload. While they were out at Dora's folks, some of the boys rode their horses to church and would race going home. He was out at the Myerses' one time shortly after he was married and some of the boys rode their horses to church, and going home Fload ran away with Curt and ran into a telephone pole, almost killing both of them. Ellis's mare was a dappled gray and was named Patsy. She got something wrong with a hind leg. I think they called it hamstrung. Dad sold her to Uncle Richard for a little of nothing and he took her to Missouri behind a wagon. I used to ride her to Wolf Lake sometimes. I cried when Uncle Richard took her away.

I don't know of any other family that was strict about their kids going to school. Even Uncle Adam and Aunt Ett let their kids miss a lot of school, just because they didn't want to go. There was no law then to force people to send their children to school. Not until much later did we have such a law. The illiterate did not care if their kids went to school

or not and some that weren't illiterate didn't care. But I thank God every day for giving me such a wise father. He did not get any schooling in a schoolhouse, but he was far smarter than the average man.

Orville was the only one of us that didn't care about school. He and John Reed left home once and went west to get a job. They ran out of money and had to turn to hoboing. They slept by a chunk fire one night and he got the back of his coat afire and burned a big hole in the back. They rode a freight train as a bum and asked for a handout, just like a bum. In those days and much later there were lots of hoboes. Mom and Dad never turned anyone away without giving him something to eat. Also, he would let them come in and sleep in the house if they asked to stay all night. Many times a stranger you never saw would come in and stay all night. There was no such a thing as robbery and murder in those days. I'm sure there was lots of it in cities, but the biggest town I knew of was Anna.

One day when we were living there Leora and I got scared at a Negro junk buyer. All but Curt was home then, and all Leora had to do was flunkey jobs. He had to keep them in fresh water to drink in the field. They were working in the field up toward Mule Hollow. (Mule Hollow was supposed to be haunted. A headless mule was supposed to come out of there at night.) They sent Leora to the house about nine o'clock to get water. There was a side porch on the kitchen and a pump outside on a platform. I was there watching him fill his jugs and a one-horse wagon drove up in front and it was a white man with the Negro junk buyer. Seems like there was a white man with him. But when he hollered, "Have you got any junk?" Leora hollered, "Mom! Mom!" three or four times and she didn't answer and Leora said, "Jade, let's go." We went through the fence and up that steep hill behind the house. We ran and we ran along the ridge. We came across a place where a log had burned and he said, "Jade, he's after us, here is his tracks," and we started running again. We ran from nine till noon. The hill we were running on curved around and took us back to the main road. If it hadn't, we would have been lost. We came out on that hilltop, this side of Mule Hollow. He made me keep my head down while he peeped over the top and it just happened the boys were going into dinner in the wagon. We ran down hollering for them to stop and we told them where we had been. Did they ever laugh. Mom had been looking every place for us, as Leora's water jug was sitting there just off the porch. He was the leader and I followed him. We laughed about that as long as he lived.

Another time I got scared was the fall before we moved to the Rixleben place, when I was ten years old. They were having an Odd Fellow and Rebekah's supper at the Lodge hall over Al Wilson's store. Mom and Dad and most everybody belonged to the Rebekahs and the Odd Fellows. Ida and Sam Latta lived where Jimmy and Wilma Schaefer lived so

long, now owned by the powder plant. Mrs. Latta didn't like kids. She was what you called stuck up, and she told Mom there were not supposed to be any kids there. Dad and the boys were batching[3] over on the Rixleben place in the old twin corncribs waiting to take possession of it, and they would be there. Mom waited till I went to bed and slipped off and went with Mrs. Latta to the supper. The Wright boys, who were batching with their father until they could take possession of the Rich place, slept in the upstairs. You would know I would wake up about nine o'clock and called Mom and she wasn't there. I cried and cried and finally I went upstairs and woke the Wright boys. We hunted everywhere for her, the chicken house, everywhere. We were still up when Mom came home. She was really mad at Mrs. Latta, as everybody had their kids there. Hardly anybody liked Mrs. Latta, as she was so stuck up and haughty.

Leora and I grew up with Uncle Adam's kids. Uncle Adam moved to the Jestes place when we left it. They had lived on the Tommy Rhodes place, near where Ray Rhodes' house stands now. Leora and I used to walk to their house on Saturday and stay all night. Mom would tell me to take my good dress off and put on one of Grace's. I wanted to put on Grace's good dress, but Aunt Ett wouldn't let me.

One time when we went, their old hound dog Sarah Jane had died and they dragged her up the field and threw her in a ditch, really a deep ravine. We all got up and went up the hill to the hollow to see old Sarah Jane. It was raining and Uncle Adam came after us with a switch. He whipped each of his kids as they came out of that ditch. I was scared he was going to whip me too but he didn't. He always had a bunch of old hounds around. Mostly fox hounds, as he liked to fox hunt.

Owl Hollow was at the left road, behind the house, and Mary Lyerla Hill was up the hollow, on the right. Mom always called her old Aunt Mary Lyerla. Nearly all elderly people were called Aunt and Uncle in those days. But now as I study the Lyerla history, I find Mary's husband Caleb was a brother to Henry Jr., who was Grandmother Ritta's father, so Mary was my grandmother's aunt [see appendix F]. I always wondered how come anyone to live on that hill, but since I've worked the Lyerla history out, that hill was just across the creek from where Henry and Zach Lyerla settled when they came from North Carolina. Caleb died young and left her with children to raise. Aunt Mary Lyerla had a big yellow cherry tree in her yard that Mom said, when she was a girl, they picked the big yellow cherries by the bucketful from it. People for miles around picked bucketsful of cherries off that tree. The yellow cherry tree that used to be in my yard was a seedling from that tree. Laten Baltzell brought these trees to Dad. He lived up there until they sold it to Shawnee National Forest.

Aunt Mary's daughter Julia Ann married Theodore Baltzell. That's why they owned that land joining Aunt Mary L's place. She in-herited it from Old Aunt Mary.[4] They cleared the land on top of that hill enough to farm and make a living and raise a family. Mr. Rendleman bought forty acres joining Theo Baltzell's and my husband Wm. J. cut two hay barn patterns off it.[5] Since then, my son Lee Roy has cut timber off it, too. Theo Baltzell was living on the Rich place when Dad rented it, and he lived on the Rixleben place when Dad rented it. Dad didn't rent him out, he had to move anyway, because they wouldn't rent it to him again. His son Laten stayed up on the hill when he was grown.

Sena Cruse was a daughter to Old Aunt Mary Lyerla also. She married Henry Cruse and had five children, Jesse, Bruno, Rufus, and Earnest, and Ethel. Henry Cruse had four boys and a girl when he married Aunt Sena. They were Bill, George, Chub, one whose name I don't know (Charles?), and Ella. Ella killed herself when they lived in the house we later lived in, the Rixleben place. She was fourteen years old. She shot herself in Mother's bedroom and fell backwards on the bed. She shot herself in the afternoon and died that night. There was a hole in the wall in the corner of the bedroom, up over Mom's bed, where the bullet went through the wall. She killed herself because her dad would not let her court/go with Bill Abernathy.[6]

There was an old log house that stood in the mouth of the hollow on the right as you went up that hollow to Old Aunt Mary Lyerla Hill. They always said it had been a school-house. We kept corn in it for the cows. It looked like a schoolhouse, but I never heard of a school near Wolf Lake, except the one that Fannie Davie made into a home.[7] Old Bennie Moore lived up on Mary Lyerla Hill when we lived on the Rich place.

Old Jim Davis lived on Mary Lyerla Hill for a short time after he took his children, Patch Eye, Arlie, and Inez out of the orphans home. Old Jim just lived off his friends. There were two or three old men that just came and stayed a week or two. Old Doc Campbell sold Saymans products. He was also a moocher, but Mom and Dad never said a word about them coming and staying. Poor Mom. She cooked for more moochers.

To the left of the big hill back of the house, where Leora and I ran from the Negro, was Owl Hollow. Bell Smith lived there with her children Hervy, Jimmy, Bertha, Nora, and Mary. They were all nearly grown. One night Leora and Bruno Cruse went up there to try to get a date and they were afraid to go up close to the house. So they hid behind a bush in the yard. The dogs barked and Mrs. Smith came to the door. They could not see who it was, and they hollered and asked her if they could take her to church. She answered back and said she didn't think so and they tore out of there, running like crazy. She laughed about that for years.

Bell Smith's brother, Tilford King, lived with them. He was nearly blind but he would ride his horse to Wolf Lake. He had to open a gate behind our house and sometimes he would miss the gate and run into the fence.

But if you ever tried to tell him where the gate was, he would snap back with, "I guess I can see."

A twelve-year-old girl by the name of Clara Nichols and her father also lived up there in a tent. She would come and get milk, butter, and eggs at our house every week. She later married Bill Allen and had several children. Bennie Moore's family carried milk, etc., from our house too. Old Benny was a blowhorn but was pretty smart also. But he was no provider for his family. Come to think of it, I don't know how they did live. Their children were Rosalia, who married Jess Thomas, Izora, Leona, who married Fred Pittman, Estee, and Alonzo was the youngest. He joined the Navy, as his parents died, and he had a high-ranking position. Mom gave milk to everybody that would come after it. I'll bet a tank car would not hold the milk my mother gave to people that didn't have anything.

Mary Hubbs, who married Jess Rogers, and her father, Fudge, and her cousin Maud, lived in a little house on the ditch bank, just a little north of where the bridge used to cross the ditch to go up to Sam Latta's.

There used to be two or three houses along the road up on the hillside, between our house and Silica Hollow. George Conaway lived in one and Martin Stone lived in the other. The Stones were so poor it was pitiful. They had six or seven other girls; namely, Nell, who married a Conaway boy, Nora, who married Levi Lyerla (Levi was Uncle Moses's son and became a minister), Eva, who married Roy

Miller, Girt, who married Oscar Chandler, Bert, who married Thof Hale, and Effie, who married Al Reed first and then John Winn. The Stones raised Ethel Stone, my friend and schoolmate. She was Nell's baby by Neri Lyerla.[8] Ethel was raised by Nell's mother, Addie Stone, and was not told until she was grown that Neri and Nell were her parents.

Mom always said Neri broke Uncle Mose as Mose had to mortgage his farm for a thousand dollars to get his son out of trouble. They said Neri told his wife to pay his father off as he died young with typhoid fever. But he only had $2,500 in insurance and that debt would have taken about all of it, so she didn't and Uncle Mose lost his farm. His brother Zachariah bought the farm and let Uncle Mose live there as long as he lived.

The silica mill was up Smith Hollow at one time. The Smith boys' mother, Susan Smith, lived a little ways up the hollow. She believed in witches. When things went wrong (like the butter wouldn't gather in a ball in the churn) she would boil a half-dollar in the teakettle and that drove the spirits away. Her husband was Wiley Smith and her sons were Andrew, Ike, Silas, and Walt. Mom and I went into her house once and it was so dark and scary we didn't stay long. I was scared half to death. I held on to Mom's dress and walked just as close as I could to her.

The silica mill was running full-time when we lived there. Ellis worked there some. A young good looking fellow from Chicago, Bill Myer, operated it. Every man that worked in the mine very long died from lung disease, including him. Bill Myer married Maud Smith. Her parents, David and Clara Smith, ran a general store in Wolf Lake. Charles Spring later bought them out. Dave Smith had two other daughters—Grace, who married Earnest Newbolds of Alto Pass when she was fifteen, and Mae, who late in years married Harry Keith, also of Alto Pass. Mae and Maud were just about the *snootiest, snobbiest* two people you ever saw. Grace was always common and friendly.

We kept an old lady named Nancy Giles because she didn't have a home.[9] Aunt Nancy, everybody called her. We had her shortly after we moved to the Rich place. She is in our family group at the Rich place. She had a son but he never cared anything about her and never gave her a dime. She had other relatives in the area but she didn't visit anybody the years she stayed with us. Mom bought her clothes. She was nearly blind and all she could do was wash dishes. Sometimes she didn't wash them clean and I would put them back and it would make her so mad she just got all over me. I had to dry them and I got so I would put them back just to hear her rave. I used to go to the toilet and stay when it was time to wash the dishes but it didn't do any good, as Mom would call me when she got some washed.

One time when she stayed with us a spectacle peddler came by and she was trying on different ones. I handed her a pair without any lens in them and she said, "Oh yes! I can see better with these," and everybody began to laugh and she got so mad at me she could have killed me.

Aunt Nancy and I used to have to churn. It was a big three-gallon, tall stone jar with a lid that had a hole in the center for the churn dasher to go through. The dasher was a wooden handle with a cross on the end of it. You just put your cream in the jar and pulled the dasher up and down till it turned to butter. I loved sour cream with cornbread but Mom wouldn't let you have a bit of it. All I got was the whey after she poured the cream off and what little cream that stuck to the whey. We would churn two and three pounds of butter at a time. In the summer, one would churn and the other fan flies with a peach tree limb. The flies were terrible.

After I married they only had one cow, as Dad did the milking, and then she got a one-gallon glass churn. After I married I had a gallon churn, too. Then the cream separator, where the cream was so thick all you had to do was stir it until you got butter.

When we moved to the Rich place and also later at the Rixleben place, there were no cellars to keep the milk cool. There was a well on the Rich place and an old cistern on the Rixleben place. Both places Mom had half a dozen buckets, with a rope to let them down to the water. Morning and evening she hung the milk down and brought it up in the morning and skimmed the cream off. She kept the cream down there until she got enough to churn. Anything that she didn't want to spoil overnight she hung in that old cistern. In 1915, when we lived on the Rixleben place, Dad had a cellar dug under the smokehouse and Mom kept her milk, butter, eggs, cream, and leftovers down there. She was so proud of the old cellar. I'll bet we made a dozen trips to that cellar a day. At wheat thrashing time I'll bet we made fifty trips a day. My name and Kyle Short's name are written on the wall of the steps. That's the day they finished it. Kyle Short was a drifter that came by looking for work and Dad hired him for a few weeks.

When we lived on the Rich place I tasted my first store-bought light bread. We traded at Dave Smith's store in Wolf Lake and he used to get it by the boxful. It was a slat box with rope handles. The box was three and a half feet long by two and a half feet wide, two and a half feet deep, and held thirty or forty loaves of bread. The bread came five loaves baked together and you just pulled off as many as you wanted. It was five cents, yes, five cents a loaf. The bread was not wrapped. Mom would buy five loaves each weekend and we would eat it for breakfast and for Sunday. She always saved everything for breakfast. When we had fried squirrel or chicken it was always Sunday morning breakfast. She always made spice cakes, stacked with apple sauce flavored with banana flavoring. I ate so many of them then that I don't like spice cakes yet today.

Mom baked light bread but we were never allowed to touch it until next day, as she always said you ate too much when it was warm. But when I married into the Rendleman family [see appendix G], Mrs. Rendleman always cut a loaf as soon as it was out of the oven and we had lots of butter and she always made enough jelly in the fall to last till the next fall. Jelly was on their table three times a day. She also made quarts and quarts of apple butter outside in the copper kettle. Mom made apple butter and jelly but it wasn't on the table all the time. But by this time we had more different kinds of food on the table than the Rendlemans did. They never bought canned goods like Mom did. Mom was really a good worker and manager. She bought all of the groceries and what few clothes we had with butter and eggs and chickens. How she always managed for each one of the boys to have a suit of clothes I'll never know, but she did. You can see them in that picture of all of us.

There was a man named Jim Minton that used to peddle beef, when we lived on the Rich place. He was from Alto Pass and he had two little bay ponies to a topless buggy with a long tail in the back. I think they call them sally wagons. And about once a month he'd come by with beef and my mother always bought some. Sometimes it was steak and sometimes boiling beef and then she would make soup with whatever kind of vegetables she had—potatoes, onions, tomatoes, corn. The onions were the most important because

it would give it a little flavor. If we were out of crackers she would make rivels. To make rivels you take two or three handfuls of flour and break a raw egg into it. Then you work big handfuls of flour into the egg and work so much in that you can't make a solid ball. You work flour in it until it becomes a little bigger around than a pea but twice as long. Then you sift the flour out of the rivels, drop them in the soup, and cook them in the boiling soup. I made them as long as I kept house.

Mom, and I later, made cottage cheese. She'd let the milk clabber in a big pan, then heat it a little bit and put it in cheesecloth and hang it on the line for that whey to drip out of it. I learned from Mrs. Rendleman to heat it up more and drain it in a colander. You'd have that with sweet cream and apples fried with sugar until they'd just scorched a little.

For dinner we nearly always ate beans— Great Northern or navy—cooked with some bacon drippings, and potatoes and slaw or, if we had it, wilted lettuce or green beans cooked two or three hours with some bacon drippings or ham hock. To make the dressing for the refrigerator slaw, you boil together about one-half cup each of water, sugar, and vinegar, for one or two minutes. After it's cool, you pour it over cabbage that you've sliced with a slaw-cutter, with about one teaspoon salt, and mix it up. It will keep about a week in the refrigerator in a Tupperware bowl. I made a cooked dressing, too, which I like better, but it doesn't keep as well. To make it, you beat two eggs until the yolk and white are mixed together. Then you add one-half cup half-and-half or sour cream and one-third cup vinegar to the eggs and mix them together. You melt two or three teaspoons of bacon drippings, butter, or margarine in a skillet and cook the egg mixture in the fat over low heat until it thickens. You mix the cut cabbage with two or three tablespoons sugar and three-fourths teaspoon salt, and when the egg mixture is cool, you pour it over the cabbage and stir it up. If it's not sour enough, you can add some wine vinegar, and if it's not sweet enough, you can add some sugar. This is good on lettuce, too. You can add shredded or diced carrots to the cabbage, also.

Mom made Spanish beans by cooking one and a half cups of chopped onions in one-third cup tomato juice and two or three teaspoons bacon drippings until they were tender and clear. Then she added one can of drained, chopped tomatoes to the onion mixture and simmered them together for ten or fifteen minutes, then added one can of drained red beans and simmered them together for ten or fifteen minutes, seasoned with three-fourths teaspoon of salt. Mom used red pepper to make them hot, but I just used black pepper.

We liked soda crackers and toasted bread baked with canned tomatoes, sugar, and butter; and macaroni and canned tomatoes cooked together. Mom would bake sweet corn she cut off the cob with sugar, salt, pepper, and butter. She would cut off the kernels, then go back and scrape off the part that's right close to the cob, for thickening. We ate a lot of potatoes, too. Sometimes I would mash them—they're a lot better beaten with the electric mixer than with the masher. Sometimes I would boil them with bacon grease and salt, or break them up after they were boiled and pour bacon grease over them, or add milk and flour for thickening to the broken-up potatoes and cook that mixture on top of the stove.

Mom and Dad were never lazy. Mom and Dad always took the lead. Dad always got up and built a fire before Mom got up. I had to help get breakfast but Mom was always up first. Then, you had a wood or coal stove and after we started burning coal, you banked the fire at night with a big hunk. But the fire died down at night and it was the same as if there weren't any fire and things froze tight all over the house. The water in the kitchen froze over. There was no heat in the house except the living room and kitchen and at night there was none in them. We were lucky enough to have feather beds, and you had to have two big heavy comforters and a blanket and two quilts to sleep under.

My Dad was a good provider. He always cut a pile of wood for the kitchen stove to last the whole year. The way they cut the stove wood was they would cut a huge pile of willow saplings (young trees), three and four inches in diameter, and haul them in. Then you would borrow a saw that you could run with the back wheel of a Model T Ford. They would take all day and cut a pile of wood as big as a small straw stack. Then they split the big ones with the ax and you had stove wood the year around.

He would help my mother with her work. If he came in from the field and the bucket was empty he would go get a bucket of water. And he would go out and hoe the garden of an evening.

Uncle Adam never cut a stick of stove wood in his life. His daughters Sadie and Grace used to have to cut their own wood out of anything they could find to cook a meal, while Uncle Adam sat in the house on his can. And Aunt Ett laid in bed while Grace and Sadie got up and got breakfast, did all the dishwashing, did the wash, and did all the work. They also had to pick spinach and beans for Cyrus Kimmel to buy their shoes and clothes. Uncle Adam was really tight. He never bought anything in the house or anyplace else, or clothes, either. He never gave Aunt Ett a penny for anything. Aunt Ett used lard can lids for bread pans.

None of the men, even my dad, ever gave their wives any money. But Mom always raised chickens and sold some and also sold butter and eggs to buy our clothes and groceries. Dad used to pocket all the money from the farm. A woman never knew what it was to have any. When you would tell him to buy some comfortable chairs, he would say, "Hell, I can sit on a nail keg." I know my mother would have liked to have had some nice furniture, but she never got a piece. And he had the finest farm machinery and the finest mules that money could buy, but he never bought one stick of anything for the house. Most of what we had was what Mom started with. We had a table with three leaves that was round when you took the leaves out, that must have been in Mom's family. Mom bought a little old cheap kitchen cabinet. Until she bought that cabinet we had the flour in a barrel in a corner of the kitchen, with the dough board on top of it and a wooden bowl inside to make bread. She didn't make light bread at that time, except when Dad and the boys were batching over at the Rixleben place, before we moved there. She made biscuits for breakfast and cornbread the other two meals. After we moved to the Rixleben place we had a nice Victrola and lots of records. I guess she bought it, too.

Dad bought a spring wagon while we lived at the Jestes place. We called it a hack. It was light, more like a buggy, only it had a bed about nine inches deep and two seats that you could unlatch and remove. Boy, we thought that was something and it really was, as we had been riding in a lumber wagon up till then. I really feel like Dad bought that to haul dead people as much as for us to ride in. He was called on all around the country. You removed the two seats and set the wooden box in the bed with the casket and corpse inside, and Dad sat up front on the end of the box and drove. Never charged a penny. He used the lumber wagon for that until we got the hack.

People died at home in those days. If there were no one there when a person died, they would send for some of the neighbors to lay them out. They would get some boards and put a folded quilt and sheet on it and stretch them out on it. They would close your eyes and put a piece of money on them to hold them shut until you got cold. They also crossed your arms. Someone would go after the casket in the wagon or hack. They would have some man to shave them if it was a man. They wrung cloths out in soda water and kept changing them all night on your face. Next morning they would have someone, perhaps the one that laid you out, to dress you. Sometimes some women would have to make you a shroud that night. Then they put you in the casket (a cloth-covered box). And they had to bury you that day as soon as possible. The neighbors would go and dig the grave as soon as possible. They were still doing that, digging graves, long after I was married.

I can't remember when they started embalming, especially in the country. When I was about fourteen, Pete Kimmel lost his only son because he would not let them take him to Cairo and operate on him for appendicitis, and they weren't embalming then. I hate to say how awful it was. It flowed out of his mouth and all over the floor and they couldn't stop it. It was so bad they couldn't open the casket at the cemetery as was the custom. But that's how silly people were about being operated on. I don't believe my mother would have given up to be operated on and she said for years she did not want to be embalmed, but in later years she knew it had to be done

and quit saying anything about it. She did not want to be taken out of the home after she died. But it was impossible to embalm in the home when she died, February 14, 1948.

We still were riding in the spring wagon for years after we moved to the Rixleben place. The Rendlemans were driving a surrey with "the fringe on top." I can remember seeing them pass, riding in that surrey when we lived on the Rich place. I suppose they were going to the Rendleman reunion, as that's the only time, except the fair, Mr. R. ever went with them. Bill would be driving. They were supposed to be rich and high above common people, all except Mr. Rendleman—he was always common and drank.

We must have really made some money, as we took a trip once to visit Uncle Jim Rogers, who had married Dad's sister Lou, and Mom's brother, Uncle Richard, and Aunt Mag in Grays Ridge, Missouri. We went on the train at Wolf Lake. Grays Ridge is just a short ways below the Cape, but I thought it was a thousand miles. To ride on a train was something. I remember the coat and tam I wore. The coat was big enough for a twelve-year-old, as you could barely see my fingers sticking out. Mom always bought everything too big so you wouldn't outgrow it. Uncle Richard had his neighbor to meet us at the train and it was a log wagon with just the bunks on it. We sat on the bunks and the mud and water were so deep your feet almost touched it. It was nothing but swamps all the way, but Uncle Richard would never live in any other kind of place. And we had to cross a small river to get to their house. There was no stock law in Missouri at that time and all the hogs and cattle ran out. You had a mark to identify them by.

Dad rented the Rixleben place in the summer of 1908 but he couldn't get possession until January 1909. George Wright rented the Rich place when we moved from there. Before we moved they batched in an old building that they called a shop, out near the road, except to sleep. The boys slept in our upstairs and their father went home to sleep. They moved seed wheat into this shop. I would often go out there when they were cooking supper. One day I climbed on these sacks of wheat and I began to itch. I beat it to the house and I was broken out all over with big red welts and they were itching something terrible. Mom bathed me in soda water and after a while they went away. The wheat had been treated with Dog Push (hartshorn) for weevil. I sure didn't get on the wheat sacks anymore.

That fall Dad and the boys batched on the Rixleben place in a slat double corncrib that stood at the corner of the road, back of the barn. They did their own cooking, on what I don't know. Mom baked light bread twice a week and cooked food that would keep without ice, as we hadn't heard of ice boxes at that time. Then in the middle of the week they would come home for food or she would have one of the boys drive Curt's top buggy to take it to them, as one of them stayed home to take care of things. Ellis and Albert were teaching school and staying at home and they would take them their food after school and on Saturday. Sometimes I went with them and I remember it was nearly all woods from Wolf Lake to the Rixleben place, except along the Bob Rendleman farm.

4 Bringing in the Harvest

We moved to the Bruno Rixleben farm January 14, 1909 [see plate 11]. It was once called Turner Brown Ford. They said Turner Brown was a Negro but it was just a tale, I guess.[1]

Plenty of the land between Wolf Lake and the Rixleben farm hadn't been cleared. All the Rixleben land on the east side of Running Lake hadn't been cleared at that time and lots of the farm I owned later [1949–89] wasn't cleared. Dad had that all cleared after we moved on it. There were always some old men that would clear for two and a half dollars an acre. I remember two old men batched in an old log house just across from the cow barn. They would cut all the small underbrush with an ax and in August they chopped a ring around a tree and it would die. It would take as long as five years for trees to die and fall down. Every spring they had to pick up the dead limbs and trees, and the first year they would plant it in corn with a one-horse double shovel. In later years they would chop the trees down and Dad would blow the stumps out with dynamite. Then they piled them and burned them.

It was mostly gum trees and along the cut there would ooze out a sticky mass we called gum wax. That was a sticky, and I mean sticky, sap that hung in drips around the edge of the cut on the trees. We kids would take a knife and pick this off and chew it. It was so sticky it would coat your teeth for days, but finally it would get where it wasn't sticky. It burned your mouth, also.

After the two old men quit living in the old log house, my Dad and Uncle Adam used it for an icehouse. Running Lake, above the barn, froze over eight and ten inches thick. All of Dad's crew and all of Uncle Adam's sawed the ice in big blocks and hauled it to

Plate 11. Sarah and Elijah Bradley at the house on the Rixleben place on Running Lake, around 1909. A year or two later Elijah built a porch across the front of the house.

this old log house. They put a thick layer of sawdust underneath it, between it, and all over it, and two feet thick around the sides. They filled that old house full to the top with ice and we had ice all summer to make ice cream, etc. Mom never made much ice cream, but Uncle Adam's family made lots of it. They did it for two or three years, around 1910 to '12.

When we lived on the Rixleben place Dad, Bob Rendleman, and Will Jones were the biggest farmers in the bottoms. When Dad lived on the Jestes Place he had one-horse walk-

Plate 12. Elijah Bradley (*far left*) with a work crew, harrowing a field after wheat harvest. A tall variety of white corn is growing in the field behind them.

ing plows and a single double-shovel. Then on the Rich place he bought two horse walking plows, and then on the Rixleben place he bought sulkies (riding plows) that had two plows behind, and later three, and cultivators. (Now, with tractors they pull five big ones.) Dad had to buy more mules, also. At one time he had fifteen.

After plowing they harrowed the land.[2] It took three horses or mules to pull the harrow, and they had to walk behind the harrows [see plate 12].

They raised more wheat than corn. Wheat is hard on the land, so they had to raise clover for fertilizer. Therefore, part of the land was laid out in clover. They also used to plant pumpkins in the cornfield. They mixed the seed in with the corn in a two-row planter. When Dad started out he used a one-row corn planter. We were using a two-row planter yet

Plate 13. Making hay on the Rixleben place. Elijah Bradley is standing on the ground. A man known as "Handsome Harry" is on the left; Jim and Bob Hubbs are on the wagon on the right.

when they—Dad and W. J.—both died in 1948. Now, they have twenty-four-row planters. After the corn was higher than your head, he used a one-horse corn planter to go between the corn rows and plant stock peas in the cornfields where my mom did not plant cornfield beans that we ate.

After the corn was gathered they hauled in the pumpkins for cow and hog feed. There was always a big pile of pumpkins over at the cow barn. We had a big long knife we used to cut the pumpkins up for the cows. We brought in the pea vines and used them for hay. You had to save one-third of your crop to feed the livestock through the winter.

Grandpa Bruno Rixleben thought a lot of Dad. He bought Dad a Duroc Jersey gilt and boar and gave them to him. They were a red hog and they were registered. We had them two or three years and they got the cholera. It wiped out nearly all the hogs he had, including the Duroc sow Grandpa Rixleben had given him. Man, that cholera used to be a dread. You would have a bunch almost ready for market and the cholera would wipe them all out but two or three. The first year I was married, when we lived on the river in the old house, we had a bunch ready to sell in the spring, including a sow and pigs Dad gave me before I was married. We lost the whole bunch but two or three. That was a hard blow, as we were poor as Jobe's turkey anyway and I was pregnant with Bud. It wasn't an easy life in those days for anybody. They had no vaccination against cholera in those days, and as sure as we had an overflow, we had a siege of the cholera to follow.

They didn't used to have these fancy hog houses, chicken houses, and cattle barns. Most of the animals had no barns to go to, no matter how cold it got. Most all the big farmers had a straw stack. This was made when they thrashed wheat, as the thrasher blew the straw out in a big pile. The cows ate straw all around the stack and made a shed to stand under. The hogs buried themselves under the straw and sometimes they had their baby pigs in under there. Sometimes the other hogs would pile in on them and kill several of them. In summertimes the sows would steal off in the pasture and have their babies. When they fed the hogs morning and night they would fill up as much corn as they wanted in a sack

and call them by saying, "Pig, *oh-ee*, pig, *oh-ee*, pig, *pig*."

They cut wheat with horse-drawn binders and shocked wheat by hand. They first had a small binder pulled by two horses and then they made the binder larger, pulled by three and four horses or mules. Dad always had two binders and each binder had two to four men following to shock the wheat. They had to cap the shocks to keep the rain from going down in it. It would take two to three weeks to get the wheat cut, according to how much it rained. They always had a water boy. He had a buggy or sled and kept them in fresh water.

We always caught a lot of young rabbits when they finished a land. We kids would always be there and the men would help us run the rabbits down. I have seen Dad jump off the binder and help us catch them. We had lots of fried rabbit during wheat harvest.

In the winter we used to ship chickens, rabbits, and furs to R. D. Haber in St. Louis. He wrote and asked Dad if he could visit us for a few days. Dad had us to write back to him and tell him that he could. He came and stayed almost a week with us. I'll bet he thought it was crude and he was glad to get back to the city. But I bet he thought the food was excellent, because Mom always set a good table. The boys, three or four of them, would go rabbit hunting and kill a whole sack full of rabbits. They would gut them and hang them up to freeze and then fill a sackful of them and ship them. They always sold.

When we lived on the Rich place, my brother Leora didn't have to work much. There was a bounty on groundhogs and crows—twenty-five cents for a groundhog scalp and ten cents for a crow, and Leora made some money hunting them. By the time we moved to the Rixleben place, he had to work with the men.

Lots of people hunted and trapped through the winter for 'coons, 'possum, muskrat, and sometimes they would catch a mink. They skinned them and stretched their hide on a board and let them dry and before spring they would ship them. People, especially old men, used to dig ginseng and yellow pukoon and other roots. They washed it and dried it and sold it by the pound in Jonesboro and got good money for it.

Lots of people ate the 'coons. Aunt Ett used to bake them, but we didn't like them and Mom never cooked one. The boys and Dad used to hunt squirrels. She cooked them for breakfast. Mom always cooked lots to eat. I remember seeing this big glass stand full of cooked prunes, peaches, apples, or pears. She made cobblers out of the leftover biscuits. She never threw a biscuit away. She'd open a jar of blackberries and split those biscuits in two and let them soak up in the blackberry and called it cobbler, and we'd eat it with cream. She never threw anything away. At one time Dad set out several peach trees south of the house on the Rixleben place, so we had lots of peaches and gave everybody peaches.

When we moved to the Rixleben place in 1909, the river had no levee, and when it got high it covered all the low places and left the ridges. It usually came out in June. They would already have the wheat cut and shocked and they would have to haul it out of the low places and shock it on the ridges and then thrash it when the river went down and the fields dried out. When we first moved to the Rixleben place, Chris Reischauer and his son Louie had a thrashing rig and would come to the bottoms and thrash the wheat. (Louie's daughter Tootie later married my son Bud.) You would just wait your turn.

Bob Rendleman also owned a thrashing machine and thrashed around Wolf Lake. He also owned half interest in a sawmill with Ran Sides. Walt Sides ran the engine at the sawmill. Then, I believe, Will Jones and Dad had a thrashing machine. After we were married, my husband, Bill, bought out Mr. Jones. They thrashed on the river. We had an engineer by the name of Herman (Swifty) Hines. He dearly loved to stay with us and run that engine. He was with us just about all the years we had it [see plates 14 and 15].

The thrasher was an awful lot of work for men and women. Mom used to have the thrasher at their house as long as two weeks, if it rained a lot, and it always seemed to. She had almost as many women and kids as she did working men. There were four to six that followed the harvest and stayed with the thrasher at night. And Dad would hire maybe three or four men. You had to feed them and fix beds for them and they were there to cook

Plate 14. Thrashing wheat, probably on the
Rixleben farm in the early 1920s.

for. If it rained they were there all the time.
Some had homes and would go home when it
rained. The men we boarded were paid sev-
enty-five cents a day; if they had a family to
go home to they were paid a dollar a day.

Carrie Custer was one that did not have a
home. He had a guitar and he always played
and sang every night. One of his songs was
about the sinking of the Battleship Maine. She
was sunk in the Harbor of Havana, which
started the Spanish-American War with Spain.
Carrie was at least forty years old but that
didn't keep us from being struck on him. He
was ugly, had kinky hair, and terribly dark
complexioned. So you can guess what people
said. Fred Stroud, Carrie's half brother, also
followed the thrasher but he had a family at
Alto Pass. Red Pittman and Swifty Hines were
others. And often there would be complete
strangers that followed the thrasher.

When we girls got up fourteen and fifteen,
we would get struck on some of them but they
never knew it. Fred Stroud took us on the
merry-go-round at the Anna Fair once and
Mom saw us and she came up and crooked
her finger at us and said, "Hoochie-hoochie!"

Plate 15. Thrashing at Roy Belcher's, across the road from Sublette School, c. 1936. Elijah Bradley and Bill Rendleman owned and operated the thrashing rig. Except for using a truck to transport the grain to the mill, thrashing technology and labor had changed very little since the turn of the century.

(shame on us). It made us so mad. She always had a way of embarrassing you.

All the families that were on the thrasher's route would help each other out. There would be eight or ten families. The men would come with their wagons to haul the bundles in from the field, and the women would help out with the thrashing dinner. Town people al-

ways liked to come to a wheat thrashing or hog killing to get a good dinner. You would have twenty-five to thirty men for dinner and half that many women and kids. And I mean, we had most everything to eat both times.

We looked forward to wheat thrashing. Everybody helped each other and all borrowed each other's dishes, pots, and pans. They fixed

Plate 16. Sarah Bradley's wheat thrashing dinner, around 1915. All the women who were involved in the thrashing came to help with the dinner. *Standing, left to right*: Sarah Bradley holding unidentified baby, Tildy Shy, Leddy Lockley, Mrs. Jones, Etta Ballance, Alice Mull, Dora Grammer, Maude Weiss, and unidentified woman. Maud Weiss's three children are seated in the front.

the best of food. They killed five or six big hens early in the morning and made a lard can over half full of dumplings. Aunt Ett was the chief dumpling maker. Mom called them *slickers*. She made them with eggs, salt, and water. They never tore up but you had to cook them a long time. Mrs. Jones was the chief cake and pie maker. She and two or three of the women would bake pies all afternoon and cakes for the next day. They made all kinds of cream pies (they called them "ball faced"), raisin pie, and two-crust pies. Mom always made apple-mixed-with-pineapple pie, cream pie, and coconut pie. Mrs. Jones made a jam cake that was always a favorite, as well as coconut, chocolate, and all kinds of cakes. They would have chicken and dumplings. And maybe ham or sausage, sometimes beef, sometimes salmon cakes, hominy, corn fresh off the cob, Spanish beans, green beans, navy beans, potato salad, slaw, kraut and wieners, and fried ham or shoulder. One of Mom's specialties was sausage with tomatoes and onions over it and baked until brown. Sliced cucumbers and onion, sliced tomatoes, macaroni with tomatoes or cheese, cooked cabbage, prunes, fresh light bread, and anything you could think of. I don't understand now why they fixed such bountiful dinners. Everyone helped each other [see plate 16].

The Rendleman thrashing didn't cook that way. They just had four or five vegetables and potatoes and things, just an ordinary dinner like you would every day. They were on the Wolf Lake run and had their own thrashing machine.

When we first moved to the Rixleben place, the wheat thrashing table was set in the yard and three or four girls stood over the table with a limb from a peach tree and fanned the flies. Dad screened in the back porch shortly after we moved, to have a place for the thrashing table. But we also fanned flies after the screened porch was done, as the flies were thick even in the house. Sometimes someone held the screen door open while three or four of us with cloths fanning tried to get them out the door. But you never got them all out by any means. Bill's brother Howard said to me once about the flies, "Jade, why don't you open the door and let them go to the barn?"

I don't think we had anything to kill the flies until we moved to the Rixleben place. That was a bellow-type container full of yellow powder. You pulled the window blinds down and closed all doors. Then squeezed the powder high in the air and got out as quick as you could. After about thirty minutes you went back and swept up the flies and burned them or swept them out. But everybody had flies, so you didn't pay too much attention to it until somebody from town came in; then you were really embarrassed. Except I don't think Mom was ever embarrassed by anything in her life. But she never was afraid of work. No matter who came for dinner, she never became frustrated and put on extra food or a tablecloth. She kept newspapers on over the oilcloth and just took the top layer off when it got dirty. She never even changed aprons and sometimes they were pretty dirty. She never changed her ways for anybody. She never knew what an inferiority complex was.

We used to have hog killings just like wheat thrashings, only there would be three or four families helping each other, and it would be in the winter, generally in December. Every farmer, except the hired hands, raised his own hogs, some to sell and some to eat. Each family butchered four to six hogs each year. You borrowed two or three iron kettles so you would have enough scalding water to scald the hogs. A day or two before, you built a scaffold and a platform big enough to hold the hog and five or six men. At the end of this platform you sank a big fifty-gallon wooden barrel in the ground and had the open end of it level with this platform. You got up by four o'clock and built a fire under the kettles and were ready to start killing them by seven o'clock or before.

Then four or five men went to the hog barn and shot a hog right between the eyes. He would fall over and someone with a big butcher knife jumped over in the pen and stuck the knife into his throat so he would bleed. The blood would squirt out. As soon as the hog quit kicking, they would load it on a big wooden sled pulled by a horse. They took him to the platform with the scalding hot water already in the barrel and three or four of them would get ahold of his hind legs and push and pull him out of the hot water,

until the hair would slip off when scraped with a butcher knife. Then they would turn the other end and scald it. Then they dragged him out on the platform and all jumped in with their sharp butcher knives and scraped him. Sometimes they had to pour more boiling water on him to loosen the hair.

When he was scraped they had a big scaffold they hung him on [see plate 17]. The scaffold would be high enough so his head would not touch the ground after he was hung up by the hind legs and long enough to hold all the hogs. They had a round stick sharpened at both ends and they stuck this in one end, through a slit they had cut in his foot, and then they all held him up high enough to get this sharpened stick over the pole and through the other foot, about where it joined on his leg. This spread the hog's legs apart so one could get in front of him to gut him. They had a wash tub sitting under him to catch the entrails (guts and liver and lungs). They would leave them hang and drain a while, and then they would lay one down at a time and cut them up. There would be two women to take the fat off the entrails while the rest of the women were getting the dinner.

They usually got the hogs all cut up by noon. There were hams, shoulders, sides (to be cured for bacon), heads, ribs, backbone, and feet. They trimmed the fat off and cut it up for lard and saved the lean trimmings for sausage. The sausage mill was like a big food grinder. It was fastened to a board, five feet long by about six inches wide, and you had a man put that between two chairs. One man turned the grinder and the other fed the raw meat into it. Later, they often ran the sausage grinder from the wheel of a Model T Ford. They would have a big wash tub half or two-thirds full of ground meat. Then you would add salt, pepper, sage, and red pepper, and some man would wash his hands and roll up his sleeves and mix all that seasoning in. In later years, after Dad bought a lard press and a sausage stuffer, some of the women cleaned the entrails and stuffed them with sausage. The lard press had a place on the bottom you could attach the sausage stuffer. It was a pipe that was six inches long and one and one-half inches wide. You put these cleaned entrails on it and pressed the sausage into them.

They took the fat they trimmed from the hogs and cut it into small, one- to two-inch pieces and rendered that in the big iron kettles. It was like the lye soap—it would foam up and run over if your fire was too hot. So two people stood there and stirred and watched the fire, as they always had two or three kettles full. When the cracklings were brown they would strain this lard through a thin cloth into five-gallon lard cans. Sometimes you would have four or five cans full. Dad bought a lard press and it was borrowed by everybody. It was a two- or two-and-a-half-gallon bucket with a steel body. The inner bucket was full of holes and it had a heavy lid with a screw top. You put the cracklings in it and squeezed the lard out of them [see plate 18].

When the butchering was done you had a

Plate 17. Hogs hung up after being scraped and gutted. *Courtesy of the Union County Farmsteads Project Papers, the Onita Davis Collection, Special Collections/Morris Library, Southern Illinois University at Carbondale.*

Plate 18. Cutting lard after butchering hogs, around 1912. *Left, front to back*: Pete Hubbs, Paul Ellis Hubbs, Elijah Bradley. *Right, front to back*: Bob Hubbs, Jim Hubbs, and Herman Lockley. *Courtesy of the Union County Farmsteads Project Papers, the C. William Horrell Collection, Special Collections/Morris Library, Southern Illinois University at Carbondale.*

big dinner for all of them and generally gave each family a side of ribs, a piece of backbone, and a big mess of sausage to take home. Then you would give your friends some of each. Oh! how I hated to cut up lard and sausage and then clean up all that greasy mess. We haven't killed a hog since 1949 and only raised chickens twice since then.

After the hogs were cut up and laid on a bench in the smokehouse, they covered it with coarse salt. Sometimes the salt didn't seep into the ham bone and the blow flies would lay eggs on the spoiled meat. They would hatch into something like maggots, which were worms that covered all spoiled or rotten meats, but they weren't as big as maggots. They would get in next to the bone. You'd be so disappointed when you cut into a ham and there it was, full of those little worms, and you would have to throw the whole ham away. Later, they had a liquid salt they put into a pump gun and they would get the salt into the joint of the hams and shoulder. They also came out with smoke-flavored salt. You would let this meat lie on the bench six weeks to take the salt, then you washed the salt off in a kettle of hot water, covered it with Borax and black pepper to keep the green flies off it, and hung it up on the rafters to smoke it. They used an old tub to build a fire in but you didn't want a fire to blaze. You used hickory tree limbs, if you could get them, and you just wanted the fire to smoke. You had to see about it pretty often to keep it from blaz-

ing. Some people made sacks out of cheese-cloth and put the hams and shoulders in to keep the flies from getting to them. It was a big job. When you wanted meat to cook you just went to the smokehouse and got it.

The day after butchering you cleaned the hog heads and hog feet. You made head-cheese out of the lean part of the head. But we wouldn't eat either heads or feet. One year I worked two or three days and made head-cheese and cleaned those feet and pickled them by cooking and packing them in a stone jar and pouring weakened vinegar over them. We didn't like either one, so I gave them away to people that wanted them. Mom didn't make it because they never would eat it. We gave the heads and feet to the neighbors or Aunt Minnie. It was a job to clean those hog feet. The head had the big jowls on them that you could salt down or put part of them in the sausage. You also used this to make mincemeat for pies, by cooking it and adding apples, raisins, currants, cider, spices, vinegar, and sugar. You could also use a piece of the ten-derloin to make mincemeat. Mom always kept some of the ears and tails. She just loved the ears and fat tails boiled. I never ate one in my life. I never liked fat meat. I used to cut the fat off the edge of ham and stick it under the edge of my plate. I did the same way with the edge of piecrust. I never liked the crust.

Mom always put the long guts of sausage down in melted lard. She packed it in two-to three-gallon stone jars and then covered it with melted lard. It would keep all year in the cellar. She sure knew how to manage and she always set a bountiful table.

Before we got electricity in 1942 you had to can everything, meat, vegetables, and fruits. Mom began using glass canning jars and cold-packing them around 1915. After I married I always canned food in glass jars.

The hog killings went on for some time, even after we got electricity. First they got a frozen food locker in Cobden and we took fruits and vegetables and meat up there. You rented a box or drawer for fifteen dollars a year. They got one in Murphysboro first, but Cobden was the first in Union County. Then Anna, and then they put up a butchering place in Dongola. Soon, people begin buying their own freezers, and later, the Anna and Dongola plant was sold to individuals. People lost a lot of money they had invested in locker stock. You were paid a small portion of your bonds. Dad and Bill only had one hundred dollars each in it and some way you were forced to buy that. Dad was afraid of it, as the one in Murphysboro didn't pay off.[3]

When I was a kid, up till I was fourteen or fifteen, Mom used to raise cabbage and make kraut by the fifty-gallon barrel. She also had a barrel of pickles. She put the cucumbers down in brine—a strong salt water—and then she would take a big panful out and soak them in clear water and then put them in vinegar. If you wanted sweet pickles you added sugar to the vinegar. They soured in this salty brine, just like the sauerkraut.

She would cut a big washtub full of cabbage and we had to cut that on the kraut cutter. That was a board about twenty-four inches long by ten inches wide, with two steel cutting-blades in the center. They were sharp on one edge and one raised just above the other, so it would cut two slices each time you ran the cabbage over it. You put a layer of cabbage about six inches thick and a layer of salt. Then you had a mall you beat it down with until the juice came up over it. A mall was a wooden piece about a foot long. It was as big around on one end as a gallon bucket and this was about seven or eight inches long. You cut the rest of it down into a handle by shaving it with a drawer knife or a pocket knife. Until they came out with a sledge hammer, they used this wooden mall to drive fence posts, etc. When the barrel got as full as they wanted it, they put a clean white cloth on top, then boards on top of that, then a big rock on top of that, to hold it down in the brine. These two barrels sat just inside the door of the little smokehouse on the Rixleben place.

You made the cabbage all in one day, but you could keep putting the cucumbers in as you picked them, every other day. You had to clean the skim off of the kraut and pickles every two weeks. You had to take the big rock, boards, and white cloth off and wash it out in clean warm water. You cleaned the scum off and sometimes the kraut would get a little soft and you skimmed that off with your hands. After the kraut had soured you could can it in glass jars. Later on, we would just make it in a big twenty-gallon crock and later on can it. We also canned pickles in the Mason jars. Then later on we cut the cabbage and put it in the canning jars and added a teaspoon of salt and a teaspoon of sugar. Then some filled the jars with cold or hot water. You put the lids on but left them loose enough the juice could run out when it began to work (ferment) or sour. You had to watch it every few days and add more water to it, as sometimes the juice would be way down in the jar and if you didn't add more water, your kraut would turn brown and decay. After it quit working you tightened the lid down and it was ready to put with the other canned foods.

Mom also made hominy, but I never made it. First she went to the corncrib and got fifteen or twenty of the finest big ears of white corn she could find. She shelled that and early next morning she would put it on to boil in the big iron kettle with some water and Merry War lye to eat the outer shell off the corn. Dad made Mom a box about fifteen by eighteen inches, with hardware cloth in the bottom. The little black ends of the corn came off in the lye and she washed them under the pump until all the black grains were rinsed out.

She never used lye made from ashes. That is what they used before Merry War lye was made. The ash hopper, as it was called, was made from boards about four and a half feet high. You nailed them together at the bottom so they were shaped like a V. This was about five or six feet long and set in a sturdy frame in the ground. You emptied all your ashes in that bin, as everybody burned wood in both stoves and fireplaces then. Then you poured water over these ashes, or left it out in the rain, and it dripped into a trough and that was lye water that they used for making hominy, soap, and scrubbing floors. The water would be a deep yellow color after it dripped through the ashes. Dora Myers's family had an ash hopper. That's the only one I ever saw. I got my first set of silverware with Merry War Lye labels. It was good silverware.

Leora loved hominy and Mom's vinegar dumplings. After he left home Mom even shipped him hominy, seasoned the way he liked it with salt and bacon drippings, cooked down real low.

Mom always used the cracklings from rendering lard to make soap. She put them in a big iron wash kettle half or two-thirds full of water and Merry War lye and boiled it down until the lye ate all the cracklings up. You would have to stand there and stir continually to keep it from boiling over. They had a fire under the kettle from limbs and chunks and when the fire got hot you would have to jerk the fire out from under the kettle and maybe pour some cold water in to cool it down. If you got the fire too hot, the grease would boil over and catch fire and maybe the fat in the kettle would catch fire. Then you left it in the kettle until it was cold. It would be hard and you cut it in bars. There was a brown soft soap you left in the kettle. She would put this in a jar and use it when you boiled the clothes.

Plate 19. Elijah Bradley and Walt Sides building a tenant house on the Rixleben farm in 1910 or 1911.

I hated this old lye soap. I never got to use any other kind, except for toilet soap for our face and hands, as long as I was at home. My cousin Grace always had store bought soap to wash with.

Do you know how people made coffee in those days? They never threw out the coffee grounds until the pot got so full of grounds there was no room for coffee. You just added your coffee to the old grounds and boiled it for a time. Mom used to boil hers all the time we were getting breakfast. When I went to visit Lee Roy in New York in 1946, when he was in the Navy, I brought a big drip coffee pot back to Dad and Mom. But Mom didn't use the grounds once, as she thought you didn't get all the strength out of the coffee in one making.

The first few years we lived at the Rixleben place we always had one or two hired hands in the house. Hammer (Arlie) Davis, Patch's brother, and Windy Ballance, who was Uncle Lummie's illegitimate son by Nora Skinner, stayed with us for years. Hammer was a lot of fun. He kept you laughing all the time with his wisecracks.

After Dad got enough money he built two tenant houses so Mom wouldn't have to keep a man in the house to cook and wash for. Mr. Rixleben furnished the material and Dad did the work [see plate 19]. He always hired a carpenter of some kind. Herman Lockley and his wife lived in one of those houses and worked for us for years. After we married, Bill loved to have a hired man in the house to wait on him, but didn't care how much work he put on me. That is one thing I hated, to always have somebody around to cook, wash, and iron for. You never got to enjoy your own family alone. The more people Bill had around, the better he liked it.

5 Farm Chores and High Jinks

I got up when Mom did, as I had to help get breakfast. Dad would call her and then he called me. I made biscuits and set the table. Leora was always hard to get out of bed. Dad would call him and maybe he would get up on the side of the bed and put one sock on and go to sleep, sitting on the side of the bed, or even lie down and go back to sleep. But when he heard Dad open that stair door again he would hit the floor, saying, "I'm up, Pa." Leora never had to work as hard as the other boys because there were enough without him, and he kept them in water and ran errands.

We had to milk two and three cows night and morning before we went to school. We all had our share of milking. The older boys did this when we were little but as soon as each one got big enough to milk, the older one dropped out, as he had to go to the field. I had it a long time by myself. It was Leora's and my job to get in stove wood for the next day, and water, kindling, and coal. We had three water buckets to fill.

Every once in a while Leora would try to make me do his share of the work. One evening late he tried to make me cut up pumpkins for his cow and I wouldn't do it. He tried to make me eat pumpkin guts and smeared it all over my face. Of course, I went to the house bawling. Dad went out and cut a big switch and when he came to the house he gave Leora a hard whipping. Leora was fifteen years old. Man, Dad had no mercy with that big switch. That was the last whipping Leora ever got. He went upstairs and wrote a letter to Ellis, saying he was leaving home. Mom got mad at me for causing him to get a whipping and Leora was mad at me for a few days. Lots of kids left home in those days because they used to whip kids, and I mean whip, for little or nothing. In those days everybody beat their kids something awful. That's why I was so scared of Dad. He really whipped hard. I don't think Dad ever whipped any of the boys except Leora and Orville. He used to whip my uncle George, when he stayed with us. But all the boys said after they were grown they were glad he was strict on them.

When we lived on the Jestes place, he whipped Leora and Orville for not picking the down row. The down row was the row of corn the wagon straddled and mashed it down, practically to the ground. There was a man on each side that gathered two rows of corn and threw it in the wagon. Orville and Leora would get to wrestling and get way behind and they wouldn't keep up. And they'd get a licking for it.

One thing I remember on the Rixleben place was having to plant cornfield beans. In those days they always plowed corn three or four times and threw all the dirt up to it they could. When the corn was about ten to twelve inches high, after it was laid by, we would go in there with a hoe and plant these seed beans in the corn ridge close to the corn. You had to take a hoe and a pocketful of beans and go along and plant them by the corn, every three feet. Leora and I both hated this job. We would get to one end of the field and catch Mom at the other, and we would dig a hole and put a handful of beans so deep they could not come up. She never did catch us. She would have given us a *licking* of our life if she would have caught us. I'll bet she had

six or eight kinds of cornfield beans. There were creasebacks, cut-shorts, and many more. You would eat these green, like snap beans. There were the big white soup beans—Great Northern—she planted to shell out for winter cooking. They lasted all winter. In the fall, after they were dry, we would gather two or three bushel sacks and stomp them and shell as many as would shell out. Then we had to finish them by hand. I don't remember Mom ever canning any green beans. No wonder none of the boys wanted to be farmers.

We would have enough cornfield beans for all the neighbors. They grew to the top of the corn stalk and would make such vines they would break the corn down. The corn then grew ten and twelve feet tall and it was a white corn. That was before they had hybrid corn. They sure were good in the late fall, especially when they had a lot of hullies in them.[1] She raised cornfield beans as long as she could get somebody to plant them. I don't think I ever had any cornfield beans after I was married.

Another job Leora and I hated was pulling straw for the straw beds. In those days we had straw beds and no mattresses. Every year, soon after wheat thrashing, Mom would have us empty the straw beds and burn the straw and wash the ticks. Straw ticks were made like sewing two sheets together and leaving a two-foot slit in the middle to put the straw in. Once in a while people would get bedbugs. One way you could get rid of them was to boil the straw ticks and fill them with new straw. After wheat thrashing, the straw would pack down in the straw stack and you just had to pull it out by the handful. It took a whole afternoon to get enough clean straw pulled. We had feather beds on top of these straw beds but most people just slept on these straw beds.

We used to have to clean lamp globes. Mom would never let you wash a lamp globe. She said it would cause it to break. She made me use a newspaper and sometimes the lamp would throw a fit and really smoke the globe, until the soot was so thick it would fall out on the floor. You blew your breath in the lamp chimney to clean it. I hated that job.

Sometimes those old coal-oil lamps would get a fire down in the kerosene. Then you'd have to throw the whole thing out the door in the yard, afraid it was going to explode, but I don't think one ever did.

And I used to have to scrub that kitchen floor at the Rixleben place with hot water and lye. We didn't have a linoleum floor for years. You just poured the water on the floor and scrubbed until you were sure it was clean. Then you swept that out at each door and then gave it two rinses the same way. That lye really ate up the floor and would make it rough and splintery, but it made it pretty and white. You had to be careful or you would get splinters in your feet if you walked on it barefooted. I did the scrubbing. I don't ever remember Mom scrubbing.

One afternoon I was scrubbing and had some kind of spell. My right arm began draw-ing up over my shoulder and I fell unconscious on the floor. My arm drew clear over my shoulder. Mom heard me fall and ran in there. She ran to the kitchen door and hollered for Dad. The men ran in from the shed and Dad had my head on his knee when I came to. They called Dr. Baysinger from Grand Tower and he came and put me to bed but didn't know what caused it. Just said it might be connected to the menstrual cycle, as I was thirteen or fourteen years old. I stayed in bed a while and never had it again.

Mom never said a word in her life to me about sex. When I was fifteen years old, if they were talking about a woman having a baby, they hushed when I walked in the room. It was almost that bad when I raised Bonnie. I am still embarrassed to talk about sex. It would shock you to know how little I knew about sex before I was married. Mrs. Lockley told me all I knew, as she was a rough talker and knew the score.

In those days, when a girl had a baby out of wedlock she and the child were ignored and nobody would have anything to do with her. And people would, especially kids at school, ignore the child. It was a stain for life. But today they have got so brazen and just have kids whether they are married or not, especially the movie stars.

There was a family of prostitutes near Wolf Lake—the mother and her daughters. They had two little girls that nobody at school would have anything to do with at all. We picked their eyes out of the 1907–8 school

picture. About once or twice a year a pro-
stitute would come to town for a one-night
stand. She used the sawmill shed as a rendez-
vous. It wouldn't be the same woman each
year. All the men would visit her, at least all
the men who weren't married.

From the time I was twelve years old, I was
making my own clothes and doing all the
housecleaning and helping wash the clothes
on a board. By the time I was fourteen, I was
doing all the washing. I never had anything
but lye soap to wash our clothes with, even
years after I was married. I always hated it.
In the wintertime, when we couldn't wash up
on the lake, we sometimes pumped by hand
a big fifty-gallon wooden barrel full of pump
water. The water from the well was hard, so
we put a little lye in it to soften it by the next
morning. We pumped water from the pump
next to the barn and carried it by the bucketful
to the chicken yard where we washed. You
rubbed them on a washboard and put them
in the big iron kettle and boiled them, then
took them back to the wash tub and rinsed
them, then hung them on the line. Sometimes
in the summer we washed up on the lake bank.

The washboard was made of wood. It was
fourteen or so inches wide and twenty inches
tall. It had a ridged piece of brass in the center,
with strips on each side, and a board across
the top to rest against your stomach as you
rubbed the clothes up and down on this piece
of brass. There was a solid piece of wood
between the brass and the top of the wash
board to lay your soap on. You rubbed your

clothes on the board and sometimes your
knuckles would bleed. Washing for a family
was the hardest work I ever did, as Dad never
believed in a woman working in the field. You
had to have all this mess in the kitchen in
the wintertime and we had to wash all these
clothes by hand. In the wintertime we washed
on the back porch, but we still had the kettle
where we boiled the clothes in the chicken
yard.

Grace Ballance and I used to do the family
wash on the lake bank, just above the horse
lot, so we could have soft water. There was
an open place where they fished and we had
our kettles up there as we boiled all of our
white clothes and washed on the board. She
brought their washing and I did ours. It would
take us till after dinner to get done. Then we
had to carry them to the house to hang them
on the clothes line. Grace and I became close
friends as well as cousins. We helped each
other with our work. We used to get on the
telephone and beg Mom or Aunt Ett to let us
stay all night with each other, for thirty minutes. We would finally outdo them.

One day we were hanging up clothes and
a caravan of Gypsies came by. There would
be eight to ten wagon and buggy loads of
them. There was always a fortune-teller in a
buggy with them. Mom wasn't home that day
and Grace and I gave her everything she asked
for to get our fortunes told. I was fourteen or
fifteen by this time and I was struck on a guy
and wanted to find out if I was going to marry
him. The Gypsy began asking for an old hen,

sugar, potatoes, etc. We had fried a stack of apple pies for dinner and we gave her all of them and anything she asked for, just to get our fortune told. She said I was going to marry this man; that was what I wanted to hear. About six months later someone who was passing on the road told Aunt Ett about the Gypsy being up there in the chicken yard in her buggy, and we owned up to it. Aunt Ett always found out everything and then told Mom. I almost got in trouble.

People dreaded to see a band of them come through. Three or four of the women would go in a store and one would keep the store owner occupied while the others picked up anything they saw. They dressed in colorful garbs with big earrings and a scarf around their head. The old fortune teller would corner a man and take his billfold without him knowing about it. A bunch came by every summer.

Grace and I began washing when we were twelve or thirteen years old and I continued washing on the board long after we moved to Sublette. I got my first washing machine in 1926. The year little Troy was born and died. I remember the first wringer I ever saw. Mom ordered it from Sears Roebuck & Co. It was a wooden frame, about four feet tall, and the wringer was at the top. It had two wooden frames, one on each side, you could set your wash tubs on. You could fold them up and it had a shelf under the wringer that you could tilt either way so the water would run back in your tub. I used this wringer for myself after I was married, as Mom had quit using

it, until I got the washer that was run by gasoline engine in the pump house, over at Sublette in 1926. Then is when I started washing for Mom.

I don't mean to say anything degrading about my mother, but she never believed in washing clothes very often. She said it wore them out. She never washed a pair of overalls in her life. And never had us change underwear or socks every week. We wore underwear (union suits to our ankles) two weeks or longer and this is the truth. I can remember wearing long, ribbed, black above-the-knee stockings when the heel and toe were out so bad there was only a strap under your foot to hold them on. You had rubber garters to hold them up. The foot would be so stiff they wouldn't bend. We got our feet wet every day when the snow was on or when it rained. And we just let them dry on our feet.

You won't believe this, but I can't remember any of us ever taking a bath until I was fourteen or fifteen years old. Then, at first, it was a spit bath. Then later, I would take the tub in my room and take a bath. The boys always had baths in the summertime, as they went swimming nearly every day. In the summertime when the men were busy thrashing wheat, there would be three or four or a half a dozen of them working. They would build the fire up to heat the water, and they would fill the kettle and use the tub on the back porch to take a bath. They would shut all the back doors so the women would stay away.

Mom used to try to raise turkeys and did

raise some, but once the old gobbler died. When I was thirteen or fourteen she made me take the old hen turkey down to Will Boyce's, on the Bozarth place, in the buggy, to mate her with a tom turkey so the eggs would hatch. Then in about two weeks I had to go back and get her. I didn't want to do it but she made me. Uncle Adam's kids teased me about it for a long time.

When we moved to the Rixleben farm in 1909, there were no levees to protect you then. The river would come out and fill the low places and Running Lake would be from the edge of our yard to the ridge the cow barn sat on. Leora and I would have to ferry corn from the crib to the cow barn. He would put three or four big two-bushel sacks of corn on the back end of the johnboat and there would only be about three or four inches of the boat sticking out of the water. A johnboat was a flatbed, oblong boat, square on each end, you made yourself. One end was so you could put things in and there was a board across the other end so you could sit on it. The water was very swift, till you had a hard time getting across, and full of logs and trees and debris. Neither of us could swim a stroke. He would do the rowing and I would sit on the front end, which would be out of the water maybe three or four feet. How Mom ever let us take such risks, I'll never know. I would never let one of my kids do that today. But I did everything he did, climbing trees and all, and Mom never seemed to worry about us.

We used the old johnboat to ferry people across and I could row the boat as good as anyone could. One afternoon Mr. Rendleman, Bill, and two other men hollered for someone to come after them. There was no one there but me and Mom, so I got in the boat and went after them. Nothing would do then but Bill oar the boat back across. He got us in the fence and I said, "Let me have it, I can get you across." I thought Bob Rendleman would die laughing. You could hear him a quarter of a mile away, laughing. He was noted for his laugh. You could hear him from his house downtown when he laughed, and he could laugh at nothing. Finally, Bill got us out of the fence and back across.

Every time it came a big rain the lake would fill up and the fish were so thick you could catch a hoop netful every three or four hours. They spilled into Running Lake from some other lake. People would come from the hills by the wagon load and take back all they wanted. There used to be a footbridge three or four feet high across the lake, so we could get across to milk. This was all before the lake was dredged in 1914 and 1915. You could stand on that footbridge and see those big carp and buffalo backs sticking out of the water. They would stand on the bridge and gig them as fast as they wanted to. In the net they would catch buffalo, carp, crappie, mudjack (grinnel), perch, and catfish; also, a few bass.

All through the summer there were campers under the big tree just across the road from the horse lot. There were lots of people from

Jonesboro and the hills that used to come down and fish. When the campers left I would go down and see if they had left anything. There used to be a drift across the lake at the big hole just above the horse lot, and you could walk on these logs and cross it. One day, my friend Ethel Cruse, her brother George, and their family were fishing at the drift. Ethel and I tried to pass each other on the logs and fell into the lake. We went clear under when we fell in.

One time, I wanted to go to her house and the low places were still full of river water and I took my underpants off and waded it. It was nearly up to my dress.

There was an island about where the bridge is now and the road went across the middle of it. A big persimmon tree was up on one side, which we climbed and shook persimmons. When the lake was low, there was a road around the island. There was woods up the north side on the lake and a big mulberry tree stood just inside the gate. We climbed that to pick mulberries. I could climb anywhere Leora did.

Leora and I often went fishing up the lake. We used to take the old johnboat and go up the lake past Abernathy's. He did the fishing. I don't know why he let me go along, as he never wanted me tagging around after him. One evening we caught two large carp fish. Mom and Dad were going to Jonesboro the next day, so we took the fish out to Aunt Minnie, who lived in an old log house, exactly where Alfred Wilson built his home on the Parmley place. They were so glad to get the fish, but after Aunt Min cooked them, they tasted like tar so bad they could hardly eat them. It so happened that Leora had just tarred the cracks in the boat and the fish flopped around in the bottom of the boat and absorbed the tar.

There was a huge walnut tree standing in the chicken yard. It was twenty feet up to a big limb that we put a swing on, using a cistern pump chain. Uncle Adam's kids and I used to push each other till we touched another limb twenty feet high. If the chain had of broken, it would have killed us. Mom never seemed to worry about us in the boat, climbing trees, or anything else we did.

The only time in my life I ever got so mad I couldn't see was in the chicken yard. Della and Dora, Curt and Orville's wives, were there with their kids, Lella and Cyril, who were about three years old, and I loved these kids dearly. Lella and Cyril had a falling out and Della and Dora were trying to make them kiss and make up. Cyril was stubborn and wouldn't do it. Della beat him with her hand and then grabbed a limb as big as your thumb and started in on him with that. I cursed her and told her I would kill her and I ran in and took him away from her. I never cursed like that and they, Mom and all, just stood amazed and never said a word.

Bill Davis (no kin to Jim Davis) used to live on Mr. Rendleman's place, just north of us on Running Lake, after the Abernathys left. They had two of the meanest kids that ever lived. They would come down to our house with their mother and you had to watch them every minute. I used to make a little garden of my own along the fence, and they would reach through the fence and pull things up. I just hated to see them come.

One caper Uncle Allen did to me I want to tell, before I leave this part of my life. They lived in a log house at the first curve on the road from our house to Sublette School. The house was just a big living room and kitchen. One day, he came back to work from dinner and I was out in the front yard. He came up to me and said, "Edith, I've got a soft tooth, just feel and see." I stuck my finger in his mouth and he bit down on my finger and then just died laughing. He was always pulling off jokes like that.

There was a peddler that came by every six months or at least once a year. His name was Peddler Sam. He was from Serbia, in the old country. At first he could only speak a few words of English. He had a big pack on his back with such things as dresses, scarves, needles, thread, lace, etc. Mom bought a lot from him. He was jolly and a lot of fun. Once he wanted to snowball with the boys. He brought his nephew over here and he married Dell Brothers and they had several children. Sam and his nephew were both good-looking, as they had black hair and eyes and real dark complexion. Sam later had a one-horse long-tailed wagon and would trade for chickens for his goods.

In 1911, when Orville and Della were first married, they moved into a tent by the old log house and he worked for Dad. Cyril was born there and Della took childbed fever. They moved her over to our house in Mom's bedroom and she was critically ill for two weeks. The doctor thought she was going to die. The fever was caused from a piece of the afterbirth being left in her and an infection setting in. You never hear of anything like that now, but many women died from childbirth then. Della lived and they later moved to Granite City, where they both went wild [see plate 20]. Della wound up running away with Earl Blay and taking their younger son, Merle, with her. Merle went by the name of Blay. We never knew where he was, for years. After Merle was married, Della and Blay brought Merle and his wife back for a visit. Orville brought Cyril down to Mom, and Bill and I took him. But he was killed by a truck when he was ten years old. The story of his accident is told elsewhere [chapter 1].

Mom thought we were ruined when Dad rented the Rixleben place. She said we would never get a crop for that river. She never wanted to move anyplace, even leave the Lester Lyerla Hill where I was born. Dad had no formal education, never went to school a day in his life. He was a self-educated man with great insight or he would never have kept moving to a little better farm. He really loved Thos. Rixleben and Mr. Rixleben loved him. He would never ask Mr. Rixleben for anything

Plate 20. Della and Orville Grammer with their children, Cyril and Merle, in Granite City, around 1918.

unless he paid half of the bill. We never asked him for paint or wallpaper for the inside of the house.

Dad and the Rixlebens had a real friendship. Mrs. Rixleben and Ann Boettner, who clerked at their store, were both common and treated my mom like royalty because she traded with them. When Tom Rixleben died in 1947, Mrs. Rixleben asked Dad's family, us too, to sit with the family at the funeral, because he thought of my dad more like a brother than a tenant. Dad lived on his farm forty years and died there. Dad was an honest man. He gave to Thomas Rixleben instead of taking all he could. And Mr. Rixleben was tight and didn't put anything extra out. He did once renovate the house. Put new windows and brown shingle siding on it, but that is all he was ever out. Dad paid for all the paint and wallpaper that was ever used. But

Plate 21. Elijah and Sarah Bradley, around 1918. Their son Leora was in the army during World War I and wanted a photograph of his parents, so they had this portrait made.

he was a good landlord. He never asked any questions or came around wanting to know anything.

Mom never wanted to improve things. But I was like Dad, I could see how other people lived and was ashamed of our house and clothes. That is why I was making mine and Grace Ballance's clothes at fourteen. I was doing the washing alone at fourteen because I didn't like the way Mom washed. I did the ironing, too. My brother used to come down from Chicago, where he was a lawyer, and I ironed his pleated shirts with those sad irons. Somehow Mom and I never did get along. Dad and Mom were so different [see plate 21]. He was dressy and looked like a Kentucky colonel, and Mom never believed in dressing up. She didn't have the figure to buy ready-made clothes. She couldn't, and wouldn't if she could have, bought a dress ready-made.

6 A One-Room School with a Potbellied Stove

When we were kids, Uncle Allen and Aunt Minnie used to take the big wagon and take all of their kids and Grace, Louie, and me to the big Anna Fair. We would get up by four o'clock and start getting ready and we started before daylight. They put straw in the back of the wagon with a comfort over it and we sat back there, with Aunt Minnie and Uncle Allen in the spring seat. Mom and Aunt Minnie cooked all day the day before and we had a picnic dinner in the fairground. We saw the sun come up in the fairground several times. We would be in there by nine o'clock so we could get a good place to put the wagon and team. Uncle Allen would take the horses loose from the wagon and tie them behind the wagon and take hay along for them to eat on. There was a watering trough in Jonesboro, just south of the overhead bridge you still cross today. We would have to water them when we started home. That is where Dad always put his team and wagon any time we went to town, which wasn't but about twice a year. Mom and Dad wouldn't start as early as we did. They went in the hack (a two-seated top-less buggy). We would all gather at the wagon at dinnertime and have dinner. And we would always eat again before we started home at four or five o'clock. We wouldn't get home till eight or nine o'clock. I'll bet we didn't have over ten cents to spend all day. As I re-member when I was twelve years old, when I went with Dad and Mom, Dad would only give me twenty-five cents. I would try to wait till we got in the fairground and catch him talking to somebody and then ask him. Then he would give me fifty cents.

One year we sure got a scare. We thought we were going to get knocked out of going, as Alice Miller was having a baby and they came after Aunt Minnie about midnight and our hopes fell. But she got home about four o'clock and started right in getting ready. It was Francis that was born.

Used to, and many years later, when a woman had a baby she had it at home. You would get the kids up and take them to somebody's house and send after the doctor and two neighbor women. Before we had doctors that would come out in the country, you had a midwife. There was usually an old woman in the community that did this. Old Granny Beaver, who lived east of Wolf Lake, was the midwife who delivered me. Alice Tweedy was also a midwife. Aunt Minnie Morgan helped deliver babies, but she didn't do it as a profession. By the time I had my babies the doctor would come, but a neighbor woman, Mrs. Johnson, was with me until the doctor came and then she helped him. All my children were born at home. We never saw a doctor when we became pregnant. I never consulted a doctor, until Lee Roy was born. Old Dutch Doc didn't deliver babies.

When I got older Grace and I went with Mom and Dad in the hack. One year I'll never forget. It was about 1911 and I was about thirteen. Orville and Della were newly married and they were staying at our house and old Aunt Nancy Giles still lived with us. They, Mom and Dad, Grace, and myself all went to the fair with Mom and Dad in the hack. I sat up in front between Mom and Dad and the rest sat in the back. We had a good time at the fair, big picnic dinner and all. We didn't

start home till late. Dad had one of his frequent headaches, a bad one, and he told me to drive and he laid his head back on the seat. Of course, I just held the lines and let old Dais and Fan pick the road, as it was pitch dark before we got to the Parmley place. You could not even see the road. There was a huge mudhole in the center of the road and a bank on each side. It was really a hog wallow and a loblolly, just after you pass the old Carroll Rich place and cross that branch. So when we came to that mudhole, old Dais and Fan decided to go up on the right-hand bank and over we went, right in that mudhole. It scared me out of my wits and I started bawling and hollering, "Oh, what have I done?" I was crying, scared of Dad. Dad had hold of the lines and he said, "I guess by G! you see what you've done." Aunt Nancy was hollering like she was killed and Dad said, "Aunt, are you hurt?" She said, "No." He said, "What in the hell are you hollering about then?"

There we were, all covered with mud on our best clothes. We were a muddy sight, scrambling around in pitch dark, trying to find our belongings. Some lost their shoes, some their things we had got at the fair, etc. Dad grabbed the lines as we were turning over and kept the horses from running away, and he and Orville turned the hack back up on its wheels. We were a muddy mess to have to get back in that hack. Grace and I got up next morning at daylight and walked back to see if we could find some of our things. We found a few trinkets from the fair. The mud stained the clothes we had on and it never washed out. Della had on a black silk skirt and it completely ruined it. I don't remember if we ever went to the fair again with Mom and Dad. Probably did, as they never missed the fair. But I'll assure you, he never let me drive again.

I went with Hattie Penrod (Wright) to the Murphysboro Fair once. We caught Billy Bryan at Wolf Lake early in the morning and rode the train to Murphysboro. Billy Bryan was the passenger train that I used to catch to ride to school in Carbondale. It went through Wolf Lake at six o'clock in the morning, going to Johnson City and back through Wolf Lake at noon. I must have been fourteen that year, as Everett Penrod was there and tried to date me. They had those sailor straw hats then and they had a piece of cloth about one-and-one-half-inch wide and long enough to reach around those hats, and they had all kinds of sayings on them, like "Yessir, that's my baby," "Everybody's doin' it, doing what? Turkey trot," "Be my baby," etc. I walked around in the fair ground with Everett, but I knew better than think about dating anyone.

Orville's wife's sister, Nellie Smith, visited Della a lot and she and I caught Billy Bryan once and went to the Murphysboro Fair. They ran a special train that night to bring people home. Mrs. Rendleman used to ride Billy Bryan to Murphysboro to do all her shopping.

Leora and I were the only ones that went to school at Sublette. I ran more to school than I walked, as Leora would say, "Jade, I'll bet you can't keep up with me," and he took steps four feet long, half running, and I had to run to keep up with him and I would be completely out of breath and sweating when we got there. He was like all older kids, mean to the younger ones. I think that was the reason he was so good to me after he left home. He often said, "Sis, I was mean to you when we were kids, wasn't I?"

None of the roads had any gravel on them. They were pure dry sand, three and four inches deep and, boy, that sand would burn your feet, as all kids went barefoot then. Kids were always cutting their feet and stepping on nails. I never went to school barefooted but lots of them had to. The roads were sand until you got to the corner going to Sublette School and then, boy, they were the worst gumbo you ever saw. It would stick to your shoes until your feet would be as big around as a lard can lid. Then it would peel off and you would step so high you would get mud on your knees. Mr. Jones graveled it when he was road commissioner, around 1930.

We never thought anything about walking two or two and a half miles to school, come rain or shine, sleet or snow. It was a lot colder then than it is now and it snowed more often and stayed on the ground. It was often eight to ten inches deep. It frequently stayed on the ground a month at a time. If it was a blowing snowstorm, Uncle Allen Morgan would come after us in the wagon. We kids would pick the biggest snowdrift and wade that drift and be wet to our waist. Then, everybody wore long underwear. When you got to school and stood up against the old potbellied stove, your clothes would steam like a tea kettle. It never made us sick. In those days everybody wore long underwear (union suits) clear down in your shoes, as everybody wore hightop shoes in those days. You later began to wear slippers in the summertime.

At first, kids used a gallon bucket and three or four would take dinner together. Then two would eat out of the same pail, and finally we graduated to a leatherlike, brownish-red, oblong box with a leather strap for a handle. That is what I took to Sublette in later years. And do you know what was in those dinner buckets? Just whatever we had on the table. Cold stewed potatoes, sauerkraut and sorghum molasses, and a hunk of cold butter and two cold biscuits. This is what I took in my lunch, even to Sublette, until I got big enough to fix my own dinner bucket.

It was customary for the teacher to go home with the pupils once or twice a year. Claud Lee, who taught there when I was thirteen years old, once came home with me to stay all night. I made a trip to Wolf Lake to get lunch meat and cookies for his lunch, but while I was gone to milk, Mom fixed his lunch like she did ours. When I got back I was astonished that she would put cold potatoes and sauerkraut and sorghum molasses in his lunch. I grabbed that out of there and fixed

it myself. I don't know how I got that much money. Mom was never embarrassed about anything. She just let company eat what she was cooking, no extras for anybody. I was always embarrassed about being poor. By then we weren't so poor, but Mom never changed with the times. She remained the same till she died. She never modernized with the times, and until she lived with me six weeks during the 1943 flood and in 1944 and used my gas stove and refrigerator, she did not want one. That was during World War II and you could not buy a stove or refrigerator of any kind. We finally did get one of each for her eighty-fifth birthday. She only got to use them about a year. I don't think they got electricity until then. They got as far as our house in 1942 and that was because Will was a director of REA.

When we started to school at Sublette, January 1909, it was a one-room building with three windows on each side, two doors in one end, and a potbellied heating stove in the center of the building. Later, somebody got the idea it was easier on your eyes to have the light coming in from the left side of the room. Then is when they put all the windows on the left side of the buildings. It had two rows in the center up to the stove. It burned coal and in cold weather it took one bucket of coal after another. The teacher would often send someone after coal during school. Everybody wanted to go. We had a pump for water and kept a bucket of water and three or four tin cups, as long as Sublette existed. I believe they did get a fountain you filled by hand and drank from a spout, just before Sublette closed. The waste water was caught in a bucket on a shelf underneath.

We sat in double seats [see plate 22]. They were just like single seats and had a shelf underneath the top to put your books and tablets, etc., in when you were not studying. The teacher had a bell on his desk that would ring once (or ding) when he struck it with his hand. The first tap was to get out of your seat and rise. The second tap was to march up front to the recitation seats, and the third tap you sat down. Each one stood and took his turn reading your lesson and then you discussed it. The recitation seats were homemade and each was about six feet long. Each class sat on them to recite the lessons. For arithmetic you went to the blackboard. They were five or six feet long and at old Sublette there were at least three, one on each side and one up behind the dais—the platform where the teacher had his desk and chair. You had to work the problems he gave you or sometimes there were problems in your book without the answer and you had to work the problems. Then the teacher looked over them to see if they were right.

There was a shelf clear across the back of the schoolhouse to set our dinner buckets on and hooks to hang our coats on; and a big potbellied stove that sat in the middle of the room. The ones that sat close to the stove burned up and the ones in the back froze.

We always opened school at nine o'clock with the Lord's Prayer and singing "America" or Stephen Foster's songs. We were dismissed at four o'clock to go home. The teacher had a small bell with a handle that he rang at the end of recess. We had a recess at 10:30 A.M. of fifteen minutes. And one hour at noon, another fifteen minute recess at 2:30. At recess we played base and stink base and drop the handkerchief and whipcracker. At noon we played scrub. It was the same as baseball. Grace Ballance, Hazel Brown, Myrtle Kimmel, and myself always played scrub with the boys. Sadie Ballance, Zora Jones, Ruth Brown, and Lizzie Kimmel were all too ladylike to be a tomboy and run and play. They stayed in the schoolhouse. The girls also played hopscotch.

The school year began in September and closed in March, with a big picnic dinner and a program of recitations and singing. We always had a spelling match or adding match or some kind of recreation on Friday after the last recess. Sometimes we had visitors from Big Barn like Claud Lee's brothers, Dan and Cecil. Cecil was the best *adder* anywhere. He learned by sight-adding. We always did the pecking kind. Somehow they never taught us the method of adding in our head, by looking at two numbers and knowing what the answer was without having to count it up. Spelling and orthography was the last thing before we were dismissed.

My half brother Ellis Grammer was the teacher when we moved to the Rixleben farm.

Plate 22. Interior of the old one-room Anna Grade School, behind what is now Davie School, 1903. All the one-room schools Edith attended looked very much like this one, although Sublette, Wolf Lake, and Rhodes schools were not wallpapered, had blackboards in the back, and varied in other minor ways. *Courtesy of Dan Wilson.*

Ellis was strict on us, as he didn't want anyone to say he was partial to us. One evening we played on the road and he almost whipped us. Then Bill Davis, Claud Lee, and Fred Fuller were the teachers. Fred Fuller was the strictest teacher we ever had [see plate 23]. We weren't allowed to whisper across the seat. He didn't whip you at the time you whispered. He waited until Friday evening and then called them all up and, brother, did he give them a licking with a big switch. Ray Kimmel and Roy Brown were two that got a whipping every Friday. Alvin Ballance got a lot of them. Alvin Ballance said he whipped him every time he turned around. He said he always swore if he ever met Fred Fuller when he was grown, he would give him a beating. But Fred died before Alvin ever met him.

When Bill Davis taught Sublette school he drew a picture of an owl holding a scroll and all of the pupils' names were written on it. There were fifty-nine pupils enrolled that year at Sublette. That picture was about twenty-four by eighteen inches.

The year Claud Lee taught there, 1911 and 1912, Zora Jones and I sat together. You could talk to your seatmate but you were not allowed to whisper across the seat. Most of the teachers would just make you stand in the corner, but Claud Lee would throw an eraser, a piece of chalk, and sometimes a fire shovel, to land on your desk or on the floor beside you.

My best friend was Grace Ballance but she was six months younger than me and that threw her a year behind. Grace and I were very close when we grew up. Uncle Adam's kids and I were together a lot, all but Dallas and Sadie. They thought they were so much better than we were. They tried to be stuck up; we were just a bunch of kids to them. And Aunt Ett and Uncle Adam always seemed to think more of Sadie than Grace. I guess that is the reason we stuck together so close.

Zora Jones was always my seatmate. We were the two smartest in the school and we were in the same grade. It was tit for tat who was the best speller, Zora or me. We stood in line at the side of the room and the teacher gave out words for you to spell. When you missed a word the one standing on your left got a chance to spell it and turn him down. Zora or I was at the head of the class most of the time. Every time you got to the head of the class they gave you a headmark and the next day you went to the foot of the class. The one that had the most headmarks at the last day of school got a prize.

I always beat Zora in spelling, as I went to the Union County spelling match two or three times. I won last prize once. Dad would always take me in the hack. We had to be there and ready to start by nine o'clock, so we had to leave home by six or seven o'clock. I would be so happy and excited I would talk continuously, and Dad would say before we hardly got started, "You talk too much," and that would just kill my soul. In those days kids were not allowed to talk, period, if there were grown-ups talking. I told my brother Albert once I had an inferiority complex. He looked

Plate 23. Sublette School class picture for the year 1912–13. Edith was fourteen years old. *Front row, left to right*: Letha Smith, Gladys Kimmel, Fannie Miller, Neely Travis, Lewis Morgan, Robert Dillow, Ellis Morgan, Alvin Ballance, Ralph Kimmel, Oliver Ragans, Louis (Buck) Hubbs, unidentified child, Harry McLain, Otis Grown. *Second row, left to right*: (?) Smith, Elma Morgan, Kate Brown, Alice Travis, August Dillow, Serena Miller, Ellen Brown, Ruth Lanham, Lura Earnhart. *Top row, left to right*: Ted (Eddie) Jones, Ray Kimmel, Roy Brown, Jean Earnhart, Louie Ballance, Alvis Whitesides, Edith Bradley, Zora Jones, Zilpha Smith, Grace Ballance, Myrtle Kimmel, Hazel Brown, Elsie Ragans, Eva Morgan. *Rear, left to right*: Will Jones; the teacher, Fred Fuller, and his wife, Dessie Fuller.

at me and said, "You? It don't show." I said, "Well, I got it anyway." He said, "And so have I. It's because we weren't allowed to talk when we were kids. We had to listen to the old folks, the grown-ups, when they were talking." Dr. Norman Vincent Peale says if a child is not loved, or feels they are not, as a kid they will grow up to have an inferiority complex and I believe it is true. When we kids grew up you were never allowed to join in a conversation with grown-ups. Kids were supposed to sit back and listen and for the least little thing they would whip you with a big switch. Dad never whipped me, as he didn't have to. I loved him so much and yet I was so scared of him, when he spoke I jumped and asked no questions. Nowadays the kids do the talking and the parents listen.

One year when I went to the spelling match at Jonesboro (the time I won last prize), Mom put a skirt and blouse on me. The skirt was made of changeable brown pongee, very soft and flimsy, and my petticoat was about six to eight inches shorter and starched stiff, until it made my skirt stand out. We always went into Rixleben's Drugstore and Mr. Rixleben always took us home with him for dinner. Mrs. Rixleben always had bananas and oranges sliced together for dessert in individual dessert dishes—a very small amount. Ann Boettner clerked in the drugstore for years and years. She took me in the back of the store and ripped all the hem and tucks out of my petticoat to make it longer. The skirt was still too long, way below my knees.

Mom never paid any attention to style. She always made everything big so I wouldn't out grow it. That is why I started making my own clothes so young. She never was embarrassed that we didn't have nice furniture. Grace Ballance and I papered our living room when I was thirteen or fourteen years old. And I begged until I got her to buy straw matting for the front room floor. That remained on the floor until after I was married. Mrs. Lockley used to throw it into Mom for having a straw-matting carpet for her daughter to have to court on and then buying an Axminster rug as soon as she was married. Mrs. Lockley was really my friend. Mom never paid any attention to what anybody said. She still lived in the 1800s when she died.

Zora beat me in our eighth grade examination, the first year we took it for the scholarship to one year at Southern Illinois Normal at Carbondale, but I won it the next. I went through the eighth grade twice, as there was no other school to go to. So did Ellis and Albert go through it twice, or maybe three times, because Ellis went until he was twenty. The year Zora won the scholarship everybody in the eighth grade could take the exam.

This is how dumb I was on etiquette. The Joneses were up in society more than I was, and Edna Rendleman, who was already out of school, invited Zora to go home with her for dinner. She came over to the schoolhouse after Zora at noon. Silly me, I hadn't been asked but when they dismissed us at noon for lunch I was with Zora, so I just tagged along with them and went over to the Rendlemans' for dinner. They treated me nice and I guess I didn't know any better. I still laugh about it yet with my friend Gussie Hessman (she did something about the same).

Another incident at Sublette was the weeds were grown up behind the schoolhouse, nearly as high as your head. We were playing base and Ted Jones was after me. I ran around the schoolhouse, or I tried to, and there was some old barbed wire in the weeds. I ran into that and cut a gash above my knee two inches long. It bled terribly and I had to go home. It healed itself but I carry the scar today.

Uncle Adam's kids missed a lot of school. Aunt Ett and Uncle Adam didn't care. We didn't ever think of missing school unless we were sick. I loved school.

In those days teachers often went back and sat in your seat while you were at the blackboard, etc. One day I had been telling mine and Charley Jones's fortune by writing his name, then mine under it, and crossing out the letters in your names. Then you had so many left over and you said, for each letter, "love," "hate," "friendship," "marry." I had left the paper on my desk when class was called and, to my sorrow, Claud went back and sat in my seat. Boy, was I scared I was going to get in trouble. He took the paper. He waited until the next evening and came back where I was putting on my coat and came up close to me, where nobody could hear, and said, "Edith, what did that piece of paper mean with those names on it?" I said,

"I was telling my fortune." He said, "Don't let it happen again."

All of my love affairs were in my head until I met Wm. J., when I was nearly sixteen. It was six months or more before I fell in love with him and I guess he was the only one I was ever really in love with. I fell in love in my head with Chas. Jones, Everett Gregory, Homer Frogge, and several others.

There was a party at Uncle Adam's house and that is one time Leora let me go with him. We walked down there. Leora wanted to walk Ruth Brown home, so he got Charley Jones to walk with me. We walked behind Leora and Ruth. I must have been fifteen. I never slept for a week, afraid Dad would find it out. Sure enough, on Friday night at the supper table, Mom said, "Did you know your little daughter caught her a feller last Saturday night?" I wished I could have gone through the floor; I was sure I was in trouble. Dad said, "I'll be G!!! D!!!, who was it?" She told him but that's all he said, as Leora said, "She was with me and Ruth Brown." Boy, was that a relief. I could sleep again.

I had a crush on Charley one time after that, but nobody knew it but me and Grace. Later on, he tried to go with me but I was over the crush by then. Everett Gregory always wanted to go with me. I had a crush on him once but nobody knew it, but Everett had a name of being fast with the girls and he was a tough guy. Leora told him to never try to go with me and I didn't care anything about him when I was old enough to go with anybody I wanted to. I had a crush on Homer Frogge at the time I started going with Bill. I went with them both for four Sundays, first one and then the next Sunday the other, before I made up my mind. Mom just had a fit about me going with Homer, as his dad was mean to his wives and sure enough, Homer was too. He later married Edna McMahan and she had a terrible life. I never had a serious date after I got serious with Bill. Had a date or two in Carbondale but that was all. Bill was known as a greenhorn but I didn't know what they meant, as I was a greenhorn, too.

I used to ride horseback a lot from the time I was thirteen, fourteen, or fifteen, until I was married. Also, we had a buggy by that time, that we got when I was fourteen or fifteen. I would drive to Wolf Lake after anything we needed. (But I walked to high school in Wolf Lake in 1914 and 1915.) I also associated with Mollie and Olevia Frogge [see plate 24].[1] We used to stop and talk to Bill, Howard, and Bill Houston when they were working close to the road. One time we were stopped talking to them and Mrs. Jones came by in the buggy and she stopped and ask me not to carry any more letters between her daughter Zora and my brother Leora (he was away in school). I said, I would "do as I pleased about that."

There weren't many places to go then—the Anna Fair, church when the folks went to take you. But the big event was the pie supper at your school. Every school had a pie supper in the fall to raise money for school supplies. All the girls and some of the women took a fancy pie and they would spend a week decorating the box it was put in. You often put bananas, cookies, or candy in with it. There was a man that auctioned them off to the highest bidder. The boys were not supposed to know who the pie or box belonged to, but the boys found out somehow. The boys would bid against each other for your pie. Sometimes, a bunch of boys would chip in together and run some fellow's girl's pie up to eight dollars or ten dollars. Sometimes, the fellow would not bid that high and let the boys have it. Sometimes, someone would buy your pie you didn't like at all, but you had to eat with them for manner's sake. Sometimes, a boy would buy your pie just to ask you if he could take you home.

They always had cakes to auction off and would have two or three cakewalks. For the cakewalk there would be three judges and they would write on a piece of paper what the object was that if you stopped at that, you won the cake. They charged ten cents a person and sometimes there would be twenty-five to forty marching around the room, hoping to stop at the right place. Later, they had a circle of chairs numbered and would pick out a number and write it down and the one that sat in that chair with the number on it got the cake. You all walked in a circle till they said stop, then you stopped.

One night, they were having a pie supper at Sublette, and Leora and I were to meet Uncle Adam's kids at the crossroad behind our house. There used to be a road between

Plate 24. Edith Bradley and Mollie Frogge (and a hog) clowning around in a straw stack on the Bradley farm, in the spring of 1916.

the blackland (gumbo) and the big field behind the house. It reached from one end of the farm to the other. Leora and I got to the crossroads before they got there and we began to holler as loud as we could, to see if they were coming, and they began to answer us back. It was pitch dark. Henry Cruse lived back next to the levee and he had a mean bull. That bull began to bellow and paw and he ran through the fence and started toward where we were. Aunt Sena Cruse ran along behind him, hollering at us, "Run, children, run." By that time the Ballances were there, and we did just that. We scattered in every direction, quiet as we could be. After he passed us bellowing and scraping the ground with his foot, we finally got together again and got to the levee and went down it, till we got to the road that turned to the schoolhouse. We were really scared and we kept quiet, too. But we were so scared at the thought of having to go home and that bull out, it ruined our evening. We went out the other way home, the way we go to Sublette now.

We had a big basket dinner the last day of school every year. Everybody in the community fixed a big basket or several boxes of food and everybody ate together and ate each other's food. All the small places like Wolf Lake School, Sublette School, Ware, Big Barn, and Beech Grove took enough food to any gathering to feed twice as many people as were there. A pie supper, box supper, or an ice cream supper was a big event in our lives. We walked there and back, until I started going with Bill.

One time, when Grace and I were too young to be courting, we went to a big baptizing at McGuire Church. They had a big revival and the baptizing was always the climax. That day was especially a big day. They had a big basket dinner at the old schoolhouse (that was where they had church, too). Sadie Wilkins and Eddie Henson were married in a public ceremony at the end of the morning service. There must have been a hundred people or more there for the wedding and the dinner. Then they had the baptizing in the

afternoon in Running Lake, at the end of our horse lot.

There used to be big revival meetings that always lasted two and sometimes three weeks and they always had a baptizing the Sunday after the revival ended, or if it was cold they would wait till warm weather. But some even broke the ice to have it. One time, they dammed up that branch at the MoPac railroad crossing in Wolf Lake and had a baptizing [see plate 25]. Ellis and the Rendleman girls, Grace, Myrtle, Edna, and Dora, were all baptized there. Wm. J. was a teenager then and he really got a chastising for laughing (you know how he could laugh). When Virgil Stone was baptized, he opened his mouth as they stuck him under the water and when he came up he squirted water ten feet, and of course the kids thought it was funny. Virgil was a good boy but he had Saint Vitus' dance.[2] The head and voice quivers. And, of course, the kids picked on him and made fun of him a lot.

Grace Ballance and I were saved at a revival in the old Methodist church house in Wolf Lake. That was in spring of 1915, the year I went to high school in Wolf Lake. We were baptized in the creek at Beech Grove, just above where the bridge stands now. That creek has had more baptizings than any other place I know. So that ended our going to dances. Now, you can square dance all you want. Even the preachers belong to the square dance club. Then you couldn't use lipstick or powder

Plate 25. A baptizing at Wolf Lake, 1910 or 1912. Baptizing required complete immersion. The people being baptized were Ellis Grammer, Warren Chandler, Virgil Stone, and Dora, Grace, Myrtle, and Edna Rendleman.

or bob your hair. At the revivals the evangelist would come in and run across the pulpit, preaching how you'd go to hell if you danced or bobbed your hair and used powder and paint. I'd rather square dance as to eat. I was the first one to have bobbed hair around Wolf Lake, after I was married. I always paid a lot of attention to style.

A bunch of the boys used to gather at our house in the winter when Running Lake was frozen over and skate all day. Grace and I were out there with them but girls didn't skate then, or at least we didn't. One Sunday morning, Everett Gregory fell on the ice and cut a big gash over one eye. Wolf Lake used to freeze over and a bunch of boys and girls used to skate at night and had a big fire to warm by, but I never was in that bunch.

Grace and Louie and I were very close. Grace and I were together nearly every day. I was down at their house every Christmas. Leora always went too, until he got big enough to go with the girls. We got a package each of those little firecrackers and some Roman candles and we would take a shovel full of live coals from the stove out in the front yard to light them with. Mom would never let us do that or much of anything else. When I was a kid, if we got an orange and a banana for Christmas we were thrilled. I usually got some kind of a toy.

One time, Grace and I rode to Wolf Lake before school for something. She was riding her old mule Pete and I can't remember what I was riding, but on the way back Bill and their hired hands were at their barn getting ready to go to work, harnessing their mules, and when I saw them I said, "I'm not going to let them see me riding astraddle, I'm going to ride sideways." And when I got in front of the barn I slid off on the ground. I thought they would die laughing. They helped me back on astraddle and I really felt little. We rode bareback and we had blisters on our rear for two weeks.

One more episode, before I leave my early teen years at Sublette. Tom Kimmel was much older than us kids and I was a year older than Eva, Aunt Minnie's oldest girl. We usually walked home together. But this certain day, Aunt Minnie's kids Eva, Elma, Ellis, and Lewis got out earlier than I did. Tom Kimmel thought he would have some fun, so he dressed up in old clothes and blacked his face and hid at the corner in the cornfield. When they came by he ran out toward them and after them and they almost ran themselves to death getting home. Aunt Minnie was so mad at him she really blew her top. Some of Uncle Adam's kids saw him but I missed him.

About the same year, Mrs. Florence (Flira) Farmer lived in the little house between the corner and the schoolhouse. She had married Will Farmer after her first husband Andrew Dillow died and had two babies at that time, by Will Farmer. They were very poor. She was Will Jones's baby sister and there was always jealousy between Flira and Mrs. Jones. Ted Jones and Flira's son, Earnest Dillow, were always fighting in school. Mrs. Farmer had a red hot temper, and this particular evening Mrs. Farmer was walking home about middleways in the lane and Mr. and Mrs. Jones were in the buggy going toward Wolf Lake. Mrs. Farmer stopped the buggy and she called Mrs. Jones everything there was to be called. She dared Mrs. Jones to get out of the buggy and when she did, Flira hit her over the head with a bucket of milk and then they clinched and Flira had Mrs. Jones down in the ditch, beating her. Mr. Jones was afraid to turn loose of the horse to separate them, but he finally did. He was hollering, "Dad Dam it, stop it!" That was his byword.

We kids came along from school and were right there at them when they went in the ditch. We started running for home. Mrs. Jones had Flira arrested and she had to pay a fine. But they said Mr. Jones paid it, as Flira didn't have enough money. Later, much later, they became friends. Flira and Andrew Dillow had lived up in an old house where Ardell Harris lives now. Mr. Dillow died up there with pneumonia and left Flira with three children, Gussie, Earnest, and Robert. They used to drive a big black horse to a long tail buggy or hack to Sublette School. Later, she moved down on Cyrus Kimmel's place.

Chub Cruse used to live on that place where Mr. Dillow died and Uncle Adam lived on Bob Rendleman's farm. We kids went up there one day and they had a pump that, if you pumped real fast, it would build up pressure and the handle fly up. Somehow it got loose from our hand and flew up and struck me under the chin and cut a gash three-fourths inch long. I bled like a stuck hog. I have the scar today. Never went to the doctor.

7 *"Jump, Edith!"*

After I went to Sublette School two years in the eighth grade because there weren't any high schools, they started a high school in Wolf Lake. When I was fifteen, I walked from home to Wolf Lake and never missed a day. Lloyd Spiller was the schoolteacher that year. Those in the ninth grade were Fannie Wright, Ben Vancil, Ethel Stone, Zora Jones, Bob Vincent, Early Tweedy, Howard Rendleman, and myself [see plate 26]. Fannie, Howard, Bob, and I all went on to Carbondale the next year. I had a good time in high school. Mollie Frogge and I played baseball with the boys. I was catcher. I could jump as high a fence as any of them. We had a pie supper up in the IOOF Hall before school started and Lloyd Spiller paid eight dollars for a bouquet for the prettiest girl, for me.

Louie Ballance got struck on me once and bought me a gold ring. Mom made me give it back to him. But I sure wasn't struck on him. I was afraid of him until he died.

The Frogge girls, Mollie and Olevia, lived in the house I moved into in 1949. Charles Ware owned that farm. It was about halfway between my parents' house and Wolf Lake. We all walked together. Olevia was a spoiled stubborn brat. She would get mad at Mollie and lag behind. Mollie and I would have to wait on her. Their father, Hean Frogge, moved here when Will Jones moved to the George Day place. Hean's wife had died and he married again to a woman named Paralee when he lived here. He was mean to his wives. I saw Paralee with black eyes more than once. She would say a stick of wood hit her in the eye. She died in the big flu epidemic of 1918, when their last baby, Jasper, was born. They let Paralee's sister in Missouri have him.

Before he died, Charles Ware's dad, Jesse

Plate 26. Wolf Lake ninth grade, 1914. *Left to right*: Earl Tweedy, Fannie Wright, Lloyd Spiller (the teacher), Ethel Stone, Ben Vancil, Howard Rendleman (holding slate board), Bob Vincent, Zora Jones, Edith Bradley.

Ware, owned thousands of acres around here and Ware. He owned my farm, the Tuthill farm, Bobby McMahan's, and the Joneses' farm. Charles Ware was president once of the Illinois Central Railroad.[1] They set his private car off here on the sideline of the Illinois Central. He had servants. They would stay a week or two here. He was wealthy but his wife died and he married a model in St. Louis and she and the Depression broke him flat. He first fixed this little house up, where George Rogers lives, and would spend two or three weeks in it every summer. Then he built a fine home back here on the lake bank. Dad bought the farm the Frogge's rented, and Mrs. Will Jones bought the Ware place after the Depression and moved there. Besides the Rendlemans, the Joneses were once the most prosperous farmers in the bottoms. He was a big wheat grower and was the first one in our community to own an automobile. And Mrs. Jones and Zora dressed much better than the rest of us, except the Rendlemans. Mrs. Jones and Mrs. Rendleman both had lovely voices and one or the other played and sang when they had an Odd Fellows or Modern Woodmen supper. Mrs. Jones always sang "As I Stood on the Bridge at Midnight." Mrs. Rendleman often played and sang at home for us.

The Joneses were very prosperous until the Depression and then, for some reason, they went broke. They lived where John Lambdin lives, but Mr. Jones just kept going down and finally had to move. He rented the DuBois farm, and finally Mrs. Jones got a little money from her brother and made a down payment on this Ware land here, in front of my house. Mr. Jones didn't live very long after they moved over here. The high water was nearly up to the roof in it in 1943. That flood ruined it. She began to lose her mind and finally was put in Anna State Hospital and died there. She used to sit in the corncrib and cut shucks day after day, trying to pay for this farm.[2] She finally joined the Wolf Lake Methodist Church and served as Sunday school superintendent for many years. For some reason she never learned to drive a car and walked to Sunday school and church every Sunday. It was sad to know how they once lived and to see how they wound up.

I'll tell you this so you will know just how

things were back then. Mrs. Jones got sick when they lived where the Lambdin's live now and she vomited so hard she got a kink in a blood vessel in her stomach. The doctor said what was wrong and they got her to Wolf Lake somehow and put her on Billy Bryan on a cot. They took her to Cairo and operated on her and she got all right. I think Dr. Gunter at Ware was her doctor, as he was a doctor for this community for years. He was our doctor only once, when Della had childbed fever.

And now, in 1994, they did five bypasses on my son Lee Roy. That's where they saw the breastbone in two and pull it back and take a vein out of your leg and use it to bypass the arteries in your heart. He was in surgery seven hours. What a difference! Of course, that was eighty-seven or more years ago when Mrs. Jones got sick. There were no hospitals then, except Hale-Willard in Anna. It was a little two-story building that joined the high school yard and they didn't do any operations, except maybe appendicitis (and then you were lucky if it didn't kill you).

When Mr. Jones was living, he bought cattle and hogs and shipped them mostly by train to St. Louis. He always brought back a barrel of apples. He took Zora and me with him to St. Louis once and he took us to a burlesque show. I'll never forget the song they sang, "Of Course the Blame Was Laid on Me." Mrs. Jones really got on him for taking us to that. Mr. Jones drank some and he had a woman in St. Louis. He and Will Boyce and Lawrence Randles would go to St. Louis every once in a while for a big time. Mr. Jones was a good provider for his family.

I don't think Mrs. Jones ever forgave Mr. Jones for going broke. She kind of looked down on him after she bought the farm. But she wished many times he was back after he died. In fact, the last time we visited her at the state hospital she said, "If Will was here things would be different."

The Rixlebens were one of the first in the county to own a car. They came down one Sunday and took us for a ride. Bob Rendleman and Andy Daisy, the ICRR operator, were the first to own a car around Wolf Lake, and the Joneses bought one not long after.

The year I went to high school at Wolf Lake was the year they dredged Running Lake, 1914 and '15. They built this drag line in the upper bottoms, near McGuire school, where Running Lake joins Clear Lake. When they got the dredge boat built they slid it off into the water. Lots of people went up to see them push it into the water, because they thought it would turn over. But it didn't. They had a houseboat they pulled along behind the dredge boat. A man and his wife slept there and cooked for the crew. One of the crew was Ben Neuman, who married Flora Tweedy. She was the daughter of Amos Tweedy, who had the name of a pretty rough guy. They had crew enough to run the dredge twenty-four hours a day and I remember hearing that old dredge

running all night. Alvin Ballance said he and Elbert took butter and eggs to them, nearly to Ware. I'll bet Mom sold them butter and eggs also, as she always had them to sell.

When they cut through the road in front of our house we had to go around it and when they got past the road they threw up a temporary bridge. It ruined the fishing with a net when the dredge boat cut the big ditch, which is now Running Lake. The old lake was just beyond Running Lake bridge. It was never very deep, except when it came a big rain or the river got up in it. It was wild and high when the overflow filled all the low places, before the levee was built. They built the first levee at the same time. It was a potato ridge compared to what we have now.

The next year I went to Southern Illinois Normal College in Carbondale [see plate 27]. At that time it was just a teachers college. Edna Rendleman was my roommate and she got sick during Christmas vacation and couldn't go back to school. I almost died from homesickness the first week of January 1916. In those days, we had chapel where all students gathered at ten o'clock each morning. I cried all during chapel and most of the time the first week. Edna never did go back.

We had a lot of fun that winter. The rooming house I lived in was run by an elderly couple named Gregg [see plate 28]. They had three boys, Carl, Ray, and Paul, in college, and that was the way they put them through college. The boys did all the work but the

Plate 27. The five girls at Gregg's Rooming House in 1915, when Edith Bradley attended Southern Illinois State Normal School. *Left to right*: Ida Lewis from Harrisburg, Edna Rendleman from Wolf Lake, Ruby Harmon from Waltonville, Edith Bradley from Wolf Lake, Lenora Schock from Pinckneyville.

cooking. The boys lived downstairs and the girls up, and the boys were not allowed upstairs. Edna's brother, Howard Rendleman, lived with about six others downstairs and they would sneak upstairs. One night, Mr. Gregg came up and they had to raise a window and get out on the porch roof. There was a large pear tree in front of mine and Edna's window, and Howard and two others climbed that tree and threw pears in at us.

Edwin and Bill Fitch took their meals there also, as several ate there that didn't stay there.

Plate 28. A Christmas dinner at Gregg's Rooming House, December 1915, given by "the boys" for "the girls." *Seated, left to right*: Edith Bradley, Howard Rendleman, Sam Bunker, Ida Lewis, Oscar Camp, Ella Gerlach, Edna Rendleman. *Standing, left to right*: Ray Gregg, unidentified man, Marjorie (surname unknown), unidentified individual, Earl Lavender, Dallas Ballance, Adlai Eddleman, Ruby Harmon, unidentified woman, Paul Gregg.

I was really a country greenhorn when I went up there. But I learned a lot. Too bad I didn't go on and finish college. It would have been an easier life than I chose. But I thought of nothing but getting married. I wouldn't take anything for that year's experience.

Until that winter, I had never kissed my mother or she me. I told the girls that and they made me promise to kiss her that weekend. When I did, she did just what she always did, make you feel like a fool. That night she told Dad and the boys, "She was glad enough to get home that she kissed me." I never kissed her again and I never kissed my dad, ever. I never was kissed by any of them. There was no kissing allowed ever at our house.

I was never kissed or hugged or allowed to sit on anybody's lap, not even my father's, when I was a child. I never sat on my mother's lap, either. I wasn't allowed to comb my brothers' hair or touch them in any way. I never saw any sign of love ever between my mother and father.

One morning, we missed Billy Bryan, the 6 A.M. train. He was just pulling out when we reached the corner of Al Wilson's store. Aunt Minnie lived in the MoPac section house one-fourth mile north of Wolf Lake, between the railroads, and Dad took me up there and made me stay all night rather than get up and take me to the train next morning. Well, I never slept any all night, as that straw in the mattresses popped and cracked every time you moved. She just had a sheet over that straw

bed. (Everett was born in that house. He weighed fifteen pounds at birth.)

Uncle Allen and Aunt Minnie were both hard workers but he just always worked by the day on the farm or on the railroad, one dollar per day then, and they had seven kids [see appendix D]. They lived on the Parmley place and worked for Billy Butcher for years. Billy Butcher had the Parmley place rented or leased. He raised asparagus, spinach, etc. They lived on top of the hill and there was no water up there. The kids had all kinds of gallon buckets and carried water up that hill from the spring, which was up that hollow behind where Al Wilson's house is now. They really had a hard life, until they moved to Granite City around 1919 or 1920, when Everett was four or five years old.

Aunt Minnie was always jealous of Mom and me. She really didn't like me. I had better clothes than they did. Mom gave Aunt Minnie lots of things like milk, butter, and eggs, etc., and helped them all she could. Aunt Minnie was greedy. She always got everything off of Mom she could for nothing. I can't ever remember them having a chicken or a cow. When they lived in Granite City and they came down in the summer, she would tell Mom she wanted to buy two or three chickens. She would fry them before she left and then say, "Sarah, how much do I owe you for them chickens?" Mom would say, "Oh! Nothing," and she never insisted on paying. But Mom didn't care.

Soon after we moved to Running Lake, Uncle Allen and Aunt Minnie lived in an old log house in the corner just below our house. Uncle Allen worked for my dad for one dollar a day. Uncle Adam's kids and Leora and I just loved to go there at night when Uncle Allen would be home. He always played games with us. Uncle Allen would rather play with a bunch of kids as to eat. He would have us singing and playing all kinds of games. Sometimes we would stay all night.

But when we went there in the day time, it would always end up somebody did something and Aunt Minnie made her kids come in the house and wouldn't let them play and we would have to go home. Aunt Minnie was so poor and so jealous of us kids she got mad nearly every time we went there and gave her oldest girl Eva a beating. Aunt Minnie used to beat her something terrible. She got the beatings for all of them. The daughter next to Eva was named Elma (called Ebbie), and Aunt Minnie thought Ebbie was the proper stuff. Ebbie laid everything on to Eva. It was terrible how Eva got the blame for everything and how Aunt Minnie beat her and never whipped any of the others. No matter what Eva did, you didn't dare say a word about it. I had to watch her like a hawk when she came to our house. One wheat thrashing, she took her teeth and tore my new dress and hair ribbons. And if you said she did it, she got another beating. Aunt Minnie always beat her for everything unmercifully. She beat her like

a dog. I guess Eva was jealous of me, as they were so poor.

They had a baby every two years. They were Ritta, who died in infancy, Eva, Elma, Ellis, Lewis, Orville, Velma, and Everett. Aunt Minnie and Uncle Allen had a hard time. Aunt Minnie was the boss but she had to be. Uncle Allen was just a good man that loved kids and worked hard but he had no management. He was just happy working by the day and had no ambition to get ahead. Aunt Minnie handled all the money. They finally moved to Granite City and he got a job that later killed him, in a creosote plant that ate up his kidneys. But he did well in Granite City.

Mom was no more like her half sister and half brother, Aunt Minnie and Uncle Adam, than nothing. They both were easy to get mad, especially Aunt Minnie. Uncle Adam would pout and go for weeks without speaking to Aunt Ett. Aunt Minnie died a horrible death. Her kids didn't want her. She owned her home, and Everett and Clo lived with her. But they moved out after she got sick and they gave Velma her house to take care of her and Velma moved in with her. They are buried on Sunset Hill, in Granite City, Illinois.

Uncle Richard, another of my mom's brothers, was a mean cruel man to his family [see plate 29]. He beat his son once so badly they got the law after him. He made everybody work but himself. One of his daughters, Edmona, ran off and got married to Walter Rogers at fourteen, just to get away from him.

Plate 29. Richard Penrod (*left*) and Mose Lyerla at Edith's house. Richard Penrod (born 1859) was Sarah Penrod Bradley's brother. Mose Lyerla (born 1845) was Sarah's uncle and married her husband Elijah's sister Martha.

He drank all of his life and when he got drunk he wanted to fight and cuss and rip and snort. Their daughter Hattie ran off and stayed at our house quite a while, when I was twelve or fourteen, and then she hired out. He and Aunt Mag came back here from Missouri several years later and they came to our house and stayed. Uncle Richard got religion after they came back and he was as radical on re-ligion as he had been mean, except he didn't change the working habits. He would make Aunt Mag read the Bible any time he got ready, no matter what time of night it was.

When Dad had the field cleared known as the pasture, Uncle Richard put it in corn with a one-horse plow. In those days, they just sawed a tree down, leaving the stumps two or more feet high, trimming the trees with an ax and burning the limbs and letting the stumps rot out. Aunt Mag had to do the plowing with that one-horse plow and Uncle picked up the roots, etc. After she plowed all day he would make her sit up till midnight reading the Bible. So one night, she got up and pretended to go the toilet in the chicken yard and she left him and went to her sister's, Ida Latta's. They lived back behind us, where Henry Cruse once lived. Uncle waited for her to come back to bed and when she didn't, he woke Mom and Dad up and they searched the chicken yard and didn't find her. So they called Sam Latta and she was there. He bawled and squalled and begged her to come back but she never went back to him.

That was 1915, when I was up at the Normal. He came to my boarding house in Carbondale and wanted me to try to get her back. I told him the only thing I blamed her for was not leaving him years ago. She stayed with her daughter, Edmona Rogers, in Carbondale, and Uncle Richard went back to Missouri. Aunt Mag stayed with my parents a lot, too. Then after she died Uncle Richard came back and lived with Edmona. They are buried in Carbondale but not by each other. Two of their daughters, Edmona and Hattie, live in Carbondale. I can't believe my mother was his own sister.

Shortly after we moved to the Rixleben place, my dad got Uncle Adam to move up on Bob Rendleman's place. He only lived there a few years and Dad rented the farm, where Wm. and I lived between 1930 and 1949, for them. Mr. Rixleben had just bought it from Charley Miller, who lived in Missouri. They built a new house shortly after Mr. Rixleben bought it. That's the same house Bud and his wife, Tootie, live in now. Uncle Adam was never very work brittle. I don't ever remember seeing him in the field at work. All the kids except Elbert and Alvin had to earn their money for shoes and clothes [see appendix C]. Aunt Ett never was too industrious, either. They did a lot of sitting.

Around 1910 to 1912, before Uncle Allen and Aunt Minnie moved to the Rixleben farm, they lived on the corner between Dad's and that farm. When Mose Abernathy's first wife, Lou, died they buried her at Morgan Cemetery.[3] Aunt Minnie often drove the hack for Mom if Dad couldn't go and they drove a span of mules, big ones. Best I remember, it was cold weather. Aunt Minnie and Mom were up in the front seat and Grace and I were in the back seat. We made it fine and went to the cemetery, but on the way home, we went around by Ware and up by Big Barn.

At that time the lake had not been dredged out and there were two bridges at Ware instead of one. The mules crossed the first bridge okay, but as they started to cross the second one, one of the mules got scared and cut the hack real short and backed the rear end off in the lake. The road was narrow and the lake bank was so steep the back end of the hack was in the water. All of us jumped when we saw we were going in the water. Mom was standing up, holding to the dash board, hollering, "Minnie! Minnie!" and Grace and I were hollering, "Jump, Mom, jump!" Well, you know how active Mom would have been at jumping. Aunt Minnie grabbed the other mule by the bits and was holding them there. A man was right behind us and he came to the rescue and made the mules cross the bridge. We sure were scared.

When we lived on the Rich place and on the Rixleben place, we all had telephones to Wolf Lake. The telephone had a central office up over Chub Cruse's pool hall. Nearly everybody in the bottoms had a telephone. Our ring was two longs and two shorts. When Wolf Lake burned in 1918, it burned the switchboard and that was the end of our telephones, until the one we've got now came through about 1961 or '62.

After Wolf Lake burned, in 1918, Charles Cruse built a nice big building with a nice big room upstairs, where the lodges met each month. They had ice cream suppers, pie suppers, and they had a farewell supper for each boy that was called into service in World War I. Leora and Leo Brothers were the first ones called. Leora was sent to France after six

Plate 30. Edith's brother Leora leaving for California, about 1925. *Left to right*: Elijah, Leora, and Sarah Bradley; Bill and Edith Rendleman.

weeks training. He was lucky. He was in the Signal Corps and got to work back from the front lines. He was gone about two years, I think. He was courting Ruth Brown very heavy when he went into service but it was all over when he came back. Then is when he went to California and liked it so much he never was back, only on a visit [see plate 30].

People used to have parties and square dances and invite everybody in the community [see plate 31]. You never had refreshments of any kind. At the parties you played games. At the square dances you generally had an ice cream supper with it, also soda you bought. Uncle Allen and Aunt Minnie had a square dance when they lived in the old log house, in the corner just below Dad's. They also had one when they lived on Running Lake, in front of my house. It was an old house that Charles Ware had built. The Houstons had lived there before Aunt Minnie and Uncle Allen, and the boys, Charles and Bill Houston, were good square dancers.

I rode old Dais over there on Saturday afternoon, before I broke out with the measles, Sunday morning. Velma, who was a little tyke about three or four years old, asked me for my chewing gum I was chewing that evening. I gave it to her and in ten days she took the measles from me and then all of their kids had them.

Very few kids ever had candy and chewing gum. When you did get a stick of gum you chewed it for weeks. You stuck it under the table when you ate and at school you were not allowed to chew gum, only at recess, and you stuck it under the top of your desk till recess. Kids would ask each other to let them chew their gum a while. You let them chew it and then they gave it back to you. I was so

Plate 31. A crowd at the Bradleys' house on the Rixleben place on a Sunday, around 1913. Edith is the young woman in the black skirt on the right; Grace Ballance stands on her right. Edith recalled, "It was nothing for my mother to cook for twenty or twenty-five people." Almost everyone in the photo is related to Edith.

particular, I doubt if I ever let anybody chew my gum, but lots of kids did. I probably gave it to them to keep, as I wouldn't have chewed after anybody.

That was Saturday evening when I gave Babe the gum and Sunday morning I woke up sick with a few red spots on me. I wasn't able to get up Monday morning and I was real sick until Wednesday. I laid in my bedroom with the blinds down. Wednesday, I was really broken out red as a piece of flannel. The way I got the measles was from getting down over Leora's trunk and breathing deep as I could. He had just come home from Valparaiso, Indiana, from going to school, and he had the measles just before he came home. So I thought I would see if they were catching and they were.

Blanche Lee stayed with us when I had the measles and Bill came to see her at our house and they sat in the kitchen. He had courted her for a year before and had decided he didn't want to marry her, so he quit her. She did everything to get him back but he didn't go back. That was a year before I went with him.

Our neighbor Will Boyce used to be a dancing fool. He had dances at his house sometimes and at every dance he and Alice Mull put on a jig for everybody. They could really dance. The Mulls lived on the farm where the Girlers lived. Then they lived where the Lillies lived so long. Will Boyce lived there before he moved to the Bozarth farm. My dad used to love to dance also. Not too many years before he died, when he got up out of his chair to

start to the kitchen, he would step off the rug on the floor and knock the back step for a few minutes.

Mom had joined the church at Beech Grove when she was young and she didn't believe in dancing and playing cards. She wouldn't allow a deck of cards in our house and she raised five boys that would rather play cards as to eat. I was never allowed to play cards. I was playing cards one night at Uncle Allen Morgan's and Dad walked in the door. I got up from that table in a hurry. I thought sure I was into it but he never said anything. That was the last of my card playing. If I knew how to play cards now, I could pass away a lot of time. But I'm too nervous and old to learn now. We used to play Flinch, Old Maids, and checkers when I was a kid and stayed all night where there were kids. We played games like slap hands and club fist.

I used to go home with Zora Jones when I went to Sublette and stay all night. Her mother always let her make taffy candy, the kind you pulled to make it white. Mom never would let me make candy. She said it was wasting sugar. Every time she went to town and left me home, which was most of the time, Grace would stay with me and we would make candy. One time, I had it in one of those old black bread pans and hid it under my bed and when I went to get it, it was covered with big black ants. I slipped it out and threw it in the toilet hole. That's where we dumped things to hide them.

I was down at Uncle Adam's once and he

and Aunt Ett were gone and we decided to clean and fry a chicken. When we had it about half-fried we saw them coming and in the toilet hole it went.

When we first got a mail route none of the roads were graveled. The road from Aldridge ran on top of the levee. We had a small levee then, about five feet high. From Aldridge to our house was like the road from the corner— pure old black gumbo. Your wagon or buggy wheels would almost bog down with that sticky gumbo. Frank Holmes was our second mail carrier and he had a buggy with a little houselike thing built on, with a little stove in it. Otherwise he would have frozen. He used to come by after dark. It took him from noon till after dark to travel ten miles in that mud. That was after I was married and back home, while Bill was in service. Jack Holder was our first mail carrier. He put somebody's check in the wrong mail box and they forced him to resign.

I rode old Dais and took up a Larkin order (that was like Rawleighs or Watkins products).[4] I got my cedar chest with the premium coupons. I also got my first buffet with Larkin coupons, after I was married. Dad didn't like for me to be out selling things. He thought that was asking people for a donation. I rode old Dais a lot. One time, I tried to open the lot gate while still on her and got my hand hung in the gate, and she went on in and it pulled me off by this one hand and almost broke my hand. I never tried that again.

When I was about fifteen, or somewhere near, we had a big bay mare named Ribbon. We drove her to the buggy and she seemed gentle enough. I drove her to Wolf Lake one afternoon and as I was going home, I was driving along so nice when Joe Evans, driving a car, came around the curve in front of where Raymond and Janette Brummit lived. When Ribbon saw it she stopped dead still, threw up her head, gave a snort, and turned, and through the fencerow and barbed wire fence we started. I jumped as soon as she turned, and she went on through the fence and all. The buggy didn't turn over until she started out into the road, through the place where they used to come into the field, and she caught one of the front wheels of the buggy on the corner post. She went right on, breaking the harness and leaving the buggy on its side. She was in a dead run, she was really scared. She ran to the barn with part of the harness dragging. Albert was home on a vacation and when Ribbon came running up to the barn with harness dragging, it really scared him and Mom. They came running to see what had become of me and I was bawling like a calf. Of course, they were glad I jumped out. I got some cuts and scratches on my arms but I sure did dread for Dad to come in. That fencerow was ten feet high in bushes and you couldn't see there was a barbed wire fence in it. It was grown up on both sides of the road. Ribbon didn't get a scratch. Dad didn't blame me for it. Nobody could have done any different, for Ribbon was really scared. So was I. Joe Evans didn't even stop to see if I was hurt or not. He lived at Grand Tower and had been down to his farm. That was the first automobile either one of us had seen on the road.

It was very common in those days for a team of horses to run away. All farmers raised their horses and mules and you had to break them to get them used to the harness. It would take three or four men to get the harness on them and they would have to do that several times before they hitched them to the wagon. So it was not uncommon for them to run away. They always tried to put a gentle horse beside them so they couldn't run away.

While I'm telling about wrecks, I might as well tell about when Bill and I had just started going together. We had started toward Wolf Lake and were driving along this same road in the evening, when all of a sudden his horses turned and ran into the same fence. One got out of part of the harness and started back down the road. I hollered, "Oh! Bill!" That's what I always said when anything happened. He hollered, "Jump, Edith!" and ran around to my side of the buggy and helped me out. He caught the horse and hitched them up again and we went on. We never did know what caused them to turn and run into the fence.

Another time I hollered, "Oh! Bill!" and just kept driving was when he was teaching me to drive his dad's old Model T. It was shortly after we were married. He was working for his dad and we were staying at my home. I had gone with him to his folks' that day and we were going home after dark and I was driving. It could have been my dad's Model T, as he bought one the fall we were married. We came to this house where Lewis Smith lives and two little kittens were lying in the ruts. I just hollered, "Oh! Bill!" and went right on over them. There was no gravel on the roads at that time and the sand was deep.

When I was about fourteen Dad bought me an organ. He said if I would wait until the next year he would buy me a piano. I couldn't wait and ordered one from Sears Roebuck. It cost fifty dollars. I took lessons from Edna Rendleman for two summers and was good enough to play for church when no one else was there. I could play popular songs like "It's a Long Way to Tipperary," "The Trail of the Lonesome Pine," "Down by the Old Mill Stream," and others. I got the sheet music in Anna. Grace, Everett, Bill, and I used to gather around the organ and sing, and when one of the boys came home we would sing, as they all used to sing in the choir at Beech Grove and Wolf Lake, too. The boys always attended church when they were growing up.

I drove the buggy to Wolf Lake to church and Sunday school. Had to go catch old Dais, hitch her up, and tie her to the hitch rack till I got ready to go. Then unharness her when I got home. That was routine if you wanted to go anyplace.

Wolf Lake at that time and before had

a pretty rough name. Bunk Anderson who worked for Bob Rendleman was a tough guy. So was Aud Travis supposed to be tough. They all drank and gambled a lot and it would end up in cutting somebody with a knife or a shooting. The Randle boys, Loge, Milas, and Harrison, were tough also. They would not fight fair. They shot Oscar Trainer down in the Cinderella Ballroom (or better, say "dance hall") like a dog. Milas and Harrison went to the penitentiary for twenty years to life, but they were paroled.[5] They went to Missouri when they got out. They were bullies and Oscar Trainer could whip all of them at one time. So they shot him down in cold-blood murder. They used to call Wolf Lake "Pistol City." But it wasn't any worse than any other small place that didn't have a police officer. There used to be shootings at dances back in the early years. They would get drunk and then wind up in a fight. There were always two or three bullies around that thought they were tougher than anybody else. Seems like in my young years there were a lot of fights and cuttings with pocket knives.

One year, Mom's half brother Lummie Ballance got drunk and was riding home with a bunch of men in a lumber wagon out west of Jonesboro and they got in a brawl. Uncle Lummie cut Herman Frick across his upper arm with his knife, and I guess he thought he had killed him. Paul McCloud said his father, Fitz, was in the wagon with them and he hadn't hurt Herm much at all. Aunt Min-nie was living in a house at the foot of Doc Rich Hill and Lummie came to see her.[6] I was staying all night there and he woke us kids up—two o'clock in the morning—and kissed us all good-bye. We were all crying. He crossed the Mississippi River that night and ended up in Louisiana and no one but Uncle Adam ever saw him again. He never even wrote to anyone for twenty-five or thirty years. Then he wrote Uncle Adam, and Uncle Adam later went to see him down in Louisiana. Uncle Adam went back again to deer hunt.

In 1941 Bill and I went with George and Mary Wilkins to the Pilgrimage at Natchez, Mississippi, where Uncle Lummie's daughter Sadie lived. By that time, Lummie was dead. We stayed with her. No one in the South did their housework and she had a Negro woman to do the cooking and cleaning. Lummie was an own brother to Uncle Adam and Aunt Minnie, and a half brother to my mother.

Chub Cruse ran a pool hall under the telephone office. My father and my uncle and two other men played pool all afternoon many days. Leora, Bill, Homer Frogge, Charles Jones, Everett Gregory, Louie Ballance, and several of the boys played pool every night till eleven o'clock. Several of the boys had a horse to ride but Leora and Homer always walked. John Robertson was the MoPac railroad agent and he lived on the corner and he had a big dog. That dog would try to get through the fence after those boys every night. They all got them a pistol and shot at him till they got to the corner. They never could hit him. Mr. Robertson would come out every night hollering at them. They just made it a joke, trying to kill the dog, but they never could hit him.

Chub Cruse would let the boys have chicken fries. They furnished the chickens and Chub would fry them. Each one would steal two chickens from his mom or wherever he was staying when they would have a fry. One Saturday night, when I was fourteen or fifteen, they had a big fry on. This night, Mr. Jones was shipping a bunch of hogs to the St. Louis market and a bunch of the boys rode their horses and mules over to see them loaded on the boat at Travis Island. Dad and Mr. Jones usually went together to have enough hogs for them to land on this side. Bill shipped in with them sometimes. The boys who had horses all went to the boat landing and were to come back and eat chicken. When they got back to Wolf Lake they all got off their horses and tied them to an iron post that held the roof of the pool hall up. But Charley Jones had his right foot on the ground and before he could get his left foot out of the stirrup, his mule got scared and ran away, dragging him down the street. His foot came loose from the stirrup in front of Fred Tucker's house or it would have killed him. But he was hurt and bruised up terrible. He and his mother, Mrs. Jones, never got along and he refused to let them take him home. Everett Gregory was staying at Everett Brown's as a hired hand and they took him there. They called the doctor that

night, as soon as it happened. Next morning, when Mrs. Jones heard about it, she was mad because they didn't bring him home and she had him brought home. But that ended the chicken fry. Nobody could eat a bite, they were scared so bad.

Leora was never in our crowd. He was older. We had a horse and buggy but he never took a girl anywhere in a buggy. I don't know if Dad wouldn't let Leora ride a horse or if he just didn't want to. I remember if the horses had worked in the field that day they weren't used at night. Long about that time, Leora asked Dad for money to go to an ice cream supper and Dad handed him fifty cents and Leora said, "If that's all you are going to give me, just keep it," and he did. You see why kids wanted to get away from home in those days.

The father carried the pocketbook and he never gave anybody but very little. Men always bought the latest machinery for themselves but never would buy any modern things for the house. They would buy stoves to cook on but that was all. You didn't have much in the house, either. Mom always raised chickens and sold eggs, butter, and milk and she bought groceries and our clothes. Mom somehow bought us a kitchen cabinet and bought a carpet made of straw for the front room. That's what was on the floor when I was married.

My Dad used to go to Waltonville and buy a team of fancy mules. He would pay as much as five hundred dollars for them. But they never thought a woman would like a piece of new furniture. The wife was never given anything, except Mrs. Rendleman and maybe other women that were in the upper bracket of society, but most people I associated with didn't get any. My mom and hardly any other woman (except Mrs. Rendleman) never wrote a check in their life. It seemed a woman never asked her husband for money. You just tried to earn it yourself. I kept boarders, school teachers, raised chickens, and everything else that was decent to make my own money. I paid for my first bedroom suit, five dollars a month. It cost eighty-five dollars at Joiners. Mom and Dad growled at every piece of furniture I bought. They would say you didn't need that, you'll never have anything, etc. They also said, "You'll never have nothing 'cause you eat it all up."

It wasn't easy, when I raised my children, for a woman to get a job. During World War II, women began working in defense plants and making money enough to live. It was good in a way but caused lots of children to be left without a home. It's a mixed-up world today, women and men just walk out and leave a good woman or man for nothing.

Dad cried after Mom died and said he never bought her any furniture or anything. After she got sick I told him Mom had to have a new bed, as hers was so high she couldn't get into it by herself. The head of the bed was seven feet high; the mattress with the feather-bed was at least four feet high. Mom didn't want it. She said she never had anything in her life and she didn't want anything now to leave for some other woman. But I bought the bed anyway. That was a year before she died.

8 Having the Time of Our Lives

Grace was allowed to go with the boys before I was. Bill took me home from an ice cream supper up over Charles Cruse's store, June 26, 1914, before I was sixteen in August. Everett Penrod got him to ask to take me home. I just liked two months being sixteen years old. I guess those next three years were the happiest years of my life. At first I couldn't tell if I liked Homer Frogge or Wm. J. Mom liked Bill (so did everybody) but she sure didn't want me to go with Homer. His dad had been mean to his wives and I guess Homer lived up to tradition.

I quit Bill three times the first six months. And the last time he wasn't so easy to get back. Then I fell in love with him and we never quit again. Bill and I courted three years, two months [see plate 32]. At first he came on Sunday afternoon, then later on, he came on Saturday night and Sunday afternoon. Then

about a year before we were married, he came on Wednesday night, also. I have been accused by Leora and others that I married him because they were supposed to have money. That was a laugh. Boys weren't paid any money for their work.

When we were courting not many of the boys had horses and buggies. There were four or five couples of us that had horses and buggies—Bill's brother, Howard Rendleman, and Agnes Choate, Louie Ballance and Hester Bridgeman, Everett Gregory and Effie Morton, Ted Jones and one of the Choate girls, and Grace Ballance and Everett Penrod. On Saturday night, we went to a dance or an ice cream supper, and Sunday afternoon about two o'clock, we went for a drive, either on the river road around by Ware or the river road around by McGuire. We always got back for church at Wolf Lake. Sometimes we went

Plate 32. Edith Bradley and Bill Rendleman,
while they were courting, 1916.

down to Wolf Lake to the ice cream parlor Joe Wilson had built onto his house.

Sometimes we would fix a picnic lunch and go somewhere and eat it. One time I remember so well, we all went on a hay wagon, eight or ten couples, to Morgan School and we stopped on the way home at Miller Pond. There is a huge rock called Miller Rock in front of Miller Pond on the side of the hill. We climbed that hill and were all over Miller Rock. There is a second ledge on that rock and Bill and Joe Gregerson were down on that ledge, where we girls couldn't see them. We girls were throwing rocks in their direction. I threw a rock the size of your fist and Bill stuck his head up just as I threw the rock. I just missed him by a split second. It scared me so bad I never threw another rock towards anybody.

Another time, on Easter Sunday, we planned a big picnic and, oh, how it poured down the rain. We had it in the old Odd Fellows Hall up over Alfred Wilson's store. That is where they used to have all the meetings until Charley Cruse built the new building, after Wolf Lake burned. At that time, there was the Odd Fellows, Rebekahs, Modern Woodmen, Royal Neighbors, etc., using the hall. But they had already quit using some of their paraphernalia and it was stored in some anterooms. How we got in the anteroom, I don't know, but we did. It was all covered with dust a half-inch thick. In the junk there was the equipment they used to get initiated into one of the lodges. Well, we had the time of our lives riding each other on that equipment that day.

Louie Ballance and Hester Bridgeman were in our crowd, also. She was one of my dearest friends. That is she with me in the overalls [see plate 33]. She was Rendleman's hired girl at that time. She was the nicest, kindest person I ever knew. She lived up on Hutchins Creek, toward Alto Pass. Wm. and I went out there for dinner. Her parents' house burned before that and burned two of their small children to death.

Everett, Grace, Bill, and I always went to the Anna Fair. One time I remember, Bill had two and a half dollars to go to the fair. We paid fifty cents to put the horses in a livery stable in Jonesboro, paid ten cents each to ride the streetcar to Anna, paid our way into the fairgrounds, which was twenty-five cents each, went out and ate dinner at the restaurant, and we had the rest of it to spend at the fair. We had to pay ten cents each to ride the streetcar back to Jonesboro.[1]

Another year Bill, Grace, Everett, and I went to the Anna Fair. You went in the morning and stayed all day. You just walked from one end of the fairground to the other. We would ride the merry-go-round. They had a Ferris wheel but we never rode it. That was the only two rides they had then. And we would meet some of our friends and stop and talk. That year I made Grace and me new dresses out of cotton crepe and a dust cap to match and we wore them to the fair. Another time we were at the fair and it came up the awfulest rain. They paid fifty cents each for us to go into a sideshow to get under a tent.

It happened to be in the middle of the fairground in a low place and the water came in from both ends, and we were standing in water over our shoe tops. We finally ran out. I was wearing a new hat with a turned-up brim and it was trimmed in pink and green ribbon. I caught a brim full of rain and when I stooped over, the water had faded the ribbon and it got all over Grace's dress and on my white dress and ruined both our dresses.

Louie Ballance, Hester Bridgeman, Bill, and I almost froze once. We drove to Anna to get our pictures made and it turned freezing cold and came the awfulest snowstorm you ever could imagine. It wasn't so bad when we started, but it lasted all day and part of that night. Bill always had heavy lap robes and had a heavy blanket for his horses. Louie just had a lap robe. We shared our blankets with them or they would have frozen. Bill always had one lap robe under the seat and let it come down to the floorboard under our feet. Bill always loved his horses and if they were going to stand tied in the cold, he covered them with their big heavy blankets. It took us till almost dark to get back home. And the snow blowed and drifted till you had to guess at the road. We looked rather frozen in the pictures [see plate 34]. That was after Grace and Everett were married or they would have been along.

Bill and Ted Jones had two ponies for their driving team. One time, we ran a race coming from McGuire. We won. Nobody could beat Bill's team.

I must tell you about the showboats that

Plate 33. Edith Bradley and Hester Bridgeman clowning around with guns, 1916. Edith and Hester dressed up in overalls and men's hats, and when approached by the hired man, Herman Lockley, they asked him how to get to Wolf Lake. Because of their dress he failed to recognize them and gave them directions. They laughed about this prank for years.

Plate 34. Edith Bradley and Bill Rendleman (*left*), and Hester Bridgeman and Louie Ballance (*right*). They drove through a snowstorm to have this photograph taken at Atkins Studio in Anna.

used to land at Cape, Grand Tower, and sometimes Neelys Landing, which was just across the river from Travis Island. Two of the boats were named *Golden Rod* and *Cotton Blossom* and there were others. The way we knew there was going to be a show, they would start playing the calliope about noon. Grace, Everett, Bill, and I went twice to Grand Tower, which was quite a ways to drive (ten miles). One of the times, Grace, Bill, and I went up and got Everett out of the wheat thrashing field. Another time, before I started to go with Bill, I walked over here to this house that I now own and Mollie and Olevia Frogge and I went over to Charles Ware's house and asked him if the Japanese boy that was working and living with him could take us to the showboat at Grand Tower. Mr. Ware had a car and the Japanese servant took us.

When Charles Ware's first wife lived, they picked the Japanese servant up as a small boy and he served as their flunkey (valet) all his life. He finally married a Japanese girl in St. Louis and they lived down here in the little house. He tried to farm. One day, he was riding the old stalk-cutter and he didn't come in for supper. They went to see about him and he was wound up in the stalk-cutter blade and cut very badly. He died that night. They had him cremated in St. Louis and his wife went back to Japan and took his ashes with her.

After we lived at Sublette Dad, Mom, Bill, and myself, and the Travises, who crossed the river all the time in a boat rowed by hand, went to Neelys Landing to a showboat. It came up the awfulest storm and big black cloud, thundering and lightning—you never saw it worse. And we had to row back across the river in that. But we got back before it caught us in that river. That was the one and only time I ever crossed that river in a boat.

Bill's dad, Bob Rendleman, owned a thrashing machine and thrashed around Wolf Lake. He also owned half interest in a sawmill with Ran Sides. His son, Walt Sides, ran the engine at the sawmill and also the thrashing machine. No wonder Bill's health broke at so young an age. He used to haul logs all through the winter in mud and water, snow and ice. It never got too bad to stop him. He always wore hip boots, as there were lots of swamps all around in those days. Russ Juden hauled logs with a pair of oxen and Bill was right in there helping him. They could go through mud that horses and mules could not. Bill started smoking at age nine (unbeknownst to his mother), which helps hardening of the arteries.

Bill was a hard worker all of his young life. But his brother Howard was just the opposite. He used to lie down at the end of the field while his team was resting and sleep for an hour. Howard used to tell Bill, "What do you mean by getting out there in the field with the hired hands and making a hand? You are not thought any more of than a hired hand." Bill never thought he was above anybody, and neither of us thought it was a disgrace to work. And we had to work to make a living.

About a year or two before I was married,

I could buy anything I wanted on a credit at Chas. Spring's store in Wolf Lake. I had a cedar chest full of pillowcases, tablecloths, sheets, etc. Dad never did say anything about me running up a store bill. I quit college a year before I was married. Those days, if you got married you didn't need to go to college. So I spent that year crocheting and embroidering, making things to start housekeeping.

We decided the winter of 1916 we would get married. Bill asked his dad if he could rent one of his farms and his dad said no, he could just go on working for him. In that day, the father kept all the money and gave it out to you as he wanted to. So Bill decided to go to Granite City, as Orville was married and had moved up there and was making big money. He left his horse and buggy (he only owned one of his horses) at our house, took the other horse home and left in the night, leaving his dad a note saying why he was leaving. That really threw Mr. Rendleman for a loop, as Bill was his mainstay. W. J. got a job at the steel mill, but he didn't like the city. We decided to get married at once so I could go with him to Granite City.

Mrs. Lockley always was for me. She would take me anyplace I wanted to go. She drove me to Grand Tower to catch the train to go to Granite City, just before Bill and I were married. I caught the train in Howerton (a small town on the MoPac Railroad) just to the right of Grand Tower, to keep people in Wolf Lake from seeing me go. I went up there and Orville's wife Della took me to St. Louis to buy my wedding dress.

We set the date for August 19, 1917, and I sent out invitations (letters) to everybody we wanted to invite. We had a big home wedding for relatives and friends. Mom and Mrs. Lockley, Aunt Ett, and others helped her fix dinner for the whole crowd. Curt and family came up from Cairo. The whole Rendleman family and lots of others were there for dinner. We were married at two o'clock [see plate 35]. Curt and Edna stood up with us and a big crowd came for the wedding. You never heard of a church wedding in those days. They were mostly justice-of-the-peace ceremonies. It was years and years before church weddings were for common people.

Uncle Dave Rendleman and family had come down to Mr. and Mrs. Rendleman's and somebody told him there was a big wedding taking place, so after the wedding they just came on over and joined in the feast. Dad had raised a big patch of watermelons that year on the island and he had the basement full of big ripe watermelons and cantaloupes. They fixed a table with sawhorses and everybody had all the watermelon they could eat. That day was the first time I ever saw a tear in my dad's eyes. Mom cried like I was dead. Guess she knew what a hard struggle was ahead of us.

We were happy and rich that day. Bill had thirty-five dollars when he came home from Granite City and his dad gave him fifty dollars for a wedding present.

I guess my teenage years and two or three years after we were married were the happiest years of my life. Too bad you can't realize what a struggle marriage was, especially in those days. And it was easy in my day to what it was in my parents' day. Each generation has had it a little easier than the one before, as you can see from my writings.

(Oh! how green and dumb I must have been. Guess that's why I fell in love with Bill, as that's what they said about him. They said it about him because he didn't try to tear the clothes off of a girl the first time he went out with one, like some I could name did. So I was dumb and green and shy with boys and didn't know they did such a thing. I had been raised so strict it would have scared me to death if one had made a pass at me. It was months after we started going together before Bill kissed me good-night.)

Mr. Rendleman knew he could not farm without Bill. So he and my dad got W. J. off and begged him to stay with Mr. Rendleman that very day, offering him one-fourth of the crop. Of course, Wm. J. didn't like the city and he took the offer. Mr. Rendleman told Bill we could move over to the Keith farm at Sublette (Mose Brown lived there) the next year. So Bill took the offer and we fixed up the little tenant house just west of Wolf Lake and moved there in the fall.

It was a mess. There was another house close by, where Lish Allman lived. His father-in-law lived with them and he was about seventy or eighty years old. He helped me felt

Plate 35. Wedding portrait of Bill Rendleman and Edith Bradley, August 19, 1917.

and paper the house and they put a new floor in it. I think they built the two rooms on the back. I did all the painting of the woodwork myself. We stayed with my folks till we got the house fixed.

We bought all of our furniture out of the eighty-five dollars and had money left over. Mrs. Rendleman bought us a complete bed outfit (bedstead, springs, and mattress). She was awfully good to us. When there was an ice cream supper or anything to go to, she would send us a check by Caroline for two and a half dollars. That was a lot in those days. Joe Wilson's wife had just died and we bought chairs and a leather couch from him. We ordered a nice range cookstove for thirty-five dollars from Sears Roebuck & Co. It had a warming oven on top. I used that stove until we bought the combination gas and wood stove, after we moved to the Rixleben place. We also bought a gray, thin, wool rug from them.

Dad bought his first car that fall, a Model T. He and Bill went to Illmo, Missouri to get it. They stayed all night and Bill drove it home next day. Somewhere along there, Mr. Rendleman had bought a Model T. The fall of 1917, I drove Mrs. Rendleman, Caroline, and Lenita over to see the new Sublette School they were building. While we were fixing up the house, Bill drove his dad's Model T to our house every night, and lots of days I went over to his house to spend the day.

One time, I helped Mrs. Rendleman and the hired girl seed some sweet green peppers for her to stuff with cabbage and they set my hands on fire. We put lard and everything else on them but it was two or three hours before they stopped burning. I walked the yard and wrung my hands, they burned so bad. They were red as flannel.

Bill got the job of substitute mail carrier and sometimes I would ride with him around the upper bottoms, until Charles Cruse, the postmaster, told him no one was allowed to ride with the mail carrier.

We moved into our house in November 1917. That was the winter of the big snow. It snowed December 6th and kept adding more to it until March, before we saw the ground. We had a little King heater stove. They were made of tin and had a hole in the top where you put the wood in. It was oblong and had four legs. You filled them full of wood and they would get red hot, and in fifteen minutes they were cold again. The lid jumped up and down. Bill and Jack Harris spent the winter dragging in logs and sawing them into wood for two stoves. The snow drifted that winter from Ted Jones's house along that bank clear into Wolf Lake, until it was level with the bank. Even horses couldn't get through. They made a road inside the fence in Mr. Rendleman's field and had to use it all winter. That was a winter to be remembered.

One time, Bill's team to the wagon ran away. He came by the house with the team in a dead run and I just waved at him and thought he was making them run. When he came in that evening he said they were running away with him and he couldn't stop them. Bill just loved to break horses and mules. So did Dick Davie. The Davies used to go down in Texas and buy a boxcar load of those Western ponies and sell them. Most every young man, especially a hired hand, had a riding horse, or a horse and buggy. You took a gentle horse or mule and put the young one in beside him and got him or her used to the harness or wagon. Nearly every farmer raised some young colts. Sometimes the gentle horse would surprise them and run away, too. It wasn't unusual for a team to run away and hurt somebody.

Wm. J. never owned both of his driving horses. He just owned the palomino. We had to use a mule with her to the buggy to go to church and the picture show at Wolf Lake. Then she went blind and the top wore out on the buggy and we had a topless buggy with a blind mare and mule for a long time. In about 1926 or '28, Wm. J. bought a Model T Ford from Ford Stone in Jonesboro. He paid two hundred dollars for it. We thought we were rich. It had side curtains with isinglass for windows, and they broke easy in cold weather and the wind came through like a storm. We were so proud of that car.

Things went along smoothly and I became pregnant in November, about the time we moved into our little house. I thought it was a mansion, I was so happy. Before I was married I liked kids so much I planned on having twelve. But I found it was a little different making a living after I was married [see appendix H].

There was nothing but routine working until late summer came. Edna Rendleman had gone to Dallas Ballance, who had been sent to Kansas by the railroad a couple of years before, and they were married in September after we married in August. She, too, became pregnant shortly after she was married. In July, when she was to have her baby, Mrs. Rendleman took Caroline and Lenita and went to Kansas to be with Edna when she had her baby, after making arrangements for Bill and me to stay at her house. She had a hired girl who did most of the work. I, also, was expecting in July and Mrs. Rendleman was still in Kansas when Bonnie was born. She was born in the spare bedroom, July 16, 1918.

Edna lost her baby boy, as Edna had small pelvis bones and she laid for two or three days before they took it and it was dead. In two years she had Maxine. She was a sectional [cesarean] baby, first we ever heard of such a thing. Mrs. Rendleman stayed two weeks longer with Edna and when she came home, I was up and ready to go home. Esther Hamilton was Mrs. Rendleman's hired girl at that time and we both got head lice from combing our hair with a comb the hired man used—at least we thought that was where we got them. I think Aunt Mag stayed with me and took

Plate 36. Bill Rendleman (*left*) and Albert Grammer in their World War I uniforms.

care of the baby. Bonnie was a fine healthy baby, so pretty and fat. We were proud of her.

World War I had been going on for three years but it hadn't touched close to home yet. Leora and three or four others had been called into service shortly before we were married and if you had been married before a certain time, you were exempted. But Bill had not been married long enough, so he was called and left, September 6, 1918 [see plate 36]. Bonnie was six weeks old. I thought the world had come to an end. I closed up our house and moved back home. I stayed at the Rendlemans' a few weeks, too. Wm. J. was sent to Battle Creek, Michigan, for training and they were all packed ready to go overseas when the flu broke out. Overnight, half of his company was stricken. Those that didn't have it were put to work in a makeshift hospital. Wm. J. was lucky he didn't take the flu, so he was put in the hospital as a nurse or flunkey. We sent Bill Vick's salve and cough drops by the box. Out of his company over half of them died. He said it was the saddest experience anyone ever saw.

It was the worst epidemic anyone had ever experienced. They hadn't discovered any antibiotics then, and they died from pneumonia. It was here and all over the U.S.A. like that. Here, whole families were stricken at the same time. Two or three would die in the same family. People were afraid to go in and help, as it was very contagious. Boge Miller lost his whole family, all but one sister. A woman with a newborn baby was sure to die if she got it. Several from around here died. The flu killed Uncle George. It was a sad time that year. We were so lucky. Neither of our families had it.

Before they got organized after the flu, the Armistice was signed, November 11, 1918. I was in Anna shopping with Mom at that moment as the church bells began ringing, horns and sirens screaming, and the whole U.S.A. went wild. You never saw such happy people. The town went wild with joy. Bill surprised us by coming home after Christmas. I never will forget that day. Herman Lockley worked for Dad and he saw him coming. He ran in the house hollering, "Bill is here." I ran out with Bonnie in my arms (no wrap on her or myself), crying with joy. He had not seen Bonnie since she was six weeks old. Now she was six months. He stayed a week and was discharged the last of January 1919.

We opened up our little house and moved back. Mr. Rendleman had just bought Mose Brown out on the river and Bill rented that farm. We moved in April. The old house sat near the river where the levee is now. That was the worst time of my entire life I think. The house wasn't fit to live in; it was about ready to fall in. It was three rooms, like most those days. It comprised a big living room, one bedroom, and a long narrow kitchen. The lower side had sunk down until it was six inches lower on that side. The floor had dropped loose from the house in the kitchen and it was so one-sided you couldn't hardly walk in it. But we were happy.

When we moved over there Dad gave us a cow. I had a sow and six pigs and Bill's Dad gave him a team of mules, harness, and wagon. Bonnie was nine months old and so fat and pretty. We were happy as a lark, as Mr. Rendleman had promised to build the new house up behind Sublette School. He started work on the house but he just had one or two carpenters working on it and they didn't get along very fast and when cold weather came, they quit working on it.

I had a narrow escape of getting hurt while we lived there in the old house. I tied the cow out to graze every evening. One day I got my foot wrapped up in the rope and the cow ran away. I was lucky I got untangled before she dragged me but it sure scared me. Bill was sick in bed with tonsillitis.

We made it fine, until the bad cold weather set in. One side of the old brick flue had tumbled off and when the wind was from the south, it blew the smoke back in the room. Wm. used to have a round of tonsillitis once or twice a year and be in bed a week with it. About the first of December, he got down in bed with a sore throat and those days there was nothing you could do but take cold tablets, grease with Vick's salve, and gargle with Listerine. Sometimes one of your tonsils would burst from infection. The weather got real cold and the wind blew from the south this Saturday and I just couldn't get enough heat out of the coal stove to keep us warm. Every time the fire started to burn, this gust of wind blew the smoke out of the stove into the room, until all three of us were all black with coal soot and no heat. There was soot everywhere. Dad came down to see about us, and there we were, no heat and even Bill in bed had soot on him. We had a bed in the living room. When he walked in he just had a fit. He cursed and said, "You can't live in this mess. Get your clothes together, you are going home with me and stay until that house is finished."

So we went up home with him, and Bud was born, December 27, 1919. Bill hired Mrs. Lockley to help Mom with the work until I got able to help. Bill's mother and Caroline kept Bonnie three weeks, which helped a lot. Della Hubbs took care of Bud until I was able. Those days, they made you stay in bed ten days when a baby was born.

It was no picnic up there at my dad's. The living room was the only room that was ever warm. Bud was about a week old and I took, they called it, a weed in your breast. The breast would get all swollen and hard and you had to draw the milk out with a breast pump, as the baby wouldn't nurse it. You would have chills with it. They said you took cold in it, but I think you had too much milk and the baby couldn't nurse it out and it would get hard and red and inflamed. It would take two weeks to get over a spell of it. I'm glad mothers don't have to have the hard times we had in those days. And on top of everything, Bud had the three month colic every evening from six o'clock until one o'clock in the morning. We sat up with him and rocked and bumped in one of those old cane-bottom chairs Mom had, until one o'clock every night. You would get so sleepy and tired you could hardly stay awake yourself. The day he was three months old he quit crying and slept like a log.

My dad got a big kick out of Bonnie. She was seventeen and a half months old. Dad would get down on his hands and knees and call it bear walking. Bonnie would crawl and try to do everything he did.

9 Bedbugs, Fleas, and Hired Hands

When spring began to come, Wm. J. just hitched up his mules to a log wagon and went to Jonesboro lumber yard, hauled enough lumber to finish our house, and charged it to his dad. They used all of old Sublette schoolhouse for lumber they could. We moved in it March 1920, when they got three rooms so we could live in it [see plate 37]. Then they finished it as they could, all but papering and painting inside. We lived in it a year or so with bare walls and floors. I did all the papering and finishing work myself as I could. Somebody, I think, helped me hang the felt paper. We sure were glad to move to ourselves again and get off of my folks, even though the house wasn't finished. Boy, those years were rough. We built our buildings as we could—a barn, corncribs, and a chicken house and smokehouse.

Bill Glotfelty worked for Wm. J. down in the old house and for a while in the new one. I always milked the cow or cows and carried in wood and most of the coal, also carried water from the barn for years until Bud, Bonnie, and sometimes the hired hands, would help with the wood and coal. But I always emptied the ashes, as I didn't trust anybody with that job because it was a dusty, messy job every time. In real cold weather there would be three pans of ashes to empty. Just think, all my life up to this time there was never any heat in our bedrooms, no matter how cold it got. But after we moved to the new house I used to open the stairway door in the evening and later we bought a floor register that Dad put in the dining room ceiling. It went clear through the upstairs floor and let the heat warm up the upstairs so it wouldn't be so cold to go to bed. But later in the night when the fire died down, it got

Plate 37. The Rendleman family in front of Sublette School, around 1921. *Left to right*: Bud, Bill, Bonnie, Edith.

ice-cold, as you banked the fire with a big chunk of coal and it just died down and had enough coals on one side to start the fire in the morning. It would freeze ice in the kitchen and everything froze up hard and tight. Wm. J. always got up first and built a fire. My dad always built the fires, but Mrs. R. always built the fires at the Rendleman home.

I believe she kept a fire burning all night, as their house was never cold like ours.

We slept under two big heavy comforters made from the legs of men's pants and scraps from wool dresses, also between heavy blankets and a quilt or two on top of that. Most everybody had feather beds those days. At least Mom did. She gave me one when I was married and I raised geese to make another one or two and my pillows.

We all four slept together until Bonnie was four years old and then I got a cot that the sides raised and made a three-quarter bed and placed it longways under the window, so their head was against our bed. Had the awfulest time getting Bud to sleep there. He would wake up in the night and over in our bed he came. I would have to get in their bed sometimes until Bud went to sleep. I always did the getting up to tend to the babies in the night. Never thought of calling on Bill to diaper one or get up with one in the night. But I've seen my sisters-in-law lie there and let their husbands see about the kids. In those days, the women did the housework and raising the kids and the men never turned a hand around the house. Even garden making was done by the women. Except my father. He always helped in the garden. He was good to my mom in that way. He kept her a good woodpile. She never had to hoe like I did. And he plowed her garden with the horse and plow. The men would plow and harrow the garden and sometimes plow it out with a double shovel. They generally tromped down more than they did good. Boy, it was a grand invention when they made Rototillers.

We had a round of bedbugs when we moved in the new house at Sublette. We had mattresses, but they were thick before I knew it. They multiplied like flies on the corners of the straw beds or mattresses. At that time, we had some kind of spray, I think, or either coal oil. They said they were in that new pine ceiling, although that was what the whole house was lined with until I felted and papered it all over. They stayed hid until you went to sleep and then they came out and ate on you. The fleas were bad, too, up till after we moved to my place. My son Lee Roy bought the first powder from MoorMan's Feed Co. that you could put in the barn where the hogs slept, that would kill the fleas. Before that, you could walk in a barn or shed and the little black devils would cover your pants legs.

I was the champion flea catcher. When one got in your clothes (which they often did, and in your bed also), when he bit me, I could just reach in and get him. They didn't mash when you caught them. You had to roll him into an unconscious state before you could crack him. And jump! They could jump a foot at a time and get away from you.

We struggled to make enough money to live on. We lost a bunch of hogs, when we lived in the old house, with cholera, which sure was a hard blow. Life was really hard at Sublette as all the chores were left up to me. I did all the garden making with a hoe, raised chickens, cooked for all of us and the hired hands, went to the hills and picked blackberries and canned them.

We had many hired hands, all young men. As long as Wm. J. lived, he had a hired hand in the house to wait on him, while I had to cook, wash, and iron for them. It made me so mad, you never had any privacy, besides all the work it put on me. Some of the young men that stayed with us when we lived at Sublette were Bill Glotfelty, Harvey Lyerla, Edward Conaway, Clarence Groves, Pete Hubbs, and many more. Bill Glotfelty couldn't talk plain. He would come in and Bonnie would be crying and he would take her out of the high chair and say, "Who said you had to set in that old chair." Harvey Lyerla was our first hired hand in the new house behind Sublette. He only worked one year. John Hill was a stranger that Wm. J. picked up. He was too lazy to go downstairs at night. I had a side room upstairs that hadn't had the floor put down, so you could see the joists. The painter had set some empty paint buckets back in there and John wet in those paint buckets. I went in there one day after he left, and there he had wet those paint buckets full of water. Believe me, I was mad. I had to haul them all out of there.

We had an old man for a while named Old Man Club. I don't know how he came to be with us. He wasn't able to work in the field. It was more like we were taking care of him. He drank hot water with cream in it and when he wanted more he'd tap on his cup with his spoon. He was real hard of hearing. There were many tramps that came by and wanted a handout. My mother always fed them. She never turned anybody away without fixing them something to eat.

Finally, Bill fixed up an old house next to the levee and Jack Harris worked for us. His wife's name was Ella and she came back from dinner with Jack every day at noon and sat there under my nose every afternoon. They had adopted a little girl, Mary Ellen, when her mother, Inez Davis, died. Inez was a sister to Patch Eye. Bud and Bonnie used to tease Mary Ellen a lot. I got so tired of Ella I almost pulled my hair, as I had work to do.

You didn't have to have much money in those days. I don't remember, but I don't think you had to have insurance on anything but your house and Mr. Rendleman had that. I boarded school teachers in those days to make a little money. They paid two and a half dollars a week for room and board, the same amount I paid at the boarding house when I went to school at Carbondale. The first was Leona Whitlock. Others that stayed with us were Dossie Burnley, Marjorie Gunn, Doris Trainer, and Nora Lilly Grant. Nora only stayed till Christmas—she was too particular. She felt all over the plate of biscuits and would grab the coffee pot off the stove. She said I boiled it too long. Pete Hubbs was working for us at that time and we used to get tickled at her and laugh in her face and we couldn't stop. We still laugh when we get together now. Dossie Burnley was one of the school teachers that stayed with us [see plate 38]. Her dad had the first sedan we ever saw.

We got our first radio when we lived at Sublette. We got the *Barn Dance* on WLS out of Chicago, and we heard Lulu Belle and Scotty sing, and George Goebel was only fifteen then, but he later went to Hollywood.

We heard the play where Abraham Lincoln helps his father make his mother's coffin and cried along with him. And then when we lived over where Bud lives now, on the Rixleben place, we got a better radio and we laughed at Lum and Abner and Amos and Andy on the radio. In later years, in the 1940s, we took a vacation and visited the Lum and Abner Theme Park in Pine Ridge, Arkansas.

Mom, and I too, after I was married, tried to raise as many chickens as we could. I also raised some geese and picked their feathers twice a year. You'd put a stocking over his head to keep him from pinching you, but sometimes they would almost pinch a piece out of your arm anyway.

I had two gardens and a strawberry patch. I used to tie Bud in a high chair and set him in front of the bedroom window and go to the garden where I could see him and hoe. One time, Bonnie ran under my hoe and I cut the top off her foot.

I never knew when I got enough work. I worked from early morning till late at night. All this time I was washing on the washboard. You had to pump your water. I tried to have a rain barrel but in winter and dry weather you pumped your water. In summer, you heated it in the big iron kettle, in the winter you heated it on top of the stove. Rubbed the clothes on the board, boiled them to get them white, and then rinsed them twice in tubs of water, and rung them out by hand, and hung them on the line, hot or cold. In winter, they would freeze as you tried to hang them up.

Plate 38. Dossie Burnley, one of the teachers who taught at Sublette School and boarded with Edith and Bill Rendleman, 1924.

It was when Marjorie Gunn stayed with us, in 1926, that I got my first washing machine. They lived in the hills where they had cisterns and it took so much water to run it that they didn't use it anymore. Her mother had it in her basement and hadn't used it for years. We gave them twenty-five dollars for it. It had two wooden tubs on a metal frame. The tubs were dried out till they had almost fallen to staves and it took us a couple of weeks to get them soaked up to where they didn't leak. It was a godsend. Bill had a pump house with a gasoline engine hooked up to the pump to pump water for the horses, cows, and hogs. He fixed the washer up to run by that gasoline engine and I didn't have to even pump the water. That was the most wonderful thing, when I didn't have to wash on the board. I began washing for Mom and Dad and washed for them up till they passed away. In the summertime, Mom always came and hung up the clothes for me, as long as she was able. Sometimes Aunt Mag Penrod came, as she stayed with them a lot after she left Uncle Richard.

Orville's ten-year-old son Cyril stayed with us at this time. His mother had run off and left him with Orville, and he brought him to Mom and Mom wasn't able to keep him and send him to school. So we took him. I have already told how he was run over by a truck in Wolf Lake, September 10, 1922. That hurt all of us very much.

When anyone dies you think of all the good things you should have done and didn't do.

When night came I would think of him out at Beech Grove, all alone and in the ground. The little fellow never knew what real love was, as his parents were interested in themselves and not in their children. His mother came back years later. She put her arms around me and said she got down on her knees at his grave and asked God to forgive her for leaving him. She took the other boy, Merle, with her, as she always thought more of him than she did Cyril, and changed his name to the fellow she ran off with, which was Blay. We didn't see him again until he was married. Then she had nerve enough to bring Blay back here with her and stayed at Mom's a week. Mom always loved all her daughters-in-law more than she did me. All she ever wanted me for was to work. I always had to go and help her cook when any of them came home. If I had of lived away from here it would have been different, I guess. Seems as though that's all anybody ever wanted with me, was to work. And I've done my share of it. So now I don't feel bad to sit down and kill time. That's the reason I like to live alone, I can work if I want to and sit down if I want to.

Troy was born in 1926, January 16. He was a fine baby, so healthy, and he was growing so fine, until he was three weeks old. Leora was here on a visit and was to leave for California on Monday. He wanted me to come to Mom's to be with them all on Sunday. I wrapped the baby up so much, so afraid he would catch a cold. And I wrapped him up too much—he was sweating when I got there. Mom didn't want me to bring him out but I didn't think it would hurt him. But on Monday he took an awful cold and never did get over it. He grew in length and was tall and blond and looked like Bonnie. Every time the weather changed, he choked up and his chest would wheeze and rattle. He never ran a fever. We took him to every doctor we heard of and none could find anything wrong. We took him to the doctor on September 3, 1926, and coming down the Jonesboro Hill I looked at him and he was ashen white. I hollered, "Turn around and take him back to the drugstore," where I could get some turpentine to rub on his navel, as they said that was good for worms. I ran in the drugstore and Ann Boettner, a lady that worked there, said, "Take him upstairs to the doctor." Dr. Lence had an office over the bank. I laid him down on a couch and he examined him and said he was dead. Such a shock. I never did realize he was going to die. One time, Mom said, "If this baby don't get better you are going to lose him." I just thought she was scared. I couldn't see it, as he laughed and played but was always thin and poor.

We never did know what killed him until many years later. Martha, Orville's second wife, said her son Hugh Dean lost a baby that was just like Troy. They performed an autopsy on it and it was cystic fibrosis. But when Troy died they never had heard of such a disease. It's a miracle as many people lived as they did. The only medicine they had was calomel and castor oil, cough syrup and quinine. I used to give my kids calomel and castor oil every time they got sick.

I thought that was the worst thing that could have happened to me. But I find there are things worse than death and that is to be dumped by your children. That is what happens to most old people when they get old and sick. Nobody wants to be knocked out of what he wants to do himself. God has been good to me to give me health and strength all these years.

There was a lapse of four years between Cyril and Troy's death. We were driving a mare and a mule to the topless buggy at this time. We used to get ready and go to church and Sunday school every Sunday morning. Also, Ted Wilson had a moving picture theater. He ran a serial every Saturday night. We went every Saturday night for twenty-one Saturday nights. It ran twenty-two nights but it rained so hard we couldn't go the last Saturday night and he ran it on Monday so everybody could see it. I can still see those boxcars running away down the side of the mountain, with people on top. And they quit each time, just as they were ready to run into a ravine or mountain. People would holler and yell like crazy, so excited. We could hardly wait from one Saturday night to the next.

Roy and Dora Belcher lived on the other side of the schoolhouse. They had four boys, Willis, Harry, Boyd, and Carrol. We all became close friends and the kids would meet at the schoolhouse and play till noon and then, as soon as they ate dinner, they would go back and play till time for supper. Willis would lead the gang, as he was the oldest. Whatever he said, that's what they did. They never had a falling out. Bud and Boyd would fight once in a while and the next minute they were playing. Roy bought a topless Model T long before we did. Roy and Dora and Bill and I all went in that car to the dedication of the Cape bridge.

The Belchers and us later on bought two ponies for the kids from George Howenstein at Saratoga. Our's was named Billy and their's Jolly. Every time Jolly would get loose in the night he would go back to Howenstein's, east of Anna. They loved these ponies and played with them for years. They made them a set of harness and hitched them up to our old buggy. Boyd and Bud were babies when we moved behind the schoolhouse. When Dora or I had to go somewhere, we would leave Bud or Boyd with the other one.

After Troy died I felt like I had to have a baby in his place, so we got Lee Roy. We all adored him. But before this, when I got pregnant with Troy, Dora and Roy decided they wanted another baby. So they got Carrol. Then when we got Lee Roy we both had babies again. But Carrol is between Troy and Lee Roy.

As soon as Carrol and Lee Roy were big enough, the older kids took them to the schoolhouse. As soon as Lee Roy could sit alone, Bonnie put a quilt in the little wagon and took him to the schoolhouse. When he got hungry or sleepy she brought him to the house and went back to play. She half raised Lee Roy. She never did get tired of taking care of him.

When Bonnie was five years old, Albert came home from Chicago in a car. He came by Ellis's place in East St. Louis and brought Dora and Ellis and their boys, Quentin and Robert, with him to Mom's. They stayed a week and when they went home they wanted the kids and me to go home with them. And we did go. That was the year they were building our first highway, U.S. 51, through Union County, in 1923. You had to make detours along the way. When we got to Mascoutah we had to go through water over the running board. Bonnie and Quentin were scared but Robert and Bud thought it was funny. I was also scared and wished I had stayed at home. We stayed a week and came home on the train.

By this time we had bought a Model T from Ford Stone in Jonesboro. Those first cars had a top like a buggy and you had to put up side curtains in the winter. They had isinglass panels in them to let in light and let you see. There were some of them always broken out. When the first cars came out with glass and metal tops, they called them sedans. Dad and Bill said they would never work because they were top-heavy, and they wouldn't have one.

When we lived at Sublette, Bill used to haul gravel in the winter for the roads and patch places in the levee. I think we had an overflow in 1926. The river broke the levee. Maybe it was 1928. But Bill got the job repairing it.

He did every odd job he could to make a little money in those days. I think it was about now that Will Jones was elected road commissioner and he graveled our gumbo road out to the corner.

By this time we had bought two or three more cows and I did the milking and had a cream separator and sold cream, raised chickens, and did anything to make an honest dollar. I wanted better things all the time. I didn't want Grandma Rendleman to be ashamed of us. She was dressy and sophisticated. She always wore a veil to church and played the organ.

My hardest work was at Sublette. I used to do the washing on the board, iron, and mop the floors, all in one day. I made mine and the children's clothes. Bonnie never had a store-bought dress until she was fifteen years old.

Lee Roy started to school when he was five years old, as it was Bud's last year at Sublette [School] and I wanted him to go so Bud could look after him. Then I made him take the eighth grade twice to keep from getting out of grade school so young. When Donald Coleman was teacher, each kid used to take a raw vegetable and they would make soup for dinner.

Bud's first year at Sublette he got in trouble and tried to run home to mamma. The teacher, Marjorie Gunn, caught him right under my dining room window. I stood there and watched her drag him back to school, but I knew if I took his part he would think he could run home every time he got into trouble. Marjorie boarded with us and she thanked me for helping her control him. He and Boyd Belcher were the two meanest ones in school. Boyd was always getting in trouble. When I lived at Sublette, my house was the place they came if they needed a Band-Aid or sew on a button or sew up a tear in their clothes.

When we lived there, we had a cat to go mad and it bit me on the back of the leg. I was washing the dining room window on the outside and I heard and saw this cat meowing but I never quit work, and when it got even with me it jumped on my leg and bit me. It also bit Bonnie and Burt Travis. Bill killed the cat and had its head sent to the lab at Carbondale and it came back rabies.

Bill took us to Anna in the buggy every day for twenty-one days and took the rabies shots (Pasteur treatments). We were taking shots at the time they had Mr. Rendleman's sale.[1] I remember the date because the day before the sale we had been to take our shots and the awfulest black cloud came up and the wind was blowing so hard we stopped at his mother's on the way home. That night we heard Gorham, Murphysboro, and West Frankfort had been hit by a tornado. That was March 18, 1925. Lots were killed in Gorham and Murphysboro.[2]

The shots never hurt either of us but later they found there were lots of side effects from them. We also had an old sow that had rabies. Just ten days before, I was out toward the barn and heard the hogs rallying around. I stepped over to the fence and a dog was going through them. It went on and I never thought anything about it, but in about ten days an old sow got to squealing and going around and frothing at the mouth and Bill had to kill her. Then we knew she had rabies. God was good to us, as none of us was bitten and we took the shots for the cat. I sure was worried.

Mr. Rendleman's drinking caused his death. He became an alcoholic after they moved to Wolf Lake in 1889 or '90. Mrs. Rendleman said the first time he got drunk was after he bought this land at Wolf Lake and he rode horseback down here every day. She had knitted him a long neck scarf for Christmas, and one evening when he came home that scarf was dragging the ground. He had a man that made a garden for him and he had a hotbed. He would be out there with him a lot until noon, then he would have the boys hitch up Bill's team to the buggy and head for the saloons in Grand Tower, where he got drunk. He usually came back around the levee by our house just before dark. One of the horses was a pacer and one a trotter and, man, they could really travel, and when they passed our house they would be going as fast as they could without running. They knew the way home without Mr. R. even holding the reins. When they went around the square turn in front of the house, we would be sure Mr. Rendleman would fall out, as he would be so drunk he would lean so far you couldn't see how he would keep from falling out, but he never did. The ponies would take him to the horse lot

gate and stop and somebody would take him to the house and then unharness the horses. When he was home sometimes for supper, he would eat out of the dishes with his fork. Except for his drinking Mr. Rendleman was a fine man.

He took cirrhosis of the liver and died from it in November 1924. He was bedfast for months. He took dropsy and his legs were swollen. There is no cure for cirrhosis of the liver and alcohol causes it. I guess his youngest daughter, Lenita, was the only one that loved him, as she was always with him when he was around the place. After he died and Bill's younger brother Howard was left to manage things, they began to go down. Then the Depression came along. They divided up his land and each child got a farm and Mrs. Rendleman got one third of it all. Then she moved to Jonesboro, in with her mother, to send Lenita to high school.

Mr. Rendleman nor Mrs. Rendleman ever did any hard work. He never worked a day in his life as far back as I can remember. They went broke, all but the land. He lost ten thousand dollars in the Grand Tower Bank one time. The cashier took all the money and skipped the country. July 25, 1930, in Lenita's junior year, Mrs. Rendleman died suddenly from heart trouble caused from an inward goiter. She died in bed about nine o'clock one night. She had been in the hospital at Murphysboro, where they found this inward goiter, but it was too late to do anything for her. She and Mr. Rendleman were both fifty-nine years old when they died. She had eight children. Three died when they were born [see appendix G].

She never had to work except to take care of the children, which was a pretty big job. Mrs. Rendleman never had a hired hand in the house. They had a house in the back where the hired hands and Bill and Howard slept. She had to cook for them, but she always had a hired girl and hired the washing done besides. Everybody that could afford it had a hired girl. They only cost a dollar and a half a week. After Mr. Rendleman died, Mrs. R. did her own cooking. Their daughter Edna never had to turn her hand to do anything. I've heard Mr. R. curse a streak because she wouldn't make the girls dry the dishes for the hired girl. Edna really thought she was something as she grew up. But it was different for Caroline. They had lost nearly everything by this time, as the Depression was at its height. She never got to go to high school, as there were none closer than Anna and they couldn't afford to send her anyplace. Edna had gone to the Catholic convent in Cape Girardeau one year and one half year to the Normal in Carbondale. She and I were roommates in Carbondale half a year. She was sick and didn't go back after Christmas to finish the year.

They divided the land between the heirs after Mrs. Rendleman's death. Bill got the forty-five acres at Wolf Lake then. Edna got the Rendleman home and nineteen acres of land, which Lee Roy bought later and turned into a subdivision. The others took land joining what they got from their father.

Roy and Dora Belcher got a chance to rent where Will Jones had lived, as Mr. Jones went broke in the Depression and had rented the DuBois farm that Harry O. Myers now owns. We tried to rent where Dora and Roy lived, but Dora was jealous of us and kept us from renting it. We fell out. I told her what I thought of them and we never visited again until Roy got sick to die. I couldn't let him die and be mad at him, so I went down to see him. Dora cried and said not to blame Roy, it was her that was jealous. So we were friends again.

We lived at Sublette on the farm from April 1919, down in the old house, and moved in the new house from March 1920, until April 1930. Then on the Rixleben [formerly Miller] place from April 1930, until May 1949.

10 My World Comes Apart

If it had not been for my dad we would have still been living at Sublette. But Dennis Howenstein, who lived where Bud lives now, wanted to sell out and my dad got after me to get after Wm. J. to buy him out. The Howensteins lived in the house Mr. Rixleben had built for Uncle Adam when we first moved to Running Lake. They had put in a light and water system and that looked good to me. Bill didn't want to move but I did, for those electric lights and water in the kitchen. So Dad and I both said yes and he finally had to do it. Dad had already rented the place for him. We moved there in April 1930. Bonnie was ten years old, Bud was eight, and Lee Roy two. But Wm. rented our farm out, when he could have farmed both of them. It was only one hundred and sixty acres on the Rixleben place (about half the size of the big Rixleben farm my dad rented) and he could easily have

farmed his place and that one, too. He rented the farm at Sublette to Dewitt Gregory and when he moved, Ira Lingle rented it. They were really nice people but after the 1943 overflow, Ira wouldn't come back to the bottoms. After Ira Lingle moved, Dad said to me and I said to Bill, "You are going to tend that farm yourself. You can easily do it." Wm. J. had no ambition. I had too much ambition and he had none. By this time Bud was married and living in Dupo and was a fireman on the railroad. He got laid off and moved over at Sublette, and he and Bill ran both farms.

Bill worked hard when we were first married but he never had ambition to have more. He was content with just what he had and no desire to have a lot. We were just about as different as two people could be. He used to wear overalls when he came to see me through the week, but I thought I could change him when we were married. But you can't change people, I found out to my sorrow.

Mom and Dad always loved Bill. In fact, everybody had to like him. He was down to earth and friendly with everybody. He would do anything for other people before he did anything for his own family. He never would take Bud with him anyplace and that hurt me so bad. I always thought you put your kids first. But he put everybody else first. If you only knew what people are inside, before you married them and found out after it was too late.

Bill worked in the field with the hired men and Bud did too, until he was elected road commissioner. Howard never worked but very little in his life. He told Bill once, "You're never thought of any more than a hired hand if you work in the field with them." Well, my dad never thought he was any better than a hired man and I never felt I was any better than an upright person with a good character.

I was tickled pink to move to the Rixleben place. Boy, did we ever appreciate those electric lights and running water in the kitchen sink. The light plant used 32-volt appliances. We also had an electric washing machine and a six-inch fan. We didn't have an electric iron, as 32 volts wouldn't furnish enough electricity to heat it. But I had a Coleman gas iron until we got electricity in 1942. It had a little tank on the back you put white gas in and pumped air in it. It was a wonderful thing, compared to the old solid cast iron you set on the kitchen stove. The first iron we had was a solid piece of iron, maybe an inch and three-fourths thick, with a handle made onto it. You had to have a pad to hold onto the handle, because it would get hot, too. Then came the one that had a detachable handle that you could fasten on and off. You had to keep the stove red-hot to heat the iron, and burning willow poles, they didn't make a very hot fire. That's all we ever had to burn, as they grew thick along the bar pits.[1] Then I got the gas iron that used white gasoline. It stayed hot, with the fire inside. Then came the electric iron.

But I cooked until 1935–36 on that old wood stove we bought from Sears Roebuck for thirty-five dollars when we started housekeeping and on a kerosene stove we bought later. First we had a two-burner and then a four-burner coal-oil range. You would put a pot of beans on that stove and go out to hoe. Then you'd come in, and that flame would have jumped up and you would find smoke and little greasy black curls all over the house, and maybe the beans all burned up. Then they came out with a combination propane gas and wood or coal stove. Rudy Weiss from Chester came down and sold us one of those. That certainly was an improvement over the old coal-oil stove. That's the only thing Bill would ever buy was something to cook on. He really loved to eat.

Grandma Rendleman's hired girl, Myrtle Thomas Baltzell, taught me how to make light bread shortly after we were married. Bill's mother made her own yeast and she always had the hired girl to make bread twice a week.

She would cut a loaf as soon as it came out of the oven and we would eat it with butter and jelly. My mother wouldn't let you touch anything until it was cold and put on the table. Of course, my mother (after she married my dad) had come up the hard way and made everything last as long as she could.

When we moved to Sublette, I also made light bread twice a week. Two big black pans full. Each had four big loaves in them, and we cut it as soon as it came out of the oven. But I remember it best the first night for supper, we had fresh light bread and blackberries with lots of sugar and thick cream. Boy, you dipped that bread down in that blackberries and cream and that was something good.

I also baked six nine-inch pies and two cakes every weekend. I still have my old pie pans yet. To get the blackberries, I would leave the kids with Mom and drive out to Uncle Moses's and Aunt Martha's and pick blackberries all day. His place was past Jake Lyerla's place; you crossed Hutchins Creek and it was up the hollow from Jake Lyerla's. I picked berries once at Harvey Plott's, on the highway going from Dongola to Anna, when my husband and Lee Roy were cutting his wheat. I almost got too hot that time; they said my face was just purple. I got a lot of blackberries, though, since nobody had ever picked them and they were thick.

One thing we always had was plenty to eat.

We had an icebox before we left Sublette, as little Troy was sick and we had to keep sweet milk for him. Tom Meisenheimer delivered ice once or twice a week. He would go to the Anna ice plant and get a pickup truckload and deliver it to those who had an icebox. We kept the icebox until we got electricity. I don't remember that we ever used it for ice tea, as it wouldn't have lasted very long and I guess we weren't able to afford it for ice tea. He still delivered ice after we moved to the Rixleben place.

When we moved to the Rixleben place we had an eight-room house and I needed a lot more furniture. I bought a new three-piece bedroom set for eighty-five dollars and paid for it, five dollars a month, from Joiner Furniture Store in Anna. Mrs. Rendleman died the year we moved to the Rixleben place and they divided her furniture up. We got her beautiful Axminster rug. She always used it in the parlor. We also got her bedroom suite she started to housekeeping with. I was still using them when we moved over here on my dad's farm.

We used aladdin lamps that gave better light than the coal-oil lamps. And then came the electric lights. They got the line up to our place in 1942, but Mom and Dad didn't get electricity until after the war ended. That was a wonderful day in our life, when we got electricity. Bud and Lee were in the field working when they came and turned the electricity on. They didn't know we had lights and they came in from the field at noon and we said something about having lights. They said, "Yeah, I bet you got lights." I said, "Well, turn them on," and they liked to flipped when

Plate 39. Lloyd Hale, Bill Rendleman, and Bill Hale (*left to right*), with rabbits, the winter of 1922–23. Photo was taken at Edith and Bill's house near Sublette School.

the light came on. Oh, it was a wonderful day. We could have a bathtub, a bathroom. And it helped the farmer so much and all his work.

Franklin D. Roosevelt was a godsend to the poor people, because nobody else had ever thought of the poor farmer. Electricity revolutionized farming and our life. I shall always love Franklin D. Roosevelt for giving us elec-

tricity. It was the greatest gift anybody ever gave the poor farmer.

We had lots of good and bad times while we lived on the Rixleben farm.

We always had a hired hand in the house, which I hated. I always liked the hired hands and treated them like one of the family. It wasn't their fault they caused me extra work. Bill Hale was one that stayed with us [see plate

39]. He used to get a kick out of Bud and Bonnie fighting. Vernon Morgan worked for us; so did his brothers Bill and Jim. Their dad, Jerry, lived in a trailer close to the levee and Bill and Jim were at our house a lot. They came over for dinner almost every Sunday. I always felt sorry for orphan boys. Vernon first stayed with Howard and went to school. Howard batched and always had a bunch of boys around. Vernon took double pneumonia and a doctor from the Cape said he couldn't possibly live. Caroline and I sat up with him for two weeks. Doctor had us saturate a flannel cloth in hot camphorated oil and keep on his back and chest. On the ninth day, his fever broke and his temperature dropped away down below normal. Doctor had warned us what to do and we filled fruit jars with hot water and placed them all around him and kept them that way till his temperature returned to normal. As soon as he was able to move, we took him to our house and kept him until he was well and able to work. The mattress he was sick on was so saturated with oil they had to throw it away. Vernon then worked for us a year or two and then went to Michigan to work. Bill [Morgan] joined the CCC camp and was boss and wound up at Le Roy, Illinois, where he later married and did real well [see plate 40]. Jim stayed with Caroline and her husband, D. G. (George Wilson), a while and later wound up with his brother Bill.

Lionel Walker stayed with us longer than any other hand. He was an orphan boy and had never had a home. I felt sorry for him. He was a good worker and he liked the kids and they liked him. He stayed with us until he decided to join the navy. He was real tight with his money and when he came out of the navy, he settled in San Diego, California. He got a good job at one of the airplane factories and made good money and saved it. He finally got married and has one daughter. He is now retired on a good pension and lives in Texas. He still comes to see us and appreciates the good home we gave him.

Carl Thomas also worked for us a while, but not near so long as the others. Swifty (Herman) Hines always stayed with us during the wheat thrashing run. I always tried to get the boys that stayed with us to buy a suit of clothes and dress up. I also tried to teach them, as well as my own, table manners. Some I helped and some I didn't.

Moving to the Rixleben place really started me working. They had the barn fixed with stanchions for cows. Stanchions were iron or steel bars the cow stuck her head in and couldn't get loose. Of course, that didn't keep her from kicking as they sometimes did. You might be milking along and she would kick your stool over or switch you in the face with a tail full of cockleburs. Bonnie was helping milk when we moved to the Rixleben place.

I was separating cream when we lived at Sublette and it only increased at the Rixleben place. First we had a small cream separator that sat on a bench, and later we bought a big one that fastened to the floor. I don't know

Plate 40. Bill Morgan (*left*) with a truckload of CCC (Civilian Conservation Corps) boys in the 1930s. The CCC camp was behind the Jestes place where Edith lived as a very young child. The Jestes place was bought by the State of Illinois for use as a state forest.

that we ever made any money off of milking cows, as you had to feed them corn the year-round. But I got the money off the cream, and Bill sure never gave me any money unless he had to. What I got I could spend as I pleased and didn't have to ask anybody.

The Howensteins had built a good chicken house and a brooder house. A chicken house was a building ten or twelve feet long and wide, with a row of hen's nests on one side

and poles set up slanting on the other so the chickens would have a roost at night. Late in the evening, they would fly up on these poles and sit there and sleep all night and they were out by daylight, scratching and hunting food. The roosters crowed at four o'clock in the morning and later, until it got daylight.

I set every old hen that went to setting.[2] The hens would lay so many eggs and then they would go to setting. If you didn't want to set the hen you put her in a coop for a week or two. That breaks her away from the nest. Then she will soon go to laying eggs again.

You swapped eggs with your neighbor if she had some kind you didn't have. You would pick out the biggest, best-shelled eggs and spot them with bluing so you could tell the setting eggs from the fresh ones. After they were sat on three days they were ruined for eating. She turned her eggs every day with her beak. As sometimes another hen would get in the nest with the one setting and lay a fresh egg, you went out every evening, late, to gather the eggs. Sometimes the hen that was setting would peck and almost take a piece out of your hand. Sometimes they would break an egg in the nest and it would get all over the setting eggs. You would have to go the house and get a bucket of warm water and wash all the eggs. Some put fifteen, seventeen, or eighteen eggs under the hen and then in three weeks, twenty-one days, they would start hatching. You usually got ten to twelve chicks to hatch. Sometimes there would be two rotten and one or two had chicks that didn't hatch.

Before I got the brooder house all the chicks were hatched by setting hens. As soon as the little ones were dry I took them in the house and put them in a box with some dirty clothes under them and covered them over. When the hen was done hatching you would put her in a little feed coop and put the baby chicks with her, until the chicks were a week old, so they would be strong enough to follow her. Many times, the last to hatch you would have to pick out of the shell. Then when they were strong enough, you would turn her loose with them. If you had two or three hens hatch at a time, you gave all the chicks to two hens so they could hover them when it was cold or rainy.

At night, you had a boxed-in coop where they could roost. It was a long box of a thing, with a slanting roof and doors on the front. It would usually be long enough for four or five doors. You would shut them up to keep the rats and other varmints, like foxes, weasels, and skunks, from eating them. When a rainstorm came up, you would try to get them protected. But if they got caught out, the old hen would try to get under something and the chicks would all get under her. She would spread her wings out and cover twelve or fifteen baby chicks. Many times, they would get caught out and after the storm you would go out and see how many drowned. Many times, you would find a bunch that was drowned or so near it. Many, many times, I picked up an apron or basket full and took them to the kitchen stove and turned the oven on and brought many of them back to life, when you thought they were dead. It was so hot in the roosting coops in the summertime, maybe you would have a piece of screen wire at the top above the door. Then when it came a blowing rain, it would blow in on them and get the whole coop wet.

I bought an incubator after we moved to the Rixleben farm—I think it was a 250-egg incubator. An incubator was a big square box,

Plate 41. Lenita Rendleman, Bill's baby sister, with a hen and her chicks, around 1914.

eleven or twelve inches deep, on legs, with one or two trays to fill with eggs and a coal-oil lamp on one side to heat them. Each tray would hold fifty to one hundred eggs or more. You bought enough eggs from the neighbors to fill it. You had to pull the trays out to turn the eggs every day and keep its light burning so the eggs would stay warm. In twenty-one days, they started hatching baby chicks. I usually got 175 or 160 chicks at a hatching.

There were always some that wouldn't hatch, although they would have chickens in them. But they just failed to pip and open up so the chick could get out. I had to pick some out of the shells.

Later on, they had big commercial hatcheries where they raised thousands of baby chicks and you could go there and buy your baby chicks or you could order them by mail. They had hatcheries all over the country.

When you ordered them by mail, they notified you by mail about when you would receive them and the mail carrier would bring them out on the route. You had your place all ready with a brooder in it.

You would have your brooder house all warmed up. A brooder was kind of like an open umbrella with a heat lamp under it. It was a big round piece of tin in a big cone shape, rather flattened out from the top, with a coal-oil lamp underneath the center that you lighted. It threw out heat from the center and the baby chicks would form a circle around the edge. When it got colder they moved nearer into the center. You put straw on the floor and had feeder and water jars all over the floor. You took the baby chicks out there and put them under the brooder. It didn't take them long to learn where the heat and feeders were. You kept feeding and watering and putting clean straw on the floor until they were big enough to eat and sell. Sometimes they would get a diarrhea and you would lose a few.

Sometimes a 'possum or weasel or skunk would get in the hen house at night and they would all make an awful commotion. If you heard them you got the gun and slipped out there, hoping to kill whatever was bothering them. The boys killed hawks if they could, because they'd come down and pick your chickens up and take them away. You could hear the chickens all go in a huddle and chatter and you'd know the hawk was near.

One time I had them in the brooder house almost big enough to sell, it got so hot on the chickens I left the door open and a varmint got inside and killed about fifteen or twenty. He just bit them through the small part of the back and left them lay. He strewed them clear to the road and over in the field, across the road toward Sublette School. I was heartsick, as I bought most of our underwear, overalls, work shirts, and blankets with the money I got from the chickens. I always ordered them from Sears Roebuck & Co. I never left the door open anymore.

Sometimes you got mites in your chicken house. These are little tiny bugs, very tiny. But there would be so many of them they would either kill the old hen that was setting on the eggs or cause her to leave the nest. You had to keep an insect powder to dust the old hen and her nest and maybe have to spray the whole henhouse. Sometimes you had to burn all the old straw in the nest and clean the whole henhouse. Boy! was that a job! I have seen hens set on a nest of eggs and the mites would kill her right on the nest. Then you would have to put the eggs under another hen or divide them up under others, if there wasn't another one setting.

This was the way it was in my teenage years at home and also the way it was in my marriage, until after Bill's death and I moved to the farm I inherited from my dad. I raised geese and ducks over at Sublette. I set the eggs under hens. Boy, I would hate to live my life over, I worked so hard. When I look back at how hard I worked and how little women or these young girls have to do today, I can't imagine what it would be like to have a new house. I have had to paper and paint and clean up every house I have lived in, except when we bought the Howensteins out on the Rixleben place. They had that one all papered and cleaned up good. That was the smartest move we ever made. Rixlebens were such nice people. They never felt they were stuck-up but they had plenty of money, but they never gave any of it to anybody. I was fortunate to have two daughters-in-law that weren't afraid of work. All three of my children were workers.

At Sublette and Rixleben place both, we always went to church and Sunday school. Bill would go to Wolf Lake and drive us but he never went to church and Sunday school. I don't know why we didn't dress two chickens on Saturday, as we had an icebox. I guess we didn't want to use that much ice. But we used to come in from church at 12:30 and we always had company or somebody there for dinner. People used to visit each other on Sunday and you didn't have to let them know you were coming a week ahead, you just loaded the kids in the wagon and go stay all day.

They would either run down or shoot two fryers and I would dress them and fry them for dinner. To kill a chicken, you took him by the neck between the head and the body and wrung the head off, throwing it around and around until you broke his neck. Then you throwed him on the ground and let him flop until he died. You had a bucket of scalding water standing by and you doused him up

and down, head first and then the feet. Then the feathers would slip off. Then you singed him with paper. When the gas stove came in, you could singe him on that. Then you scraped all the dead skin off and cut him up. Some people chopped the head off, but I never did. It would be two o'clock before I'd have dinner ready.

On the Rixleben place, I had a big garden and I had to hoe it all by hand. Bill would plow it once in a while with one horse and a double shovel. He sometimes did more harm than good, as he would cover up lots of plants and the horse would step on things. You had to follow along behind and uncover everything. He never hoed one row of anything. He was always working in the field. I always put out a strawberry patch and was always trying to raise rhubarb, blackberries, and fruit trees. But I didn't have much luck with fruit trees. I'll bet I've set out a dozen cherry trees and never got one to grow.

Farming when Dad and Bill lived was never as good as it is now. Now, they have fertilizers and herbicides that keep weeds out of your corn and beans. They hadn't started raising soybeans yet around here, when they were living. You raised red clover for fertilizer, then. You had to raise a field of clover and cut it for hay and then put corn there the next year. They just started using fertilizer (anhydrous ammonia) the next year after we moved over to my farm, after my mom and dad and Bill died. Lee Roy and Rodell Rhyne used to sell it and put it on the ground for people. That caused Lee Roy to neglect planting his own crops.

We still had the thrashing outfit when combines came in and forced the thrasher out of business. Dad had bought two combines when he died, in 1948. When they first came in, Dad and Wm. J. said they wouldn't work, but they did, to everyone's advantage: We didn't have to have the big thrashings anymore. I think we still used the thrasher in 1948, the last year Bill lived. Dad and Bill said the same thing about rubber wheels for tractors, that they wouldn't work. They thought the tires would pack the dirt.

After Bonnie got into high school, they had a three-year high school at Wolf Lake. You can give George Wilkins and E. J. Dillow credit for that. George even brought kids from Cobden and kept them, to have enough kids for a basketball team for two or three years. And I know it was a hard struggle for them to make ends meet. We became close friends of theirs and have remained so ever since. George Wilkins was a man with character and integrity. There was nothing but honorable deeds in his life. Wolf Lake owes him, a lot of which they never appreciated.

We had lots of good times going to basketball games. From the time Bud was ten or eleven years old, he played basketball at Sublette and we went to every game. Then when Bonnie went to high school at Wolf Lake, we went to Thebes and to all the games everywhere. We—Ted Jones's family and us—followed them everywhere to ball games. And

then when Bud got in high school, we really followed them everywhere, and the Joneses and the Wilkins and us became close friends. We would fix after-games eats. Lots of times I baked two big two-layer cakes, baked in a long bread pan and a chocolate icing or coconut on them. When we got beat we would always blame the referee and Ted Jones would always get mad at the referee. One summer after George and Mary Wilkins left Wolf Lake, Jeff and Peggy Marquardt, the Joneses, and us cooked dinner in Pine Hills. We would fry chicken or fish and have salads and desserts.

Bonnie went to Anna and finished her senior year of high school [see plate 42]. She stayed with Bill's sister Lenita and Artus[3] and we furnished groceries. By the time Bud graduated, they had a four-year high school at Wolf Lake.

Bonnie started to college in Carbondale and played around and flunked out at the end of the first semester. She later went back and took courses and graduated. She was smart and could have made good grades, but she got to running around and that ruined her grades. If only you could make kids see how important it is to study in school, whatever school it is. But you can't put an experienced head on a young person who has never had any responsibility. I did the same thing when I went to Carbondale, because I knew I was going to marry Bill and live on the farm and thought you didn't need an education, but to my sorrow I found out different. Teaching school

Plate 42. Rendleman family portrait, 1936. Bonnie and Bud (*back*), and Bill, Lee Roy, and Edith (*front*). Bonnie is wearing her graduation dress that was bought ready-made.

would have been easier than milking cows and raising chickens. Those days, you never went back to school after you were married.

Bud didn't want to go to college and Lee Roy didn't have a chance, as Bill died when Lee Roy was in the navy. Lee Roy went in the navy when he got out of high school in 1946.

In 1943 we had one of the worst floods ever. It just rained and rained for weeks. We only had a small, small levee. I don't think it was over six or eight feet tall. My husband was a levee commissioner at that time and he felt so responsible he made himself sick by staying up on the levee. All the men in the community patrolled it. Groundhogs just in-

Plate 43. *Left to right*: Elijah Bradley, Sarah Bradley, Edith Rendleman, Bonnie Rendleman Rushing (holding her daughter Sue Ann), Etta Ballance, and Curtis Grammer, at Bonnie's home south of Anna, about 1940.

fested the levees, and they would find these groundhog holes that they would have to sandbag. School kids and everybody would come from far and near and fill up sandbags and sandbag the levee. Sometimes it would break out a hole at the berm and if they caught it in time, they could stop it. Bill walked the levee for two or three weeks. It would break through here and there and yonder, and they'd

patch it up. It finally got to where it just ran over the top, the levee was so low.

I nearly got caught in there, me and my mother and father. My husband hustled me for a week to get things and get out. And I said the levee wouldn't break. I was sure it wouldn't break. That night, my mother and father and I got in Dad's Buick about 9:30 or 10:00. I said, when we got in the car and

Plate 44. *Left to right*: Tootie and Bud Rendleman, Julie and Bill Phillips at the Log Cabin, a
tavern east of Anna on the Lick Creek Road, in
the 1940s.

Plate 45. The 1943 flood, at the Rixleben place.

sat there a few minutes, "I just have the good notion to go back and go to bed." And I said, "Oh, I better not, he wants us to get out so bad, and I'd better take them out." I never did go against what he said. We got just to the Rendlemans' barn gate at the edge of Wolf Lake, when we heard this terrible roar. It was the water that had broken the levee and it roared like a steam engine coming right through the car.

It broke through right behind where we lived, or just a little north of there. They thought it had ruined those forty acres of ground, so much sand washed in, but it helped it because it was that black gumbo and the sand made it good. The men working on the levee had their cars parked up on it and they had to leave them there until the water went down.

The water was thirty-two inches deep in my house, and it was up to the top of the window sash in Mother's house [see plate 45].

It just about covered Mrs. Jones's house—the one Charles Ware built on the bank of Running Lake. It ruined her house, because it was all plastered. Mr. Ware was a city man and he knew about plaster. But the people were poor down in here and the people that owned the farms lived mostly in Jonesboro and Anna and they weren't going to put out money for plaster when they could seal it with lumber. If you got it papered, you had to paper it yourself. The water washed a hole under the house Sam and Ida Latta had lived in and it was never liveable again.

My mother and father had been at my house for several days before the levee broke, because they had hauled all their furniture out over to where I lived. We got all the furniture in my house upstairs except the cookstove. They put the cookstove on barrels and didn't punch a hole in the barrels, so the water couldn't get in and they floated and turned the stove over in the water. They hauled my chickens out to Bill's sister, Lenita Dillow's, in Jonesboro, but they didn't get Mom's chickens out [see plate 46]. She had a big long coop of old hens with the baby chickens and they all washed away. Only the old laying hens survived, although some of them fell off the roost into the water and drowned. That must have been a blow to Mom because that was her income.

Dad had the mules and hogs and everything at the house I own, which is up on a hill. (Dad had bought that farm when the bank foreclosed on Charles Ware's widow, but he stayed on the Rixleben farm and rented his farm out.) A lawyer from Jonesboro almost got drowned when he got a boat behind the motor boat they were using to swim the mule out, and the mule almost turned the boat over. They got the hogs up in the barn and then word came that the water was going to raise and cover all the ground between that house and Wolf Lake. Dad wasn't there and I said, "Well, we'll just have to let the hogs out." That really aggravated Dad, because they could have come in there yet with trucks and got them, but we turned them out and they just went everywhere. They rounded them up later and got them back.

I went back to look at my parent's house when the water was still up in it and I found pieces of the organ my dad bought me floating in the water. It was too big to move upstairs and they had to leave it. It came unglued with the water and it was just floating around the living room. Mom had an old round buttermold she left in the cupboard and it split in two in the flood.

We stayed with my husband's sister Lenita in Jonesboro for three weeks. Then we came back and stayed in a little country motel that Fannie and Dick Davie owned. That motel was on the place where the old Wolf Lake School had stood, the one that my brother Curt and Dora lived in. There were eight or ten cabins. They weren't fancy but they were clean and nice. Each family had a cabin and then we had one for our kitchen. They weren't going to charge us anything, but Dad and

Plate 46. During the 1943 flood, at the Rixleben place. Elijah Bradley had to cut a hole in
the roof of the hen house to rescue the chickens.

my husband made them take twenty dollars apiece, because we used their electricity and they gave us food. They barbecued a goat for us while we were there and had friends in. They were so nice to us; she was so good to my mom. I never liked her much before, but after that we became good friends and remained so until she died.

After the water went down it was a mess. It was a long time before we could move in.

The water got in all the cabinets and everything that we couldn't get out. Mom had her suitcase packed and she left it lying in the middle of the bedroom floor and it washed away. We first began to come in on the tractor, and Dad and my husband and the boys and other people came in with them. They took shovels and shoveled the mud out and then washed it out, over and over. The didn't have electricity up at Dad's, so they had to pump the water and carry it to the room to wash the mud out. All the paper was off the wall. Every bit had to be taken off. I helped felt and repaper it. It was months before we got back and made things look normal again.

My parents hired a jackleg carpenter to put wallboard on their house and he didn't know how to do it. He put strips over the cracks where the plasterboard meets and he didn't smooth them down. That turned me against plasterboard, so I had my house plastered when I moved over there.

We didn't have a crop that year or the next. It flooded again in 1944. It lacked six inches getting in my house, but it got in my mother's house and it washed my father's double crib away, with several hundred bushels of corn in it.

Bonnie's husband, Ray Rushing, and his brother put out a big field of green beans after the water went down, in 1943 or 1944, because you can plant beans later. The price went down or something and they didn't pick them all. When the shell got yellow, the beans were nice and soft and we canned so many beans. I was Matron of the Eastern Star in Jonesboro that year and we honored three of our fifty-year members and I cooked a big cooker full of those green shelly beans.

My world crumbled under my feet in 1948.

In 1947, Mom and Dad took the flu. They were still sick in March 1947. Dad took a relapse and had pneumonia. His fever got so high about midnight he became delirious.

Mom had no way of calling for help until the next day about nine o'clock, when the hired man came by and she sent for me. I begged every doctor in Anna to come but they wouldn't leave their office until closing time. Finally, Dr. Rife agreed to come at one o'clock. He came and said Dad had pneumonia. That was on Monday. We had spent the day there on Sunday and Dad was up and pumped water, etc., but that's how quick you can take pneumonia. But his lungs had opened up and he had spit on newspapers and it was old thick yellow stuff. He soon got better. Then Mom's heart gave way and we thought she was going to die, but they both pulled through and Dad seemed all right but Mom could not get around very good after that. She would get her a stick to use for a walking cane and go to the barn and look for eggs. She would walk a little piece and rest, until she made it.

The first sign of Bill's breakdown was high blood pressure. We went to a doctor at Cape and he gave him high-blood-pressure medicine, but Bill was aggravated at my dad, as he called on Bill to help him more and more. So he just threw the medicine aside and said there wasn't any use to take medicine if he had to help Dad all the time. He could have sent men to work for Dad, which he did most of the time. He didn't help him that much anyway. We didn't realize Bill was seriously ill, until a few months before he died.

In March when Dad was better, he wanted Bill to take him to a sale. Bill caught the flu

Plate 47. Bradley family celebration of Sarah Bradley's eighty-fifth birthday, 1946.

from him and had this congestion in his chest, which caused a blood clot in his heart. He came up to Mom's when the doctor came to see them, but Dr. Keith just told him he was scared. That was in March 1947. In June, we took him to Dr. Rendleman in St. Louis and he had a light coronary heart attack. In those days, there was nothing to be done. He went back and forth the next year and kept getting worse. We got Lee Roy out of the navy on a hardship discharge because of Bill's bad health. He came home in October.

That winter, we were in St. Louis and Bill was in the hospital and Dora Esther, a nurse at Missouri Baptist Hospital, told me they were expecting him to die. I thought she meant right then and I got on the phone and called Bud and Howard to come up there. They drove through the awfulest snowstorm to get there that night. It scared me out of my wits. He lived on until June 17, 1948.

Mom drug around the whole year. Aunt Minnie and Uncle Allen came to stay with them, but Uncle Allen took real sick in June. They took him to the hospital in Granite City and he died in a few weeks, with kidney trouble. Aunt Minnie helped me out a lot, as she stayed with them and did the cooking. But I had to go and give Mom a bath every day when she was in bed and they wanted me there every day, so I went every day.

That was one hard fifteen months in my life. I really had a hard time. Bonnie had left her husband, Ray Rushing, and was at home to help me out, and Bud helped out a lot, as Bill had to go to the hospital in St. Louis every three or four months and stay a week and I had to go with him. There wasn't a decent hotel or place to stay close to the hospital and Bill made me stay at the hospital until nine o'clock at night. There was nothing but colored people all around the hospital and you never saw anything on the street but colored people. The street between the hospital and hotel was nothing but taverns. I was so scared I walked out in the middle of the street. The hotel was the awfulest looking place you ever saw. I was afraid to go to sleep at night. If I could have left the hospital when visiting hours were over at eight o'clock, there were other whites on the street. But Bill was so afraid he

made you stay as long as possible. Bill was so afraid at night he made you sleep with your feet against his. Lee Roy was good enough to sleep with him most of the time, as I was so overworked going to see about Mom and Dad and cooking for hired hands and the family and having tension headaches, I had to have some rest at night. Some days I didn't think I could make it another day. But God was good to me and let me take care of all three of them, and with the help of Bonnie, Bud, Lee, and Aunt Minnie, we made it through.

Mom had been sick with this hurting in her chest when we took Bill to the hospital in early February. She was in that old cold kitchen as I stopped to see them as I went by and she said, "Edith, what will we do and you gone?" I said, "Mom, I'll get Bill to the hospital and I'll come back." We brought Aunt Minnie back to stay with them and I came back, too. I went to Anna and bought her a low bed and springs and mattress (Dad paid for it), as the one she had was so high she couldn't get in it by herself. This was the first week in February, as we were in St. Louis with Bill when Darryl was born, February 3, 1948. Bud had to leave him and Tootie in the hospital, as he was up there also and was helping take care of Mom and Dad at home.

We had just got back home from St. Louis and Bud brought Tootie and Darryl home and Mom died that night. She had this hurting in her chest and it went up in the top of her head for a week. Dad came after me, about nine o'clock. It was February 13, the second worst night anyone was ever out. It was snowing and blowing like a storm. When I got there she said, "I have to have a doctor, get me a doctor." I went to Wolf Lake and called every doctor in Anna and not one would come out in that snowstorm. It was snowing and blowing, till you couldn't see the road. I went back and said, "None would come." She says, "I have to have a doctor." I said I would go back and see if I could get Dr. Hughes from Grand Tower. He said, "Yes, I'll be there." She said, "I want him to give me something to stop this pain or kill me, one way or the other." It took him forty-five minutes to one hour, as you could not see the road. He gave her a shot and she began to get better. After about fifteen minutes she got better and said, "I believe I will get in bed." We helped her to bed and I was getting the bedclothes around her and she said, "Edith, tuck the cover in to my back." I went behind the bed and tucked them in and I had just got back to the foot of the bed, when she gave a loud snore. I ran and turned back the cover and such a sight I never saw. I screamed and Doctor and Dad and Aunt Minnie ran in there and Doctor said she was dead. He said it was the second quickest death he ever saw. I got in the car and ran after Bud, as I didn't want to scare Bill. He came with me and we went and called the funeral director, Cecil Norris. That was February 14, 1948.

In September, when Dad was staying with me, he cried because he had never given my mother any money. I said, "Yes, you should have given her money." I only saw him cry three times, the night she died, and that night, and then when I got married tears came to his eyes.

I went home next morning and told Bill and Bonnie and Bud. Bill wouldn't go up there. I had to phone all the boys. I think Curt came. All the rest did (what an awful time). She died Tuesday morning, a little after midnight. We had to keep her till Thursday for Curt and Leora to get here.

We didn't know there was anything wrong with Dad until after Mom was buried. Leora slept with Dad one night and he heard him straining to urinate. So we took him to a doctor in the Cape. He put him in the hospital and Dad got worse. They told me they thought he had cancer of the kidney. We took him to St. Louis, to Missouri Baptist, and they found he did have cancer of the kidney. They operated on him and he was in the hospital three weeks. Leora and I stayed with him. We stayed at Ellis's in East St. Louis. It doesn't seem like Ethel was here at first but I think she came.

Dad was delirious part of the time and one morning I went in and he had gotten out of bed in the night and had messed all over himself. So we hired a nurse around-the-clock to stay with him. I think Orville stayed with him a couple of nights before we got the nurses. He began improving and we brought him home at the end of three weeks. I dressed his side. Ethel and Leora and Aunt Minnie stayed with him and he got stronger and in two months he was driving his car. That was in April.

Leora and Ethel went home and in June, Aunt Minnie went to Washington State to see her kids and Dad stayed with me while she was gone. He was staying with me when Bill died, June 16, 1948.

I was sleeping with Bill the night he died. Lee Roy wanted to go somewhere and when he came in, he went upstairs to bed. We had been asleep. It was about two o'clock and Bill was smoking his pipe. He reached over to lay his pipe on the table and I heard it hit the floor and he slumped on the side of the bed. I raised up and put my arm under him and lifted him back on the pillow. I knew he was dying. I jumped out of bed and screamed for Lee and Bonnie and Dad, and they all came running down the stairs. Lee ran after Bud and almost turned the car over, he was scared so bad. I was really shocked, as I didn't believe he was going to die, as he was up all the time. His death didn't hit me for three or four hours.

I kept putting on a good front for Dad when Bill died. I was hurt and stunned too deep to cry. And Lee Roy and I had to have a home. So we carried on with Bud and Bonnie's help. I didn't have much to live on. Bill had a life insurance policy, which paid his funeral expenses and bought a monument. Lee Roy and Bud took charge of things and Lee Roy raised two thousand dollars worth of hogs the summer Bill died.

Things went on after Bill and Mom died. All of us lost, but trying to carry on. And then in September, Dad took sick again. I called Dr. Glenn in St. Louis and he sent me some more medicine. The first dose made Dad so nauseated he was deathly sick. He got so bad I had to call Dr. Ashworth and he had him sent to Anna Hospital. That was on Saturday. He remained deathly sick and Monday morning we took him to St. Louis Hospital in an ambulance. Shep Weiss took us and I think Bud went with us in the ambulance. Shep did not know the shortcut in St. Louis and I thought Dad wasn't going to make it. After we got Dad to the hospital, Shep dumped me out at a dump called a hotel. I never was so scared in my life. I didn't sleep any, I was so afraid.

Dad was so sick I didn't think he was going to live to get him there. They like to have never got the vomiting stopped. They finally got it stopped after a few days and he seemed to get better and we talked of coming home in two or three days. By this time, Ellis had come and he took me home with him to stay at night.

The next morning, Thursday, they called me from the hospital and told me Dad had a heart attack. Quentin drove me to the hospital. Dad was better but he had given up. He said, "Edith, you and the boys will have to carry on." I tried to tell him he would get better, but he didn't. I called all the boys. Leora and Ethel and Albert came and he died on Saturday morning, October 17, 1948. He became unconscious two or three days before he died. I was experiencing the most difficult time in my life [see plate 48].

Plate 48. Bradley family portrait taken the day after Elijah Bradley died, 1948. *Standing, left to right*: Curtis Grammer, Orville Grammer, Leora Bradley, Ellis Grammer, Albert Grammer. *Seated:* Edith Bradley Rendleman.

When he died, Curt could get off but he didn't try, till it came time to see what he was going to get. I let Leora and the boys settle things. Leora and I were the only legal heirs, as Mom's name wasn't on anything, but we bought out the Grammer boys. Leora wanted me to have the farm, as he thought Dad wanted me to have it. I offered him cash for his share but he wouldn't take a dime. He was the dearest, most wonderful brother a girl could ever have.

I gave up the dearest friend and Dad anyone

could ever have. I think I was in a trance for three to six months. My world had crumbled. All the burden was on my shoulders. Three of them died in eight months. I bought the best caskets Cecil Norris had for all three. God was with me to guide and take care of me, or I couldn't have gotten through.

After Dad died, the boys gave me power of attorney to settle Dad's estate. He had twenty thousand bushels of corn to sell and we had a sale, the eleventh of March, 1949. It came another terrible snowstorm the night before the sale and it was cold and four inches of snow on the ground. We went on with the sale, but it was a mess. My brother Albert and his daughter Barbara had come down the night before the sale.

I decided Lee Roy and I would move on the farm Dad left me, and Fred Rixleben trusted me enough to rent Bud the farm Bill and I had farmed. We started remodeling this old house and it took till the next May to get it done. Lee Roy did all the plumbing in this house, also sanding floors, and we all painted and varnished until we were sick of it. Dad had started to remodel before he died. He had a basement dug under two rooms of the house, or I might have built a small new one. We had a stove in the basement. After Lee and

Bud carried Bill upstairs twice to take a bath, we put in a bathroom on the first floor at the Rixleben farm. It cost seven hundred dollars and Fred Rixleben would only pay one hundred and fifty dollars on it. It was just finished that spring Bill died. I didn't realize he was going to die so soon or I wouldn't have spent that money. But I never thought about Dad dying either, so soon.

Lee Roy married Roberta Forrest, October 22, 1950. They moved down in the little house after two or three years. He fixed up the little house and paid for it himself and then he fixed up the Tuthill house, after he bought Sam Morgan out.

My life has been very lonely. But there was no way out of it. It would have been worse to marry someone I couldn't stand and I couldn't live with my children and ruin their lives. As I think back to when I was small and grew up, I loved my dad more than anybody on earth, and yet I was so afraid of him that my life was miserable. It wouldn't hurt him, he's been dead so long, so I think I should say that I almost hate him now for giving a twelve-year-old girl twenty-five cents to go to the Anna Fair all day and fifty cents to his sixteen-year-old son to go to a pie supper and never giving my mother one dime.

11 Carrying On

We moved over to the farm I inherited, May 5, 1949 [see plate 49]. I only raised chickens one year after I moved here. But I made a big garden and nearly hoed myself to death in the garden and flowers. Overwork caused me to have bad headaches but no doctor could tell me what was causing them. I went to Chicago, St. Louis, and all around here trying to find the cause of my headaches. I finally realized it was overwork that caused them. Also, my eyes are weak and cause a headache if I read very much.

We had traveled some before Bill died. In 1941 Bill and I visited Natchez, and then when Lee Roy was stationed in New York when he was in the Navy, I spent a week with him there, in September 1947. After Bill died I made quite a few trips. I went to visit Leora and Curt in California in 1949 and 1953 and stayed three weeks with each one. Curt lived

in National City, near San Diego, and Leora in Burlingame, near San Francisco. Leora's wife liked to show off San Francisco because she was raised there and she loved it. The first time I visited Leora we went to the old Ogden-Mills estate in Redwood City. It had been a showcase in the 1860s. Ogden and Mills financed the Southern Railroad from Chicago to San Francisco. Ogden, Utah, was named after him. The old horse-carriage house and stable were there, the tennis court, and the most beautiful shrubbery and two of the most beautiful holly trees I ever looked at. They were ten or twelve feet high and they had been pruned until they were as round as a can and so dense with berries and leaves you could hardly get your hand in it. They had a circular brick driveway where the horses and carriage drove up right to the doorsteps. They used it, at first, for an entertainment center, but it got

Plate 49. Aerial photograph of Edith Rendleman's farmstead in the 1950s. Elijah Bradley bought this farm, once owned by Jesse Ware, during the Depression; Edith moved to it in 1949.

too expensive. And they just sold the whole thing and built a subdivision there. The bulldozers were there, just about to tear it down. Everybody on the street was carrying shrubs and dirt and everything from the old Mills estate to their house. The next time I went back, in '53, it was all subdivision. There wasn't a vacant lot left. It was all new houses.

I took four tours with Wayman Presley's tours, with my friend Gilda Hessman. I went on the first trip he made when he chartered a whole train to Miami. And then I took his tours to the World's Fair and to Washington, D.C. and Mount Vernon and the places around there, and another to the Grand Ole Opry in Nashville. We went to New Orleans one Christmastime, and I never saw such beautiful Christmas decorations as they had in that hotel. We came back by Vicksburg and visited the old cemetery and found my grandfathers' names in the Illinois building in the cemetery—all the Illinois soldiers that fought in the war, their names were in bronze on the wall around the building. There was my grandfather Penrod and grandfather Ballance. And some of my husband's folks were there. It was so exciting to go through that cemetery and hear that guide tell how they fought, sometimes right against each other.

I belonged to the Eastern Star. Bill and I joined in 1941 and I was elected Worthy Matron in 1944. In 1943 I had to finish Mary Wilkins's year out, as they moved to Madison, Illinois. I loved the OES and met many nice people and made a lot of new friends. I still belong to the OES.

I also joined the Anna-Jonesboro Garden Club. Fannie Davie and I belonged to that until I got to where it was too much to drive to every meeting, once a month, so I quit. We attended lots of flower shows everywhere.

I was a charter member of Home Extension that began in 1948. We met every month for a lesson or a meeting. I still am a member.

Bonnie and Ray's daughter Sue Ann stayed with me a lot when she was little, and then I took care of Bonnie's and her second husband Amon Lee Jackson's three children a lot, too. Bud and Tootie's children often stayed with me on Saturday nights when they went out [see plate 50]. Lee Roy and Roberta lived at the end of the driveway, so I saw their children a lot, but I didn't take care of them too much.

After Sublette School consolidated, we began having square dances in the old schoolhouse. At first it was just people from Wolf Lake, but then my friends from Jonesboro and Anna started coming and the Wolf Lake crowd stopped. We bought records and danced with the records. And then at midnight everybody'd fixed nice things to eat and we'd have a big feast at the end of the square dance. One of the men would buy a ham and he'd charge it to each one.

I bought a television in 1956, when they put the TV station in at Cape.

I have always been interested in history. In 1976, when we dedicated the Shawnee Valley Water and Sewer District, I wrote the history of Wolf Lake, and it ran two weeks in the *Anna Gazette-Democrat*. I helped with the bicentennial celebration and rode on the float in the Anna parade.

I got started on the Lyerla history when Bernice Freer wrote me from Midland, Michigan, and wanted to know if I knew anything about the Lyerlas. I answered her letter and that started a lifelong friendship. Then I talked with Gladys Randles, whose mother, Daisy Wilson, is a Lyerla, and she told me about the book John Doty wrote about the Lyerlas, so

Plate 50. Edith's daughters-in-law and grand-children in front of Edith's house in the fall of 1953. *Left to right*: Bill, Tootie, Bonnie Lee holding Brad, Darryl, and Roberta.

I wrote him, and then one thing led to another. It took us five years to unravel who Zachariah Lyerla was. Lawanda Wiley, Bernice Freer, and I wrote a lot of letters. But I had the best opportunity because I lived where the Lyerlas settled when they came from North Carolina. I joined the Daughters of the American Revolu-tion in 1975, when I wrote the Lyerla history. My ancestor Zachariah was in the Revolutionary War. I couldn't attend their meetings because they were in Vienna, and I wasn't able to drive to Vienna.

Then two of my granddaughters, Janet and Sue Ann, Bonnie's oldest and youngest daughters, asked me to write what it was like when I grew up. So after I finished the Lyerla history, I sat down and began writing what it was like. I hope this book will let them know how much things have changed.

Wolf Lake as I knew it is no more. Now Schaefers is at one end with a salvage business, which, they say, employs lots of people, and Randy Myers's fertilizer plant is at the other end of town. Lee Roy still owns a building that houses a beauty shop and an apartment, and there's still the post office and two churches. All the rest is houses. There used to be three grocery stores, three gas stations, three restaurants, the grade school, and the high school. All that is gone.

Those men in Anna that had money owned all the land in the bottoms, when the bottoms first opened up for farming. Now the Rixleben place where Dad lived is the only place owned by Jonesboro people and she—Thomas Rixleben's granddaughter—lives in Oklahoma. Lots of the people who were tenants own their farms now. In fact, most of them do.

Starting around 1950, people stopped raising chickens, milking cows, and raising hogs. They just buy it at the store, ready to eat. A lot buy a steer and have it processed in Dongola and put it in their freezer. What a difference! What a change! Girls have got it so easy now. They don't even know what it was like to start out. And I guess my mother's life, when she started out, was as hard again as mine, because they had to make everything by hand. I don't know if it could get any easier for these girls. But they don't know what it was like, and they never will. Everything is packaged. All you do is go to the store and buy you a package and cook it. Automatic washers and dryers. I'm glad they don't have to work like I did. Very glad.

Appendixes

Notes

Selected Bibliography

Index

Appendix A:
The Family of John and Mary Curtis Bradley

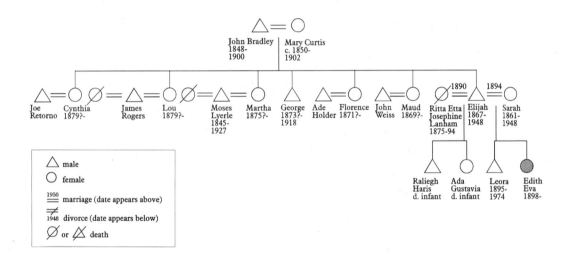

Appendix B:
Descendants of Zachariah Lyerla (1755?–1847) Relevant to Edith Bradley Rendleman

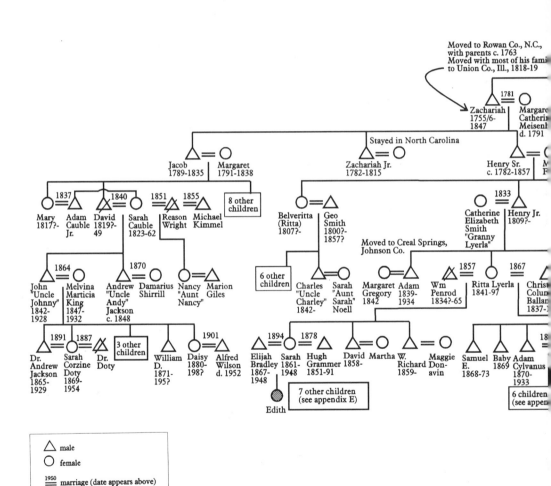

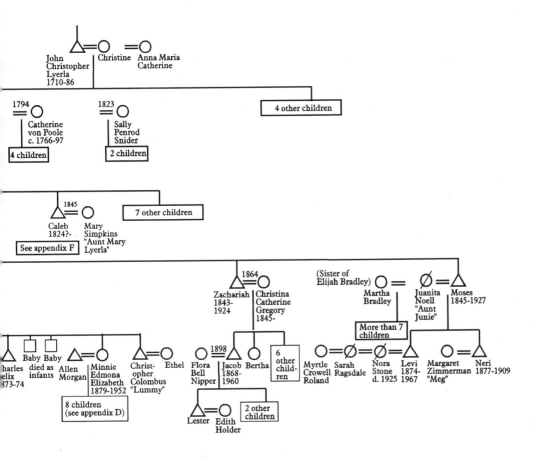

Appendix C:
The Family of Adam and Etta Bittle Ballance

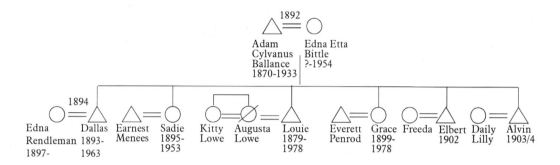

Appendix D:
The Family of Allen and Minnie Ballance Morgan

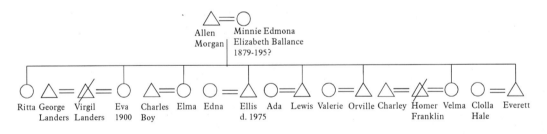

Note: Except for Eva and Ellis, the Lyerla genealogy does not give birth,
         death, or marriage dates for Allen and Minnie Morgan's family.

△ male

○ female

$\overset{1950}{=\!=}$ marriage (date appears above)

$\underset{1948}{\neq}$ divorce (date appears below)

⌀ or ⨉ death

Appendix E:
The Family of Sarah Penrod Grammer Bradley

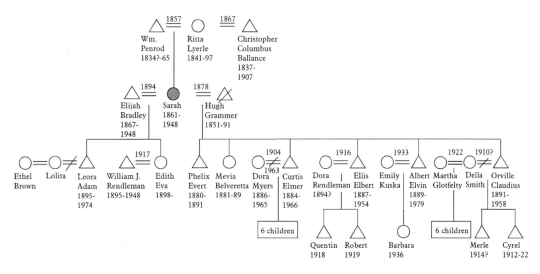

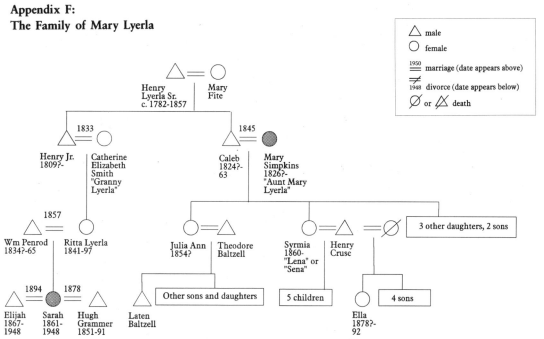

Appendix F:
The Family of Mary Lyerla

Legend:
- △ male
- ○ female
- ⚌ (1950) marriage (date appears above)
- ⚌̸ (1948) divorce (date appears below)
- ⌀ or △̸ death

Appendix G:
The Family of Robert and Hallie Crowell Rendleman

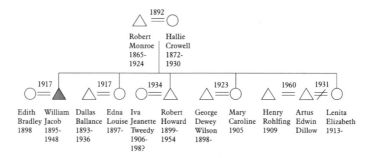

Appendix H:
The Family of William and Edith Bradley Rendleman

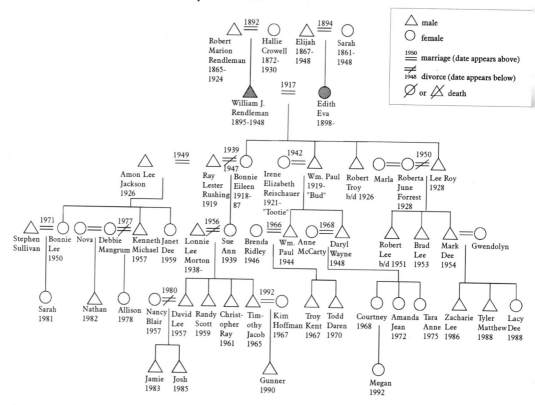

Note: Some dates are from memory and may be slightly inaccurate.

Notes

Introduction

1. I have written an extended study of the area: *The Transformation of Rural Life: Southern Illinois, 1890–1990* (Chapel Hill: University of North Carolina Press, 1994).

2. See Darrel Dexter, *A House Divided: Union County, Illinois, 1818–1865* (Anna, IL: Reppert Publications, 1994).

3. For accounts of the Dunkard and Lutheran migrations to Union County, see David B. Eller, "George Wolfe and the 'Far Western' Brethren," *Illinois Historical Journal* 80(summer 1987), 85–100; and E. Duane Elbert, "The American Roots of German Lutheranism in Illinois", *Illinois Historical Journal* 78(summer 1985), 97–112. See also W. J. Boatman, "The Sesquicentennial, St. John's Lutheran Church, Near Dongola, Union County, Illinois, 1816–1966: Illinois' Oldest Lutheran Congregation: Brief History" (unpublished manuscript in

Adams's collection, 1966, photocopy); and Q. Maurice Hunsaker and Gwen Hunsaker Haws, eds., *Hunsaker Family History* (Salt Lake City, UT: Deseret News Press, 1957). On the Clear Creek Baptist Association, see Gale S. McMahan, ed., *The Southern Baptist Churches in the Clear Creek Baptist Association*, (Utica, KY: McDowell Publications, 1988); also Darrel Dexter, comp., "Clear Creek Baptist Church Minutes, 1818–1848, Union County," *Saga of Southern Illinois* 20(fall 1993), 24–39. These minutes document tensions between Clear Creek Baptist Church and the Dunkard Church (as well as the Methodist Church). On the naming of Union County, see William Henry Perrin, ed., *History of Alexander, Union and Pulaski Counties, Illinois* (1883; reprint, Utica, KY: McDowell Publications, 1990), 286. On the Jonesboro Masonic Lodge, see Edward I. Oliver, "Ancient Free and Accepted Masons, Union Lodge No. 10, Jonesboro, Union County, Illinois," *Saga of Southern*

Illinois 20, no. 2 (1993): 6–11. For preemption records (the records of squatters in Territorial Illinois who were given rights to claim land as it was surveyed) see the "Squatters Report of 1807" and "Squatters Report of 1813," *Illinois Libraries* 59(May 1977), 328–44; 345–82. Note that *Wolf* is spelled in a number of ways, including *Woolf* and *Wolfe.*

4. See "Abstracts of *A Gazetteer of Illinois . . .* , 1837," *Saga of Southern Illinois* 17, no. 2 (1990):34–46; no. 3 (1990): 21–26; no. 4 (1990): 29–38. Population figures are from U.S. Bureau of the Census, *6th Census of the United States, 1840* (Washington, DC: GPO, 1841) and *4th Census of the United States, 1820* (Washington, DC: GPO, 1821).

5. The name Jacob Hudggens appears in the preemption record of application number ten, dated September 3, 1807, claiming 320 acres of land "Situate on the West fork of Clear creek. Bounded by vacant land. Supposed Range 3 West, Township 11 South" ("Squatters Report of 1807," 330). This site would have been along the branch that was later called by his name (also spelled *Hudgeons, Hutchens,* and *Hutchins*) and was probably a mile or two north of Edith's birthplace. The land where Edith lived when she was five, known as the Jestes place, appears to have been claimed on the 1807 preemption report: Robert Tweedy, Nathaniel Green, and Thomas Green settled adjoining parcels ("Squatters Report of 1807," 330). In the 1813 preemption report ("Squatters Report of 1813," 378), Robert Tweedy is listed as owning the southeast quarter of section 12, town 12 south, range 3 west, at the junction of what is now Beech Grove and the State Forest roads, known to Edith as the Parmley place,

where her mother and her mother's first husband lived.

6. The family name *Lyerla* is spelled in a wide variety of ways: In Union County records I have found variants including *Leyerele, Leyerle, Leyerley, Leyerlie, Leyerly, Leyrle, Leyrley, Lyerle, Lyerley, Lyerlie,* and *Lyerly.* John Hubert Doty lists a number of other variants in his genealogical publication, *Vancel and Lyerly Families in America* (privately published, 1991, photocopy), 44. Originally compiled in 1980, this revised edition of the booklet is available from J. H. Doty, 225 Moline St., Aurora, CO 80010. These additional variants include *Lirely, Lirele, Lireley, Lyerla, Leyerla, Lierle, Lierly, Lierley, Liarly, Lyarly, Liley,* and *Lyley.* The 1994 Union County area telephone book lists only *Lyerla,* while in contrast the Salisbury, North Carolina, directory lists only *Lyerly.* Following the contemporary Union County usage, I have standardized the spelling in the text of Edith's memoirs.

7. Quoted in Doty, *Vancel and Lyerly Families,* 45.

8. Doty, *Vancel and Lyerly Families,* 78.

9. For a sketch of the Honorable John Grammer, see Perrin, *History,* 271; and Darrel Dexter, "John Grammer of Union County," *Anna Gazette-Democrat,* Sept. 24, 1992.

10. Billie Snead Webb, comp., *Randleman, Rendleman, Rintelman Reunion, 1981* (privately published, 1983), 11. Compiled with the assistance of members of the Randleman Research Committee (Rendleman, Rintelman), this 1,070-page book is available from B. S. Webb, 651 Sherwood Way, NE, Corvallis, OR 97330. See also Doty, *Vancel and Lyerly Families,* 44. I have made the spelling of the names consistent with current Union County usage.

11. Fithian (1854–1921) had been a U.S. congressman (1889–95), served on the Illinois Railroad and Warehouse Commission (1895–97), and operated farms in Newton, Illinois, and Falcon, Mississippi (John Clayton, *The Illinois Fact Book and Historical Almanac, 1673–1968* [Carbondale: Southern Illinois University Press, 1970], 123).

12. B. N. Griffing, *An Atlas of Union County, Illinois* (Chicago, IL: D. J. Lake & Co., 1881). Other early atlases of Union County are Guy Beauman, *Map of Union County, Illinois* (Vienna, IL: Guy Beauman, 1899); George A. Ogle, *Standard Atlas of Union County, Illinois* (Chicago, IL: Geo. A. Ogle & Co., 1908); and *Atlas of the State of Illinois* (Chicago, IL: Union Atlas Co., 1876). The Illinois Central Railroad issued maps during the 1860s showing the lands they had for sale, and these maps sometimes include county-by-county sectional maps. Current maps are available from the Illinois Department of Transportation and the U.S. Geological Survey. Another useful source is the *Johnson and Union Counties Plat Directory* (Dayton, OH: Great Mid-Western Publishing Co., 1993), which is updated about every four years.

13. See Joseph Yeager, "Geographical, Statistical, and Historical Map of Illinois, 1822," in *Indian Villages of the Illinois Country*, vol. 2, comp. Wayne C. Temple (Springfield, IL: Illinois State Museum, 1975), plate 86. Perrin, writing of the early settlement period, notes that Hamburg Landing "was about five miles below Willard's Landing and our nearest point to the Mississippi River" (*History*, 358).

14. See the *Jonesboro Gazette*, Feb. 23, 1867 ("Mail Route to Preston," and Aug. 3, 1867 ("New Post Office" [at Big Barn/Willard's Landing]).

15. Perrin, *History*, 436. See also *Jonesboro Gazette*, Sept. 3 and Nov. 26, 1870.

16. Perrin, *History*, 435.

17. This story was covered in the *Jonesboro Gazette*, Mar. 19, Apr. 2, and Apr. 16, 1892; Mar. 3, Mar. 10, Mar. 24, Mar. 31, and May 12, 1894. The records of the Clear Creek and Preston Drainage Districts are housed in the Union County Circuit Clerk's Office, Jonesboro, Illinois. Both the 1899 and 1908 atlases (Beauman, *Map of Union County*; Ogle, *Standard Atlas*, 39) indicate a ditch (labeled "Old Ditch" in the 1908 atlas) linking the south end of Miller Pond to Clear Creek, draining land that, in 1899, belonged to Robert Goodman (section 14, town 12 south, range 3 west).

18. See Union County, *Corporate Record* 1 (1876–98) and 2 (1898–1927), housed in the Union County Clerk's Office, Jonesboro, Illinois; and Ogle, *Standard Atlas*, 39.

19. The application was filed Feb. 16, 1912 (Preston Drainage District, *Drainage Records*, vol. 1, p. 10). Due to resistance by a number of residents in the district who were members of the Clear Creek Drainage District (formed in 1908), the petitioners went to court and, eventually, the Preston District was permitted to condemn the land necessary for constructing the levee and for dredging Running Lake. Bids were let in January 1914 for construction of the levee and ditches (Preston Drainage District, *Drainage Records*, vol. 1, pp. 20, 30–31, 47, 56–58, 91, 115–23, 161, 189, 305).

20. Edith Rendleman, "History of Wolf Lake and Ware" (unpublished manuscript in Adams's collection, 1976, photocopy). See also

Joseph McMahan, "Past and Present Needs," *Illinois History* 37(fall 1983), 54–55; and Union County, *Corporate Record* 2, Union County Clerk's Office, 321.

21. The Lyerla genealogy compiled by Doty gives only nine children; Edith, however, recalled that her grandmother bore eleven children, of whom seven survived past infancy.

22. For an account of the Rendleman family, see Webb, *Reunion*. For the Lyerla family, see Doty, *Vancel and Lyerly Families*. Edith Rendleman contributed to both works.

23. Perrin, *History*, 413.

24. See Dexter, *A House Divided*, 63–65; G. McMahan, *Southern Baptist Churches*; and the *Jonesboro Gazette*, July 6, 1870, p. 3.

25. Department of Agriculture, Report No. 103, *Social and Labor Needs of Farm Women* (Washington, DC: GPO, 1915), 11. The report goes on to say, "On the other hand, many women writing from much the same States express complete contentment with farm life. . . . Apparently, the complaint about the loneliness of farm life is more or less closely connected with other statements regarding overwork and long hours of farm women, which make afternoon or other visiting almost impossible, and therefore keep the women at home. Several point to the fact that the farmer, in carrying his produce to market, comes into touch with the outside world, and that even this opportunity for change of scene, seeing new faces, and talking with other people is not afforded to the women."

26. U.S. Bureau of the Census, *13th Census of the United States, Population, 1910* (Washington, DC: GPO, 1913); *16th Census of the United States, Population, 1940*, vol. 1, pt. 2 (Washington, DC: GPO, 1943); and *Census of the Population, 1990: Summary Population and Housing Characteristics, Illinois* (Washington, DC: GPO, 1991).

27. U.S. Bureau of the Census, *10th Census of the United States, Agriculture, 1880* (Washington, DC: GPO, 1883); *11th Census of the United States, Agriculture, 1890* (Washington, DC: GPO, 1895); *13th Census of the United States, Agriculture, 1910*, vol. 6 (Washington, DC: GPO, 1913).

28. For an in-depth study of inheritance processes in central Illinois, see Sonya Salamon, *Prairie Patrimony: Family, Farming, and Community in the Midwest* (Chapel Hill: University of North Carolina Press, 1992).

1. The Hard World I Was Born Into

1. A slat double crib is a corn crib. Each crib was about twelve feet wide by twenty-four feet long, with the sides covered by approximately four-inch-wide slats about two and a half to three inches apart. The cribs were joined by a common roof with a passage between them wide enough to drive a wagon through.

2. The record of original land entries (Illinois State Archives Computer Conversion Project, Springfield, Illinois, hereafter ISACCP) shows that Henry Leyerle bought eighty acres, the southeast half of the southwest quarter of section 25, town 11 south, range 3 west, in 1832, adjoining land taken out by George Smith in section 36 that same year. Both farms lay astride Hutchins Creek. Lyerla Cemetery is located in the northeast corner of this land. People locally refer to this area as the "Smith settlement."

3. Charles Smith was George and Belveritta

Smith's son and the first cousin of Edith's grandmother, Ritta Lyerla.

4. Government land records (ISACCP) show that Henry Leyerle Jr. bought thirty-four acres in section 6, town 12 south, range 1 west, in 1837 and another thirty acres in 1840. Henry Leyerle (Jr. or Sr. not noted) bought the thirty-four-acre segment between these two in 1848. According to Edith, they eventually acquired 440 acres.

5. In addition to considerable acreage, Henry Sr. left an estate that sold for $338.75, plus growing crops and outstanding loans and other accounts due him totaling $757.20. He appears to have been a blacksmith, as his estate included a set of blacksmith tools appraised at $25.00. In addition to an assortment of farm and household tools and equipment, he had two lots of books valued at $9.00, a clock, hogs valued at $60.00 (including six wild hogs), nine head of sheep valued at $9.00, a horse valued at $20.00, a mare valued at $75.00, and one cow and yearling valued at $20.00. The sale bill included a rifle gun that sold for $5.40 and a variety of other items not specified in the appraisal (Sale bill for Henry Lyerla dated Jan. 14, 1858; Appraisement signed Jan. 13, 1858, Union County Circuit Clerk, Probate Box 19).

6. Much of this information is from Edith's chapter, "The Family of Zachariah Lyerly (1756–1847)," in Doty, *Vancel and Lyerly Families*.

7. Edith insisted that Lum was from Vicksburg and wondered how someone from the South came to fight on the side of the North. Perrin says he was a native of Union County, "a son of Samuel and Vina (Steiner) Ballance, who came to this county from Louisiana" (*History*, B93). Samuel Ballance bought 265 acres in Union County from the federal government in 1836, 120 acres in section 30, town 11 south, range 3 west; and 155 acres in section 24, town 11 south, range 4 west (ISACCP).

8. According to family tradition the baby was two years old when the fatal accident occurred, although the birth and death dates (July 21, 1868 and October 9, 1873, respectively) given in Doty (*Vancel and Lyerly Families*, 89) indicate he was five.

9. Edith was unable to determine which Henry Lyerla operated the gristmill. However, family tradition recounted only one Henry Lyerla, and Henry Jr. abandoned his family while his father was still alive, suggesting that the gristmill was operated by Henry Sr. or by both father and son.

10. The school was located in the southwest quarter of the northwest quarter of section 6, town 12 south, range 2 west, on the west side of Hutchins Creek, in the field just east of Willis Rhodes's house. Information about this school came from Laura Rhodes via her daughter, Fannie Rhodes.

11. Julius and Robert Rendleman, Edith's future father-in-law, were somewhat distantly related: Julius's grandfather, Henry (1805), and Robert's father, Jacob (1808), were brothers. For genealogical information on the Rendleman family, see Webb, *Reunion*.

12. Despite the fact that Hugh and Sarah did not own any land, they owned a considerable amount of property. The appraisement bill of Hugh Grammer's estate, entered in probate, lists housewares including a cookstove, a heating stove, a safe (kitchen cupboard) and dishes, two bedsteads with bedding, a sewing machine, a

table and six chairs, a baby crib, a clock, three pictures, one looking glass, a trunk, and a bureau; a shotgun and a rifle; a sugar bucket and a molasses barrel; farming equipment including a two-horse wagon, two rolling cutters, two harrows, seven plows, a mower, a binder, a saddle, two pairs of doubletrees and single-trees, three pairs plow gear, and one pair wagon harness; various tools including a post auger, a brace and bits, chisels, sheep shears, a mowing scythe, a cutting box, and a log chain; draft stock including a horse, a mare, and a mule; livestock including fifteen head of hogs and a cow and calf; and crops including four acres of corn in the field, fifty acres of growing wheat, two hundred bushels of corn, twenty bushels of wheat, and two stacks of hay. All of these combined brought a total appraisal of $776.98 (Appraiser's Warrant signed Dec. 4, 1891, Union County Circuit Clerk, Probate Box 123-G). Sarah was named administratrix of the estate; in the administrator's bond that was filed, she was the only one of the three signers who could sign her own name. The other two, her stepfather, Columbus C. Ballance [sic], and a neighbor, Jacob R. Rhodes, both signed with an *X*. Since the widow's exemption was set at $840.00, Sarah appears to have inherited the entire estate.

Sarah's fight to retain her binder appears in the Union County Circuit Court Record (*Common Law Order Book Q*, March 1893 term, p. 565, March 24, 1893). The record indicates that a judgment was entered against Sarah Grammer for $25 and the costs of the suit and "that the note now held of plaintiff by W. Deering and Co. dated June 22, 1891 for $40 due Sept. 23, 1893, be surrendered to Plain-

tiff and that W. Deering and Co. keep the binder." Under the widow's exemption, Sarah should have been allowed to keep the binder; in any event, Sarah lost the implement, valued at $80 in the estate appraisal, and had to pay $25 plus the cost of the suit. It appears to have been an instance of the "poor widow" being taken advantage of by more powerful and well-connected merchants, a situation that is amply documented in the oral tradition.

13. Harvey Plott was indirectly related to Edith: Her daughter Bonnie and his daughter Elaine married Rushing brothers and were, therefore, sisters-in-law. The Plotts lived in a hamlet named Balcom, on the ICRR, south of Anna.

14. Beech Grove was organized as a Christian (Cambellite) church and the first church house was built in 1878 (Perrin, *History*, 413).

2. First Memories of Home

1. Jacob Lyerla and Edith's mother, Sarah, were cousins. A search for title for this farm suggests that Elijah and Sarah attempted to buy her parents' farm after her mother died in 1897; that year Elijah bought out the interest "Gen. C. Ballance and wife" had in the farm for $100. However, except for a small strip of ground Sarah and her siblings granted to their father/stepfather for $100, the land was sold in two parcels, in 1897 and 1898, to their cousin Jacob for $1,065 and their uncle Zachariah for $925. See title books in Union County Clerk's office, vol. 46, pp. 215, 406; vol. 47, pp. 170, 205. Edith believed that the estate was sold to pay off debts; however, as her memoirs recount, around that same time Elijah and Sarah began buying a farm, suggesting that some of the proceeds may have been distributed among the

heirs. A search of the titles shows the transaction between the Bradleys and the landowner was never recorded in the county clerk's office.

2. Edith spelled the name *Justice*, but was unsure of the spelling. The 1881 atlas of Union County shows a J. P. Justice owning land near this farm; the 1899 plat map and 1904 atlas show Alice J. Jestes owning the farm the Bradleys rented. I therefore use the spelling *Jestes*.

3. The Jestes place was subsequently owned by Dr. A. J. Lyerla, by Zeph Hale, and by Roy Whitlock and is currently the site of a State of Illinois tree nursery. It joins the Parmley place now owned by Ted Wilson. See map 3.

4. These are the names by which the sites are now known. This was, of course, before the state forest had been created or picnic tables had been placed in the hollow.

5. Raising Angora goats must have been a relatively popular scheme around this time. Margaret Harris recalls that the Hines farm, which was a few miles north of the Dodd farm on the Bald Knob pasture range, began raising two thousand Angora goats in 1909: "The goats were out of their habitat and did not do very well as a money making project, but we had them on the farm for two years" (Harris, "Lawnetta Acres" [unpublished manuscript in Adams's collection, n.d., photocopy]).

6. Eva's father, Mastin Lyerla, left home because, according to a family tradition, he got in trouble during the Civil War and had to change his name to Liley. As an adult, Eva and her husband came back and raised their children here.

7. *Vina* is pronounced "Viney," and *Malvina* is pronounced "Malviney." After the state bought their land, Johnny and Vina

Lyerla's house was moved to the northwest corner of the State Forest Road and Route 127 and enlarged, says Edith, for the "big shots out of Springfield to take a weekend vacation."

8. This is Mary (Skinner) Lyerla, wife of George Lyerla, not the much older Aunt Mary (Simkins) Lyerla, wife of Caleb.

9. "Yonkee pins" is a name that was commonly given to the seed pods of the American lotus.

10. The 1908 atlas of Union County (Ogle, *Standard Atlas*) shows a 120-acre tract owned by the Egyptian Hunting Club on the west side of the lake and, south of there, a clubhouse on land owned by D. W. Karraker. The Egyptian Gun Club of South Pass (Cobden) was organized in 1895 (Union County, *Corporate Record* 1, Union County Clerk's Office).

11. This must have happened before 1881; the 1881 atlas of Union County (Griffing, *Atlas*) shows the man's estate, indicating he was deceased.

3. Spice Cake and Fried Squirrel

1. "Uncle Carroll Rich" was William Carroll Rich (1819–1915); Bill Rich was probably his son, William J. (1860–1948), since the 1899 map (Beauman, *Map of Union County*) shows both farms owned by W. C. Rich. As indicated on map 3, the Bill Rich place was in the next hollow east of the farm the Bradleys rented. William Carroll Rich was a prominent citizen of the county. He was a large landowner and farmer, and at different times a merchant, president of the First National Bank of Cobden, sheriff, county commissioner, and justice of the peace. He was also a prominent Democrat and served in the state legislature. See George E.

Parks, *Reaching for Riches: Rich Family Genealogy* (privately published, 1980, mimeographed); and Perrin, *History*, B142–43.

2. Bill Rendleman, her future husband.

3. When men "batched" they cooked for themselves and, generally, slept in makeshift quarters; they lived like bachelors, without a woman to keep house for them.

4. This land appears in nineteenth-century atlases and plat maps in section 35, town 11 south, range 3 west. Theo Baltzell bought eighty acres in section 36 (the northwest quarter of the southwest quarter and the southwest quarter of the northwest quarter) from the Illinois Central Railroad in 1886 (ISACCP).

5. This is the northwest quarter of the southeast quarter, section 35, town 11 south, range 3 west. Mr. Rendleman is Robert Rendleman, Edith's future father-in-law. A hay barn pattern is the milled timber sufficient to frame a hay barn.

6. The August 13, 1892, edition of the *Jonesboro Gazette* tells the story:

A daughter of Henry Cruse, living in the bottoms seven or eight miles west of Jonesboro, shot herself last Sunday evening with suicidal intent. She used a 32 calibre target rifle, lying down upon a bed and discharging the gun with her toes. The ball entered the left breast and passed completely through the body, burying itself in the pillow. Dr. Lence was called and upon investigation at once recognized that the case was hopeless, but she lingered until Monday evening, when death came to her relief. This was a most deplorable case. Ella, the girl in question, is said to have been bright and beautiful and more than ordinarily intelligent. She was only fourteen years old, and had a pleasant home. But it seems that some time ago she left and went somewhere in company that did not meet her father's approval, and he went after her and gave her a talking to. A few days later she repeated the offense for which he punished her. Immediately after receiving the punishment she went upstairs and committed the rash act. It is rumored that a woman in the neighborhood had been instrumental in poisoning the child's mind against her father and this terrible ending of her mischievous work excites the indignation of all who believe that the home should be sacred from all outside interference.

7. The 1881 atlas shows a school at that site (Griffing, *Atlas*). It was probably the Abernathie School, as there was a school by that name in the precinct (Perrin, *History*, 436); and a man named Abernathie first owned that piece of land (ISACCP).

8. Neri Lyerla was a cousin to Edith's mother, Sarah (see appendix B).

9. Nancy Giles was distantly related by marriage to Sarah Bradley: Nancy's mother married David Lyerla, whose father was a brother to Sarah's great-grandfather (see appendix B).

4. Bringing in the Harvest

1. The "Jonesboro News" in the *Jonesboro Gazette*, July 30, 1887, reported that "Bruno Rixleben last week purchased the Turner Brown and Mrs. A. P. Jones farms in the Mississippi bottoms. They are adjoining and are among the best farms in the county."

Turner Brown was listed in the 1860 census

as a mulatto living in Preston Precinct. Dexter, in his survey of African Americans in Union County (*A House Divided*, 63–65, 68), traces Turner Brown's history: His father, Beverly Brown, came to Union County from North Carolina via Tennessee and Kentucky around 1829 and was listed as a "bright mulatto" on the papers that proved his freedom. Turner was born in North Carolina and first settled in Missouri where, according to his son, he married a white woman. He moved to Union County around 1850 and became one of the larger landowners in the upper bottoms. He died in 1869.

Bruno Rixleben died a few years after the Bradleys moved onto the farm, and his son Tom inherited the land. Tom and his wife operated a drugstore in Jonesboro and became valued friends of the Bradleys. Edith recalled that Tom died in 1947 and his sons Bruno and Fred inherited the land.

2. Lands were established at plowing, so that the team did not have to travel over a great stretch of already plowed ground. Beginning about twenty feet (a rod or a bit more) from the long edge of the field, the farmer plowed a long middle furrow, working outward from it. When the land became thirty-five feet wide (around two rods) the dead time traveling across the already plowed ground and the danger of compaction at the end of the rows increased. The farmer then shifted across the short end of the field and repeated the process, creating another land. Space between lands was then plowed so that the dirt from the last furrow of the land was thrown back into the land, leaving an open furrow that would have to be plowed in the following year. Laying out lands and plowing the initial furrows was skilled work, which could be followed by less skilled or attentive plowmen. (This description provided by Edward L. Adams.) For detailed instructions, see Jonathan Periam, *The Home and Farm Manual* (1884; reprint, New York: Greenwich House, 1984), 63–65, 73–74.

3. Beginning in 1945, the Union County Cooperative Extension Service annual reports show that the agency promoted the building of lockers. In 1947 the Union County Locker Service was organized with $76,000 in stock sold and a $75,000 loan from the Federal Bank for Cooperatives. It opened units in Anna, Cobden, and Dongola. One of these units contained slaughtering facilities, one could handle carcasses, and one was only for storage (*Annual Reports*, 1945–47 [Anna, IL: Union County Cooperative Extension Service]).

5. Farm Chores and High Jinks

1. Hullies are mature beans that are shelled and cooked before they dry.

6. A One-Room School with a Potbellied Stove

1. The Frogges lived in the house Edith's father bought in the 1930s. Elijah rented the farm out; after his death, Edith remodeled the house and lived in it and her youngest son, Lee Roy, farmed the land.

2. The affliction was a chorea, a term that means "dance."

7. "Jump, Edith!"

1. According to George E. Parks, Charles Ware was president of the Missouri-Pacific Railroad; subsequently he writes that Ware was vice president of the railroad (*History of Union*

County and Some Genealogy Notes [privately published, 1988], vol. 1, 350; vol. 2, 535).

2. There was a tamale factory in Jonesboro that bought corn shucks from farm women in the area. An advertisement for it appears in E. G. Lentz, *The Spirit of Egypt: Southern Illinois* (Carbondale, IL: H. B. Keller, L. R. Colp, and F. C. Bastin, 1927), 106.

3. Morgan Cemetery is located north of what is now Route 146, about one mile east of Dug Hill. Edith noted that a lot of people from the bottoms are buried there.

4. Larkin products were flavoring extracts, powdered puddings, cleaning products, and brushes.

5. The *Jonesboro Gazette* (April 2, 1925) reported on the trial:

The Randle brothers, Logan and Harrison, were convicted of the murder of Oscar Trainer and received penalties of life imprisonment and twenty years in the penitentiary respectively. . . . The crime for which the Randle brothers were convicted was committed in October last at a dance in Wolf Lake, when Oscar Trainer, a young school teacher, was shot and killed. The evidence showed that Logan Randle fired two of the shots that took effect in Trainer's body, but also showed that Harrison was the chief instigator of the trouble. Another of the Randle brothers, Milas, was implicated but disappeared and so far has succeeded in evading arrest. It is said that he really fired the shots that were fatal to Trainer. He is about 42 years old. [Edith recalled that he was eventually caught and served time.] Logan Randle, the one who drew a life sentence, is 50 years old and

is very illiterate. Harrison, 36, has some education. They are single men and had no occupation save working on farms in the neighborhood of Wolf Lake. . . . The court room was jammed with spectators, particularly to hear the closing speeches of the attorneys.

6. Doc Rich Hill is located in the southeast quarter of section 18, town 12 south, range 2 west, on a road that linked what are now known as the State Forest Road and Route 146. The 1899 plat map shows 263 acres in sections 18 and 19 owned by Lafayette Rich (Beauman, *Map*). Edith recalled that the hill was so steep that their Ford Model T automobile would usually stall and they would have to turn it around and back up the hill. In the Model T the gas tank was located under the front seat and gasoline flowed by gravity to the carburetor. On a steep hill, the car had to be reversed so that the tank would be higher than the carburetor.

8. Having the Time of Our Lives

1. The streetcar track ran from a depot across Market Street from the courthouse in Jonesboro, crossed the Mobile and Ohio Railroad on a high trestle, then ran down Mary Street to Heacock Street, and from there to Main Street in Anna, and then to the State Hospital. The 1908 atlas indicates its route as the "Fruitgrowers' Refrigerating & Power Co's. Electric R. R." See plats for Jonesboro and Anna in Ogle, *Atlas*, 10–11, 14–15).

9. Bedbugs, Fleas, and Hired Hands

1. Edith is referring to the estate sale for Robert M. Rendleman, who died November 19, 1924 (Webb, *Reunion*, 473).

2. For an account of the tornado of 1925, see Peter Felknor, *The Tri-State Tornado* (Ames: Iowa State University Press, 1992). This tornado was one of the most destructive ever recorded in U.S. history. It remains a recurring topic of local recollections, along with other natural catastrophes like the Ohio River flood of 1936, which was documented by the Farm Security Administration photographers, and the Mississippi flood of 1943. The summer-long flood of 1993 will undoubtedly be remembered much the same way. Although in 1993 the Mississippi did not breech the levees in the immediate area, it swept away the Fayville levee just

south of Union County. A large area of the bottoms flooded because rain water could not drain into the swollen rivers, and the entire bottoms were evacuated due to the threats to the levees.

10. My World Comes Apart

1. Bar pits (barrow pits) were the holes left when dirt was taken out to build the levee.

2. "Setting" means to incubate eggs. Hens normally lay a number of eggs, then stop laying until the eggs hatch.

3. Lenita married Artus Dillow in 1931 (Webb, *Reunion*, 474).

Selected Bibliography

"Abstracts of *A Gazetteer of Illinois* . . . , 1837" [John Mason Peck]. *Saga of Southern Illinois* 17, no. 2 (1990): 34–46; no. 3 (1990): 21–26; no. 4 (1990): 29–38.

Adams, Jane. *The Transformation of Rural Life: Southern Illinois, 1890–1990.* Chapel Hill: University of North Carolina Press, 1994.

Atlas of the State of Illinois. Chicago, IL: Union Atlas Co., 1876.

Beauman, Guy. *Map of Union County, Illinois.* Vienna, IL: Guy Beauman, 1899.

Boatman, W. J. "The Sesquicentennial, St. John's Lutheran Church, Near Dongola, Union County, Illinois, 1816–1966: Illinois' Oldest Lutheran Congregation: Brief History." Unpublished manuscript in Adams's collection, 1966. Photocopy.

Clayton, John. *The Illinois Fact Book and Historical Almanac, 1673–1968.* Carbondale: Southern Illinois University Press, 1970.

Dexter, Darrel. *A House Divided: Union County, Illinois, 1818–1865.* Anna, IL: Reppert Publications, 1994.

———. "John Grammer of Union County." *Anna Gazette-Democrat,* Sept. 24, 1992.

———, comp. "Clear Creek Baptist Church Minutes, 1818–1848, Union County." *Saga of Southern Illinois* 20, no. 3 (1993): 24–39.

Doty, John Hubert, comp. *Vancel and Lyerly Families in America.* Rev. ed. Privately published by J. H. Doty, 255 Moline St., Aurora, CO 80010, 1991. Photocopy.

Elbert, E. Duane. "The American Roots of German Lutheranism in Illinois." *Illinois Historical Journal* 78(summer 1985): 97–112.

Eller, David B. "George Wolfe and the 'Far Western' Brethren." *Illinois Historical Journal* 80(summer 1987): 85–100.

Felknor, Peter. *The Tri-State Tornado: The Story*

of America's Greatest Tornado Disaster. Ames: Iowa State University Press, 1992.

Griffing, B. N. *An Atlas of Union County, Illinois.* Chicago, IL: D. J. Lake & Co., 1881.

Harris, Margaret. "Lawnetta Acres." Unpublished manuscript in Adams's collection, n.d. Photocopy.

Hunsaker, Q. Maurice, and Gwen Hunsaker Haws, eds. *Hunsaker Family History.* Salt Lake City, UT: Deseret News Press, 1957.

Illinois State Archives Computer Conversion Project (ISACCP). Computer file of original land sales in Illinois from federal land office ledgers, state auditor's files, and county swampland sale records. Springfield, IL: Illinois State Archives.

Lentz, E. G. *The Spirit of Egypt: Southern Illinois.* Carbondale, IL: H. B. Keller, L. R. Colp, and F. C. Bastin, 1927.

McMahan, Gale S., ed. *The Southern Baptist Churches in the Clear Creek Baptist Association.* Utica, KY: McDowell Publications, 1988.

McMahan, Joseph. "Past and Present Needs," *Illinois History* 37(fall 1983): 54–55.

Ogle, George A. *Standard Atlas of Union County, Illinois.* Chicago, IL: Geo. A. Ogle & Co., 1908.

Oliver, Edward I. "Ancient Free and Accepted Masons, Union Lodge No. 10, Jonesboro, Union County, Illinois." *Saga of Southern Illinois* 20, no. 2 (1993): 6–11.

Parks, George E. *History of Union County and Some Genealogy Notes.* 3 vols. Privately published by G. E. Parks, Anna, IL, 1988.

———. *Reaching for Riches: Rich Family Ge-* *nealogy.* Privately published by G. E. Parks, Anna, IL, 1980. Mimeographed.

Periam, Jonathan. *The Home and Farm Manual.* 1884. Reprint, New York: Greenwich House, 1984.

Perrin, William Henry, ed. *History of Alexander, Union and Pulaski Counties, Illinois.* 1883. Reprint, Utica, KY: McDowell Publications, 1990.

Rendleman, Edith. "The Family of Zachariah Lyerly (1756–1847)." In *Vancel and Lyerly Families in America*, compiled by John Hubert Doty. Privately published by J. H. Doty, 255 Moline St., Aurora, CO 80010, 1991. Photocopy.

———. "History of Wolf Lake and Ware." Unpublished manuscript in Adams's collection, 1976. Photocopy.

Salamon, Sonya. *Prairie Patrimony: Family, Farming, and Community in the Midwest.* Chapel Hill: University of North Carolina Press, 1992.

"Squatters Report of 1807." *Illinois Libraries* 59(May 1977), 328–44.

"Squatters Report of 1813." *Illinois Libraries* 59(May 1977), 345–82.

U.S. Department of Agriculture. Report No. 103. *Social and Labor Needs of Farm Women.* Washington: GPO, 1915.

Webb, Billie Snead, comp. *Randleman, Rendleman, Rintelman Reunion, 1981.* Privately published by B. S. Webb, 651 Sherwood Way, NE, Corvallis, OR 97330, 1983.

Yeager, Joseph. "Geographical, Statistical, and Historical Map of Illinois, 1822." In *Indian Villages of the Illinois Country.* Vol. 2. Compiled by Wayne C. Temple. Springfield, IL: Illinois State Museum, 1975.

Index

EDITH BRADLEY RENDLEMAN, born in
1898, is a retired farmer-homemaker from
the Wolf Lake area of Union County.

JANE ADAMS is an associate professor of
anthropology and of history at Southern
Illinois University at Carbondale and the
author of *The Transformation of Rural
Life: Southern Illinois, 1890–1990*.